P9-CBW-279

THE TRUTH OF AUTHORITY

THE TRUTH OF AUTHORITY

Ideology and Communication in the Soviet Union

THOMAS F. REMINGTON

University of Pittsburgh Press

Series in Russian and East European Studies No. 9

Published by the University of Pittsburgh Press,
Pittsburgh, Pennsylvania 15260
Copyright © 1988, University of Pittsburgh Press
All rights reserved
Feffer and Simons, Inc., London
Manufactured in the United States of America

Library of Congress cataloging-in-publication data

Remington, Thomas F., 1948–
   The truth of authority.

   (Series in Russian and East European studies, no. 9)
   Bibliography: p.
   Include index.
   1. Political socialization—Soviet Union.
2. Propaganda, Communist—Soviet Union.   3. Public
opinion—Soviet Union.   4. Communication in politics—
Soviet Union.   5. Mass media—Political aspects—Soviet
Union.   6. Ideology.   I. Title.   II. Series.
JN6581.R46   1988   303.3′2′0447   88–4745
ISBN 0–8229–3590–2
ISBN 0–8229–5408–7 (pbk.)

Chapter 6, "Politics and Professionalism in Soviet Journalism," first appeared, in
slightly different form, in *Slavic Review* 44:3 (Fall 1985):489–504.

303. 32
R 388 t
238979

TO THE MEMORY OF MY FATHER

In the monolithic parties a peculiar kind of cognitive relativism prevails. The truthfulness of any new idea is evaluated according to its author's position in the party hierarchy. Therefore, the party is interested not primarily in *what* is said, but in *who* says it, when, where, about whom, with what motives, in what form, before whom, what is "behind" it, who will profit by it, whose interest it reflects, and so on. The substantive content of what is said, which is the sole matter of relevance for its truthfulness, is completely pushed into the background. The center of attention is assumed by the author and the situational context of the statement. That which *surrounds* the truth becomes more important than the truth itself. In such circumstances "the most embarrassing thing of all is when the wrong person says the right thing." The truth of authority replaces the authority of truth.

—Svetozar Stojanovic
Between Ideals and Reality

CONTENTS

CONTENTS

TABLES

of stops and starts in ideological policy, during which a dramatic change of leadership occurred, and culminating in a sweeping turn toward openness and pragmatism in ideology, affords a detailed view of the alternation of policy impulses and developments in the organization of ideological effort. In addition, some reference will be made to the structure and process of ideological work in earlier periods of Soviet history.

Chapter 1 explains the rationale for including extensive descriptive detail about the structure of ideology and communications. The pioneering studies of Alex Inkeles, Gayle Durham Hollander, Mark Hopkins, Ellen Mickiewicz, and others remain important but need to be updated. Moreover, as will become clear, this book argues that the essential clue to the persistent centrality of ideology lies less in the content of the doctrine than in the organization of its dissemination, through which the privileged and leading members of society are made into partners of the party apparatus, thus relieving the burden on the party's own small full-time staff and diffusing responsibility for the stability of the political system. Chapters 2 through 6 discuss particular components of the oral propaganda and media systems and the characteristics of the groups that run them. The seventh and final chapter focuses on the target of ideological work, the Soviet populace itself, and reviews existing data about how people use channels of information to meet their particular needs for information and opinion. It speculates about the differential impact of party ideological work on different segments of society and singles out the elite groups coopted into ideological activism as a category of special interest and importance.

The research for this study has occupied several years and has incurred obligations to a number of institutions and individuals. In particular, I would like to note my appreciation of the University of Illinois's nonpareil Summer Research Laboratory on Russia and Eastern Europe and of its Slavic Reference Service. The comprehensiveness of the University of Illinois library holdings and the expertise and helpfulness of its staff have been critical to the research. In addition, research leaves from the Emory University political science department and support from the Emory University Research Fund made possible much of the research and writing. Among readers of early drafts of portions of the study, Ellen Mickiewicz and Fred Barghoorn were particularly helpful. Conversations with Vladimir Shlapentokh have been invaluable sources of stimulation and insight. Research assistance provided by William Stowe, Catherine Scott, Gregory Haley, and Andreas Sobisch was most useful. Finally, I am deeply grateful for the patience and encouragement of my wife, Nancy.

THE TRUTH OF AUTHORITY

1 IDEOLOGY IN A NEW KEY

THE "MIGHTY COMPLEX"

On 17 April 1979, Mikhail Suslov, secretary of the Central Committee and a Politburo member, addressed a plenary session of the Central Committee of the Communist Party of the Soviet Union (CPSU).[1] Although the newspaper report on the plenum did not indicate the topic of his remarks, they almost certainly concerned a major Central Committee resolution on ideology that was about to be promulgated. Published on 26 April, it was probably circulated first to lower party committees before being printed in the press on 6 May. Suslov played a prominent role in overseeing the subsequent publicity campaign surrounding implementation of the resolution until he died in January 1982.

The resolution consisted of a lengthy call for major improvement in the quality of "ideological, political upbringing work" carried out by party committees and other state and public institutions. Criticizing the existing state of ideological work for having become stale, formalistic, and ineffective, the resolution also emphasized the higher levels of information and cognitive skill among the Soviet population, pointing out, for example, that a majority of families were now receiving three newspapers as well as watching television and listening to radio. The resolution demanded therefore that all organizations involved in ideological work, the "whole mighty complex of information and education" including the large corps of trained ideological cadres and the large and modern "information-propaganda apparatus" of the mass

3

media, renew their efforts to "arm the Soviet people—each new generation—with the invincible weaponry of historical truth, a deep understanding of the laws and perspectives of social development, relying on the unwavering foundation of Marxist-Leninist teaching."[2] Then, following the standard procedures for conducting a publicity campaign, the press followed up this resolution with editorials repeating its major themes, dispatches about related decisions adopted by local party organizations, and articles invoking the resolution in discussions of ideological problems.[3]

Promulgation of the 1979 ideology resolution was the culmination of two long-term trends that were especially pronounced under Brezhnev: the co-optation of the country's rapidly growing managerial and technical intelligentsia into party ideological work and the inability of an increasingly hollow, ossified propaganda system to reverse the trends toward declining productivity and rising anomie in society.

The recruitment of much of the country's social elite to the propaganda system resulted in an immense expansion of activist participation in mass political work, both in areas in which party ideological work had been done for decades, such as agitation and adult political education, and in others introduced in the 1960s and 1970s. A 1971 Central Committee resolution singling out the Cherepovetsk metallurgical factory, and accompanying party instructions, made it clear that party committees were to recruit *all* managers and engineering-technical personnel (ITRs, in Soviet parlance) to ideological work. A 1977 resolution criticized those party organizations that were doing too little to recruit managers and specialists to mass political work. At the same time the complexity of political work grew appreciably. Throughout the 1970s, it is clear, party policy sought to incorporate members of the social elite from every institutional sphere into the ideological *aktiv* and achieved considerable quantitative success.[4]

With expansion, however, party ideological work grew impossibly bureaucratized. Paper organizations—ideological commissions, councils, and public bodies of various kinds—flourished while attitude surveys, particularly the party's own confidential studies, testified to the erosion of effectiveness in inculcating collectivist values, dedication, self-sacrifice for the socialist cause, mastery of doctrinal theory, and faith in the future. By late 1978 mass indifference to the sterile, ritualized diet of official propaganda had become the subject of top-level concern, indicated in Brezhnev's harsh criticism of the state of ideological work at the November plenum in 1978.[5] The ideological resolution itself sharply attacked the deficiencies of ideological work, the "commonly encountered traits of formalism, inclination to idle chatter, all sorts of propagandistic clichés, a dry 'official' style of materials, the frequent mechanical repetition of general truisms instead of thinking them through creatively and searching for a vivid and accessible form of expression." It noted as well the pomposity, superficiality, and pedantry of much propaganda and demanded that "all this must be decisively eliminated from practice."

Predictably, the response, a call for a return to orthodox fundamentals, could not overcome the numbing routines of a new campaign, which quickly dissipated its force in a cascade of showy reorganizations and meetings. Because the resolution simply triggered more of the very kinds of bureaucratic behavior that it condemned, its effects were self-limiting and even counter-productive.

Yet the call for a return to basic principles that it embodied represented one of the impulses that result in periodic shifts in the direction of party ideological policy between orthodoxy and pragmatism. In the fundamentalist's view, the task of party ideological work is to instill understanding of and commitment to the basic tenets of Marxism-Leninism, thus sharpening the sense of opposition between socialism and capitalism, increasing loyalty to the party and its goals, and rousing antagonism to liberal democracy. The orthodox response regards ideological indoctrination as the principal defense against forces such as capitalism, nationalism, liberalism, or religion. One of the axioms conservative writers repeat most frequently is Lenin's warning that any weakening of socialist ideology must inevitably lead to a strengthening of bourgeois ideology.[6]

Underlying the pragmatic impulse, in contrast, is the desire to harness theory to efficiency and productivity. Ideological pragmatism tolerates greater differentiation of interests and a lower concentration of power to enforce social solidarity. Usually born in reaction to a phase in which ideological policy has been particularly orthodox or stagnant, the pragmatic impulse is also historically associated with a reduction in political controls over the expression of political opinion.

It is this periodic oscillation of ideological policy between alternative value sets that one misses when one talks of Soviet ideology as a fixed doctrine, or what the 1979 resolution termed the "unwavering foundation of Marxist-Leninist teaching." Still less does one think of the "mighty complex" of institutions conducting ideological work, including the media, the agitation-propaganda establishment, education, science, culture, and the corps of professional ideological cadres, in structural terms. One generally thinks of ideology as an intellectual system rather than as an organized network of institutions imposing a measure of doctrinal coherence over the stream of communications in Soviet society. As a result, when one asks, "What are the functions of ideology in the Soviet system?" one usually means "What are the functions of doctrinal teachings?" And this question in turn divides naturally into two, the two dimensions of any doctrine: Is it consistent, and therefore a usable basis for action? And is it believed, so that it in fact forms the basis for action?

Regarding content, one is often led by the logical inconsistencies in the doctrine to conclude that there is no specifically Marxist-Leninist teaching any more: that though lip service is paid to the existence of a doctrine, its content has been reinterpreted so often that it is devoid of meaning. There is undoubtedly a good deal of truth to Jerry Hough's observation that "in fact, there is no coherent, uniformly agreed-upon Marxist-Leninist ideology. . . . Ideology has become much more ambiguous—no doubt deliberately so. . . . Many of the most central ideas are open to challenge and debate. In the more propagandistic treatments for the broad public, the ideology can be a summary of generally accepted clichés, but for those in the intellectual establishment, broadly defined, it becomes the medium of discourse."[7] Other observers believe that the socialist, class-internationalist orientation of doctrine has been displaced by a sotto voce Soviet-Russian great power nationalism in the doctrine's content.[8]

Parallel to the argument that the doctrine no longer possesses any definite content is a competing view that the decline of ideology poses a serious threat to the stability of the system. Some, such as Robert C. Tucker, go so far as to speak of a "crisis of faith" in a political system so structured as to require a mobilizing creed.[9] Other analysts point out that, though many of the tenets specifically associated with the party

and its justifying ideology have failed to transform Soviet mass consciousness, the political system retains features broadly congruent
with deeply rooted values in Soviet—or Russian, at any rate—political
tradition. Such are the conclusions Stephen White reaches, on the basis
of careful study both of Soviet surveys of the effectiveness of party
political work and of interviews with émigrés. However, he does warn
that, coupled with the decline in the performance of the economy,
upon which the legitimacy of the system depends to a growing degree,
the relative failure of Marxist-Leninist indoctrination could turn out to
have serious consequences.[10]

Both viewpoints leave us without a sensible explanation for the
survival, indeed growth, of the machinery for propagating Marxism-
Leninism and controlling communications.[11] We tend to imagine that
only inertia can explain the hardiness of a doctrine that corresponds so
poorly to the political system's needs or the populace's interests. The
same perspective also leads analysts periodically to discover a secular
trend toward de-ideologization, or, alternatively, toward the "modernization" of Marxism-Leninism. By treating the ideological complex as
a dynamic political subsystem, closely linked to party management of
social change, one is led to inquire into its functions for social integration, and particularly the consolidation of a general political elite
formed of managerial, specialist, and professional elites.

Proceeding from this perspective, the present book argues that the
indispensability of ideology to the political system becomes more
evident when one moves away from the ideological message apart from
the larger society and looks instead at the means by which a relatively
small core of professional politicians maintains itself in power. The
weight of evidence indicates that their success in generating political
authority depends on their ability to draw society's elite groups into
the work of disseminating and applying doctrinal theory, sharing with
them a measure of power and privilege. Although the diffusion of
ideological responsibility strains the coherence and credibility of the
doctrine's content, it is through the recruitment of the ideological
aktiv that the regime broadens and consolidates the political elite on
which its power rests.

This book concentrates on two main forms of party ideological
work: direct political work with the populace by activists through

agitation, propaganda, and their related forms; and the operation of the print and broadcast media. Though many other arenas of culture and communications are also objects of party ideological supervision, the print, broadcast, and oral media are the vehicles of most political communication in Soviet society. A third field of ideological authority is theory, where we *can* identify a stable, albeit slowly evolving core of teachings. Theorists work in a politicized organizational environment, since the CPSU leadership can intervene in theoretical disputes before they develop into competing ideologies. In the remainder of this chapter, I will survey the process of the formation of theory, and in chapter 3 I will discuss the propagation of theory through the adult political education system.

The scope of the book is selective; it passes over channels of communication in which artistic, educational, or entertainment content is dominant, such as cinema, music, art, theater, literature, schooling, and publishing, and is limited to the more directly political media. Since existing accounts of the structure of such institutions as the party ideological sector, journalism, agitation, political education, and related institutions contained in earlier studies are by now somewhat out of date, this book includes a good deal of descriptive information based on the voluminous Soviet literature on this subject. The study considers, therefore, both the structure and the process of ideological work. Before turning in the next chapters to the setting of ideological work, however, let us consider some views of how Soviet ideology operates in the political system.

THE PLACE OF DOCTRINE

It might be best to start from Soviet theory itself. N.B. Bikkenin, in 1987 named editor of *Kommunist* and before that, deputy head of the Propaganda Department of the Central Committee, reminds readers of his 1983 treatise on socialist ideology that all persons are ideological in their thought and action; ideology is a category of theoretical consciousness that is reflected in the ways people comprehend and act on their surroundings. Distinguishing between ideology's roles as a theoretical system and as a social phenomenon, Bikkenin argues that its effectiveness in spurring the advance of society depends on the degree of correspondence between the two functions. In each society ideological institutions are an inseparable part of the political superstructure, the main function of which is to secure the intellectual foundations of the ruling class's political domination. Only with Marxism does ideology acquire a scientific character, as the forms and categories of comprehension that reflect the false consciousness of exploiting classes are progressively rejected by the proletariat. To be sure, Marxism opposes vulgar reductionism, Bikkenin claims, which would deny the complexity and even contradictory nature of cultural and spiritual development of society by reducing spiritual values to the simple reflection of material interest. Nor is ideology the same as science, although in the case of Marxism it combines scientific objectivity with the defense of class interests. While not impartial, the ideology of the proletariat coincides with—and reinforces—scientifically determined truth. (Recall that, according to George Lukács' early, somewhat Hegelian formulation, when the proletariat's consciousness rises to the point at which it grasps the dialectical process of history, the proletariat itself will become "the identical subject-object of history whose praxis will change reality."[12]) Ideology gives expression to the proletariat's programmatic goals and at the same time unites the diverse interests of different groups of the proletariat into a common class interest made possible by the integration of the class and the rise of its political consciousness.[13]

But orthodox conceptions of the correspondence of Marxist theory with the fully realized class interest of the proletariat must then be fitted into the procrustean bed of official conceptions of Soviet society. The historically privileged position of the proletariat as Marxism's "carrier" must be shared with "the popular masses" more generally and with a party specially endowed with theoretical insight.[14] The fundamental premise defended by Soviet doctrine is that ideological theory rests on science rather than power. The notion that science and ideology might diverge, that ideology derives from dogma rather than independent inquiry, is ascribed to a crisis in bourgeois ideology, and recognition that ideology serves instrumental needs for the party must be reconciled with the assertion that Marxist-Leninist theory guides the party.[15] The authority of ideology stems, according to the theory, from the correspondence of truth and knowledge in awakened proletarian consciousness. The political power of the party, however, is based on "its recognized authority as the leader of the Soviet people." This authority enables the party to conduct ideological work as one of the three principal branches of its activity—the others are political and organizational—with the aim of forming a Marxist-Leninist world-view among the Soviet toilers.[16] Like Escher's famous picture of a hand drawing itself, the inconsistency here—that the party's power is drawn from the same enlightened and united self-interest that it is forever establishing—arises from a logical impossibility. It reveals the contradictory demands on theory: the need to preserve the Marxist doctrine of historical materialism as the explanation of the coincidence of subject and object, and the need to justify the party's independence and even superiority vis-à-vis theory.[17]

The competitive relationship between ideology and power explains the circularity of Soviet formulations, according to which theory guides the party, which in turn maintains, develops, and disseminates theory. Not a few Western scholars have attempted to resolve this paradox. Few doubt that party theorists treat official doctrine manipulatively for the sake of legitimating policy changes, but some hold that the doctrine retains a central core of assertions, too fundamental to be revised without excessive cost, some residue of which influences the outlooks of leaders and citizens.[18] Some go farther and argue that the ideology is both a ruling doctrine and an instrument of power. For example, in a recent essay, Carl Linden, following the tradition of Nicolas Berdyaev, presents the Soviet political system as "ideocratic." That is, it is ruled by a doctrine (Linden refers to "the ideology that rules the rulers"[19]) that at the same time serves as an "instrumentality" to justify and rationalize the enormous power exercised by the leaders. A similar version of the same paradox is offered by Robert Daniels in his recent synoptic history of Russia. Daniels argues that Marxism-Leninism supplies a vocabulary, but not an intellectual content, for justifying all aspects of the political system, including the exclusion of alternative belief systems. It does not guide policy, since it lacks any firm content; as policy changes, doctrinal ideas are reformulated. Since, however, the political leadership's power to reformulate and propagate doctrine requires a monopoly over the means of political expression and over the content of ideas circulated in society, it cannot dispense with ideology as a tool of legitimation. "The resulting control system must then be justified by even greater ideological rigor."[20] Of course, a tool of legitimation must have some intellectual content. Though Daniels helps one to appreciate how doctrinal legitimation imposes costly constraints on expression, the Orwellian evisceration of content should not be overstated. Elements such as the stage theory of history, the leading role of the party, democratic centralism, state ownership of at least the commanding heights of production, collective farming, and hostility to religion, have been constant features of doctrine as well as practice.

Emigrants have generally stressed the indispensability of ideology while also insisting that, both as a doctrine with content and as a creed, ideology is dead. For Leszek Kolakowski, however, "vague and indefinite" the faith, "ideology is not simply an aid or adjunct to the system but an absolute condition of its existence, irrespective of whether people actually believe in it or not. . . . The apparatus is essentially ideological and internationalist in character and could not be replaced by the police, the army, or any other institution."[21] As an ideological institution, the party has no other means of legitimating its power. However, Kolakowski has also questioned how long such a system, in which neither party nor populace believes in ideology, can survive.[22]

In his impassioned "Letter to the Soviet Leaders," Alexander Solzhenitsyn makes several basic points about the doctrine. First, as a theory of society, it is "discredited and bankrupt," false in its assertions and disproved through its predictions. Second, realizing the goals it set forth—the collectivization of the peasantry, the nationalization of all trade and services, overdevelopment of military power, irrational forms of industrial administration, and particularly the persecution of religion—entailed deeply destructive consequences. Third, its preoccupation with international revolution prevents the regime from activating the one force that can strengthen Russia in the face of its enemies: patriotism. (He writes, "And the whole of this letter that I am now putting before you is patriotism, *which means* rejection of Marxism.") Fourth, the effort to preserve the ideology drowns the leaders and country in lies, which impose a terrible burden on the moral and intellectual life of society. Finally, Solzhenitsyn asserts that it is only through the "sheer force of habit, tradition and inertia" that ideology has survived, not out of any conviction on the part of the leaders. Once the leaders find the courage to cast off Marxism, allowing it to compete freely with other doctrines, the state can begin to regain its vitality. At that point, it is not so much authoritarian rule per se that need be rejected as an authoritarian order that rests on lies.[23]

A more analytical treatment of the indispensability of communist ideology to the Soviet political system is offered by Alexander Zinoviev, formerly a professor of mathematical logic at Moscow State University, in his book *The Reality of Communism.* Calling the Soviet Union an "ideological society," Zinoviev draws attention to both the behavioral and the normative aspects of ideology. Ideological work "is one of the most important, if not *the* most important, aspects of Party work in general," he points out, and he adds that it is not only party professionals who perform duties in the ideological sphere. "The number of people employed professionally in the ideological field is enormous. The number of people who in one way or another are forced to carry out bits of ideological work is innumerable. Every official is one way or another the transmitter of ideology." Finally, he notes the vast scope of ideology's target: millions study in "universities of Marxism-Leninism," and even more attend circles, seminars, and lectures. Sports, science, and culture are pervaded with ideology. As a domain of activity, then, ideology absorbs a large proportion of the society's time, energy, and material resources: as Zinoviev puts it, "ideology is not only doctrine. An ideology is kept alive by the everyday activity of people in the ideological field." Their responsibility is to "preserve this teaching, to adapt it to people's current lives and to impose it on the population of the country." They see to it that the population knows and accepts the basic tenets of the doctrine and continually manifests devotion to it through "ideological heel-clicking." The ideological apparatus watches over culture, excluding ideas that are inimical to the doctrine and encouraging that which is helpful and interprets current events in the light of doctrine. It activates citizens to play out ceremonies that reaffirm the faith; citizens are to be active rather than passive participants in the community of Soviet people; this requires them, in Zinoviev's terms, to "masquerade seriously and with deep feeling."[24]

At the same time, ideology is of course a doctrine prescribing a particular set of beliefs and behaviors. In this respect, too, Zinoviev takes Marxism-Leninism seriously, although there are contradictions in his treatment. On the one hand, he claims that, with time, the higher levels of information and analytical skill among Soviet people increase the discrepancy between public opinion and the prescribed doctrine, with the result that the doctrine loses credibility. As ideology erodes, popular demand requires "less oppressive forms of ideology," less fantastic and demeaning to believe. The "thaw" of the post-Stalin period, therefore, is continuing in a gradual way, despite the resistance of the deeply conservative ideological establishment.[25] On the other hand, Zinoviev considers ideological training to be highly successful in inculcating internalization of prescribed modes of thought and behavior. Most members of the scientific and cultural intelligentsia "are themselves elements and mechanisms in society's ideological apparatus of power." Accordingly, he sees little likelihood that, in the absence of the external yoke of ideological control, the arts would evolve in a liberal direction. Ideology, in his view, is too deeply internalized in the consciousness of most members of the cultural elite for such a development to occur: even the most "critical" works of literature, for example, benefit the ideology by masking the true extent of ideological control.[26] Zinoviev considers most Soviet people to be adept at playing expected public roles and thinking in standard intellectual patterns while readily expressing quite cynical private views. How, therefore, dissonance between ideology and the values, goals, and beliefs absorbed from other sources erodes doctrine over time is a question Zinoviev leaves unanswered.

Another, more novel view of Soviet ideology is that of Alain Besançon, who compares Soviet doctrine in its structure and attitude to gnosticism, that is, neither religion nor philosophy, but also not quite science, though dependent on faith in science. Besançon points out, however, that in its "field of action" ideology is political: indeed once canonized, it becomes power. This has characterized not only Leninism, but also Hitlerism: elsewhere the beliefs of intellectuals were detached from the militant state in the life of civil society. In Besançon's view, ideology strains to be realized in action, and, whereas in Europe ideology struggled to form areas of thought and action free of dogmatic religion, in Russia, certain strains of nineteenth-century ideology reawakened religion, giving the intelligentsia a purpose. The already weak civil society was finished off by World War I and the Bolshevik revolution, and the Communist party, realizing its ideological mission, replaced it instead of rebuilding it.[27] Besançon's treatment at times comes close to regarding ideology as an autonomous and self-sufficing force, neither the product of social behavior nor a codified system of values and beliefs. However fanciful his account may appear—and this rendering cannot do justice to its depth and subtlety—it is useful in focusing attention on the essentially political objective of Lenin's adaptation of Marxism.

The dynamic, power-generating role of ideology also formed the central element in Brzezinski and Huntington's classic comparison of Soviet and U.S. politics. Defining Soviet ideology as comprising both a fairly immutable doctrine (statements about first principles) and an instrumental action program (statements about policy priorities), Brzezinski and Huntington see it as giving the society, particularly the political elite, a common goal demanding internal unity in the face of a constant struggle against obstacles and enemies. The stress on change, progress, achievement of goals, and struggle serves to justify unity of leadership and a political monopoly by the CPSU. The goal-directed nature of ideology explains the need for political leaders constantly to restate ideology according to the current policy program, while framing all policy goals in accordance with the militant terms of orthodoxy generates a feedback effect: political language is constrained by doctrinal jargon while the ideology's emphasis on struggle and conflict reinforces the militant style of thought and action of the political elite. In contrast to much of the received wisdom then and since, Brzezinski and Huntington do not predict an ineluctable erosion of ideology in favor of pragmatism. In fact, they consider ideology, for all its intellectual ritualism and restrictiveness, a source of strength for enabling the leadership to politicize the consciousness of the elite around Soviet nationalism, class conflict, and goal achievement.[28] Technological progress, although it generated strains between ideology and the need for innovation, would not fundamentally require a change of the political system toward liberalization. Early on, therefore, they rejected convergence theory.

Although Brzezinski and Huntington's definition is essentially normative—that is, it refers to ideology as a doctrine or system of codified beliefs—they also analyze the relationship of the ideological establishment to other sections of the political elite. Their analysis of the dynamics of party politics derives from their distinction between the philosophical and programmatic roles played by the doctrine. Much of the job of the party's agitation-propaganda specialists consists in preventing tendencies of degeneration and instrumentalization that might naturally set in with an unestablished faith. By the same token, the work of these specialists inevitably contributes to the ritualization and routinization of ideological work and leads to predictable bureaucratic tendencies, such as self-aggrandizement. Yet the ideologists are needed, since the party is both an ideological and a managerial organization. However, ideological specialists rarely achieve the highest positions of power regionally or nationally (Chernenko's brief ascendancy may be the very exception proving the rule), since it is generalists who can adapt the ideology's "action program" to current policy needs; by orientation they are innovators of a more pragmatic bent than those whose professional duties call on them to preserve the orthodoxy against secularization and heresy. It is these "action-program generalizers," according to Brzezinski and Huntington, who will likely continue to lead the party. Surely, in view of the rise of Brezhnev, Andropov, and Gorbachev, their prediction has been borne out by events.[29]

MODERNIZATION THEORY AND THE MODERNIZATION OF THEORY

Modernization theories place society rather than politics at the center of theories regarding the relationship of ideology and power, and they emphasize the long-term impact of social change on political structures. According to modernization theory, technological advancement spreads a pragmatic worldview at odds with revolutionary and consummatory value orientations. It follows that the political order must institutionalize decision-making procedures capable of generating legitimacy in a highly differentiated society, which only institutions based on reason and consent can achieve. In a particularly strong version of this position, Talcott Parsons asserts that only democratically organized political institutions are capable of generating legitimacy of the system. "No institutional form basically different from the democratic association can, *not* specifically *legitimize* authority and power in the most general sense, but *mediate consensus in its exercise* by particular persons and groups, and in the formation of particular binding decisions. At high levels of structural differentiation in the society itself and in its governmental system, generalized legitimation cannot fill this gap adequately." Parsons goes on to predict therefore that communist political systems will prove unstable in the long run and will either evolve toward electoral democracy and multiparty competition or will fail to advance.[30]

In his analysis of the transformation of one-party authoritarian systems, Samuel Huntington also argues that the viability of the regime requires strategies for incorporating intellectuals and other potential sources of dissent through legitimate channels of expression—these, while necessarily marking a decline in ideologically grounded integration, increase the legitimacy and capacity of the system. The very erosion of ideological faith, therefore, "is a sign not of decay but of stability" because the intense, overriding political cleavages of the revolutionary era have given way to a multiplicity of group interests mediated by the party. In the established one-party regime, accordingly, "ideology is less important in shaping its goals and the decisions of its leaders; pragmatic considerations are more important."[31]

Arguing against this view, Richard Löwenthal questions whether Communist party regimes have been willing to evolve in the direction of nonideological, demobilized authoritarianism. Addressing the problem of reconciling the system's needs for rationality and efficiency with the political elite's need for a justification of its power, Löwenthal points out that no Communist party has been able to dispense with a doctrine specifying an ideological threat to its continued tutelary authority, however much this spells conflict with the rising level of political demands upon it. He therefore takes a more pessimistic view than does Huntington about the likelihood that a de-ideologized, demobilized, and inclusive authoritarianism can gradually replace the present decayed system of party-ideological rule. Löwenthal concludes that, "while a further evolution of Communist regimes ruling mature societies toward an acceptance of ideological erosion may be conceivable, it would also be an evolution leading away from the monopoly of the party—a step on the road toward democracy."[32]

It is true that in Poland, Czechoslovakia, and Hungary, external intervention has prevented the realization of democratic change resulting from the release of long-suppressed social pressure. But these are also regimes where communist rule was imposed from outside. If only indigenous communist revolutions are compared, one might point to China in the 1980s, where the radical turn to market-oriented reforms and the partial intellectual thaw indicate the potential for a decay of Marxism-Leninism. But however dramatic, the reform phase in China represents a strategy for rapid growth in an impoverished society rather than the evolution of ideology in an economically mature system. Under Deng the leadership has been careful to limit political activity outside the party and government. The selective repression of reformist intellectuals and the warning, which occurred in early 1987, that intellectual debate proceed exclusively under "Marxist guidance" signaled the Chinese leadership's insistence on retaining control over the reform process. Neither China nor any other case so far, therefore, refutes Löwenthal's observation about the dependence of Communist party regimes upon ideological legitimation. It is also worth noting that all Communist parties incorporate references to Marxism-Leninism as the fundamental source of their ideological authority in their statutes.[33]

Whereas the predominant tendency in the 1960s and 1970s was to regard Soviet doctrine as an impediment to modernization that either gave way to more inclusive and nonideological bases of legitimacy or persisted at high cost to the effectiveness of the regime, a new line of argument has emerged in the last several years that holds that the doctrine has itself been modernized and become a strategy for political and social development. Scholars such as Erik Hoffmann, Robbin Laird, and Donald Kelley have argued that Soviet formulations such as "developed socialism," "scientific management of society," and "scientific-technical revolution" reflect a fundamental change in both the content and the functions of Soviet ideology.[34] To be sure, these theorists recognize that doctrine performs multiple services in the Soviet political system; Kelley lists those of providing a language for discourse and analysis, legitimating both the system and a particular leader's policies, and serving as a guide to action.[35] Therefore, although the new theoretical ideas helped to justify the Brezhnev leadership's more "cautious and thoughtful problem-solving approach,"[36] this was only one of its functions. In Donald Kelley's terms, the new armory of ideas developed from the mid 1960s onward was a reform program in search of a political base; in Hoffmann and Laird's terms (referring specially to the concept of the scientific-technical revolution), it was a reformist program early in the Brezhnev era and gradually became a conservative strategy.[37] As an agenda for change, it was adopted by theorists and officials pressing for a wider role for experts in the policy process and a more scientific approach to decision making as well as greater popular participation, improved coordination among branches, closer integration with advanced capitalist economies, and pragmatism rather than utopianism in setting goals.

Hoffmann and Laird observe that party officials and experts compete among themselves to define and apply the new concepts, and that, indeed, such theoretical openness is a characteristic of the post-Stalin system.[38] They insist, however, that the conceptual innovations are much more than mere tactical adjustments. The new theory reflects and guides a process of rationalization in policymaking, although in somewhat contradictory ways. While it emphasizes the expanding importance of information, particularly scientifically generated knowledge, as a force of production, the wider flow of information through society also reinforces the position of the political center in coordinating the more complex society. The new theoretical ideas can therefore justify either reformist or conservative action, but they can help produce new attitudes by "proposing novel strategies for development for the USSR."[39] In becoming more pragmatic, ideology has become a more significant force for change.[40] Donald Kelley indeed argues that the theory of developed socialism "affected the actions of the brief-lived Andropov and Chernenko administrations" and predicts that "it will be enshrined in the new party program to be approved at the 27th party congress in February 1986."[41]

Like most propositions about Soviet ideology, the ideas of the "technocratic socialism" school about the influence of the new theory on policymakers cannot readily be tested. After all, knowledge of how policymakers might have acted under different circumstances is lacking. Kelley's prediction, however, that the concept of developed socialism has become an essential political formula and would therefore find a place in the revised version of the third party program can be tested. Its fate will serve as a test case indicating whether the new theoretical concepts of developed socialism and scientific-technical revolution represent an irreversible step in the development of party ideology or simply a tactical adjustment rationalizing post-Khrushchev conservatism.

"DEVELOPED SOCIALISM" IN SOVIET THEORY

Without question, Konstantin Chernenko attached great significance to both the developed socialism concept and the adoption of the new party program. Indeed, the two were intimately connected since, in the speeches and articles published under his name after he became general secretary, the concept was made into the pivotal theme of the impending party program. Chernenko had already attached his own authority to the concept in his major address on ideology at the June 1983 Central Committee plenum, where he emerged as Andropov's ideology secretary. Here he offered the basic dictum, which was to be repeated frequently by him and in commentaries during his reign, to the effect that Soviet society had entered into a prolonged stage of developed socialism, and that perfecting it was the strategic task of the party in the current phase. The concept was to be made integral to all ideological work, so as not to permit an "oversimplified" view of the transition to the highest stage of communism, "as was done in a certain period." The unity of word and deed was paramount.[42]

After he became general secretary, Chernenko remained his own ideology secretary.[43] He continued to call for a "reorientation of social consciousness," presenting it as one of the most critical party tasks. Meantime, work on the new edition of the party program was given added prominence, and the press carried a series of articles devoted to various theoretical issues germane to the framing process. Correctly conceptualizing the present stage of society's development and the tasks for the party deriving from it was said to be essential. Chernenko's lead article in *Kommunist* in December 1984 on the party's current tasks asserted that the country was at the beginning of the stage of developed socialism and that this fact determined the further course of social development. This thesis, he indicated, lay at the basis of the new draft party program to be discussed and adopted at the coming party congress. The main theoretical point he made about the link between the concept of developed socialism and the party's present policy goals was that before undertaking to build communism, it was necessary to finish out the "historically lengthy" phase of developed socialism.[44]

A *Pravda* commentary on Chernenko's article observed that a "sober, scientifically grounded" view of current reality enabled the party to avoid the mistakes of the past, when there occurred "leaps ahead in theoretical and political thought." Therefore, the CPSU had concluded that only the term *developed socialism* properly defined the party's course. Moreover, it was essential to understand that the construction of communism could begin only after the successful completion of the present phase, developed socialism. "Mastery of this conclusion, to which our party has come, should be the heart and soul of the whole process of reorientation of social consciousness."[45] Chernenko still was fighting the ideological battles of the mid 1960s when the Brezhnev leadership had to undo the damage of Khrushchev's utopianism.

By February 1985, Chernenko had grown too feeble to appear in public, so his speech to the voters of the district he represented in the Russian Republic Supreme Soviet was delivered in his stead by Viktor Grishin, Moscow city party chief. Here once again he emphasized that the "strategic course of the party" is "the course toward the all-round perfecting of the socialism we have already built." The new edition of the party program to be adopted at the coming party congress would be "a program for the perfecting of developed socialism." Even this, Chernenko worried, might be considered too utopian. "Someone might, perhaps, say: aren't we too distracted by long-range tasks, when by no means all the current problems have been solved on the level of the demands of developed socialism?" He answered the hypothetical query by assuring the voters that the party's tasks were entirely realistic.[46]

Chernenko died two weeks after this speech. Immediately it became evident that the theory of developed socialism, which by now had become a fetish, was a political liability, indeed embarassment, to Gorbachev and his allies. With Gorbachev's election as general secretary, the term suddenly disappeared from *Pravda* editorials and other authoritative sources of ideological guidance. This eventuality might have been predicted, in fact, from close study of Gorbachev's December 1984 address on ideology at a Kremlin conference on ideological work, a condensed version of which appeared in *Pravda* the next day, and a fuller version in pamphlet form separately. In this address, although he loyally paid tribute to the ailing current leader, Gorbachev spelled out the major theoretical issues and policy goals that became major themes of his own leadership after March 1985. It is worth examining this speech closely, therefore, to grasp the differences between Gorbachev and Chernenko vis-à-vis ideological theory and policy.

In the first section of the speech, Gorbachev cited Chernenko's greeting to the conference, then the June 1983 Central Committee plenum on ideology—Chernenko's brief moment of ascendancy—and the important work that had been done to reorient ideological work in its name. He also praised the "deep and principled postulates" Chernenko had set forth on the crucial problem of perfecting developed socialism and other weighty tasks. Much of the first quarter of the speech recapitulated demands Chernenko had posed in much the same terminology.

Then Gorbachev shifted gears, dropping the term *developed socialism*. Asserting that "the most important field for exerting effort in ideological work, as in all activity of the party and people, was and remains the economy," he implied that forming a Marxist-Leninist consciousness in the toilers was not the most important task of ideological work. From this point in the speech to the end, the term *developed socialism* was entirely absent. Indeed, Gorbachev introduced the phrase that he made an early motto of his own leadership. *acceleration of scientific-technical progress.* This was now to be the party's strategic course (not the "perfecting of the present stage of developed socialism"). "Priority should be given to fundamentally new, truly revolutionary scientific-technical solutions, capable of raising by many times the productivity of labor." Near the end of the speech he praised the agitators, propagandists, lecturers, teachers, cultural workers, and others who comprised the corps of ideological cadres. Immediately he then went on to praise the scientific and artistic intelligentsia, who had been under renewed ideological pressure in the Chernenko interregnum, for their services to the people. He even offered them a promise: "Our intelligentsia may be sure that everything significant, honorable, truthful that is created by their talent will be supported by the party and with gratitude will resonate in the hearts of Soviet people." This had the sound of a campaign commitment to a segment of the populace resentful at the reign of mediocrity in the Chernenko and late Brezhnev years, and it was a strange and novel note at a conference devoted to ideological work.[47]

Moreover, sections of the speech omitted or reworded in *Pravda*'s condensation raised certain theoretical issues that foretold major changes in the emphasis of ideological policy. Gorbachev called for recognition of the need to bring productive relations into correspondence with the deep qualitative changes that had occurred in society's productive forces, a theme central to the writings of a number of reformists, such as Tatiana Zaslavskaia and M. I. Piskotin, who have called for economic decentralization under this theoretical rubric.[48] Second, *Pravda* omitted Gorbachev's call for better use of money-commodity relations, a term referring to greater use of measures of value determined through market competition, another central theme of the reformists. Third, he emphasized the importance of *glasnost'*—a policy of greater openness and disclosure in political life. On it, he asserted, depends the "persuasiveness of propaganda, the impact of upbringing work, ensuring the unity of word and deed." Finally, concluding an appeal for greater attention to social matters, Gorbachev linked the quality of recreational and health care facilities directly to ideological activity. Concern with this sphere, he said, "must find its proper place in the political upbringing work of party organizations."[49] *Pravda* reworded this portion of the speech, not merely condensing Gorbachev's text. Dropping his direct link between party ideological effort and social services, the newspaper version instead shifted responsibility for attention to public services to "state, economic, and public organizations, central and local organs." The party's role was not mentioned, an omission that indicated an area of direct disagreement over the proper duties of the ideology sector between the Chernenko forces, who still controlled the Propaganda Department, and the Gorbachev camp.[50]

Between Chernenko's death and the time the draft party program was published for discussion on 26 October 1985, many further changes must have been made in the program's content and tone. The concept of developed socialism survived, finding a place twice in the text: once, in bold-face type, toward the end of the introduction, where the program stated, "The country has entered the stage of developed socialism," and again in the last sentence of the first section of part 1.[51] When the final version of the program was adopted at the Twenty-seventh Party Congress, however, the second reference to the concept had been dropped, and the paragraph in which it occurred was totally rewritten, eliminating the language that had suggested that it was the "stage" of "developed socialism" that generated the tasks currently before the party. Other concepts associated with the Brezhnev-Chernenko era of ideological theory were also dropped, such as the scientific-technical revolution and "real socialism."[52]

That these changes were not accidents was confirmed in Gorbachev's address to the congress. He himself raised the question of why the term *developed socialism* had been sharply deemphasized, and he supplied a candid answer.

Those postulates of the program that characterize the stage of social development achieved by the country and those frontiers that we must reach as a result of attaining it have attracted considerable public attention. In connection with this, various opinions have been expressed. Some propose entirely deleting those postulates dealing with developed socialism; others, on the contrary, believe that they must be elaborated more fully.

In the draft is laid out a judicious and realistic position on this question. In the basic conclusions about contemporary socialist society, it is affirmed that our country has entered the stage of developed socialism. With understanding we accept the posing of the task of building developed socialism in the programmatic documents of the fraternal parties of the socialist countries.[53]

At the same time it is appropriate to remember that the thesis of developed socialism was disseminated among us as a reaction against oversimplified conceptions of the paths and terms of solving the tasks of communist construction. But subsequently the accents in the interpretation of developed socialism gradually shifted. Often matters boiled down simply to citing our successes at the same time that many vital problems tied with moving the economy onto the rails of intensification, growth of labor productivity, improvement in supplying the populace, and overcoming negative phenomena were skirted and remained without due attention. Whether we willed it or not, it became in its own way a justification for slowness in solving problems that arose. Today, when the party has proclaimed and is carrying out a course toward accelerating socialist economic development, such an approach is unacceptable.[54]

Gorbachev rather frankly indicates the compromise nature of the wording in the draft and the political reason for first introducing the concept and then dropping it. The concept, or, more precisely, the commentaries *(traktovki)* explicating it, were expedient as apologetics for a stagnant leadership and therefore interfered with the attempt by a vigorous new team to set its own stamp on policy. In turn, therefore, Gorbachev has replaced the terminology associated with developed socialism with a set of semantic pivots of his own, to be associated with his leadership and the policy program for which he is mobilizing support. Much as U.S. presidents find it helpful to repeat ringing phrases summarizing their particular programs to make media publicity an instrument of public relations, so Soviet leaders rely on theoretical key words to distinguish their leadership from that of their discredited predecessors and to focus propaganda on their policy programs.

To be sure, Kelley, Hoffmann, and Laird recognize the instrumental value of ideological theory, but their belief that the role of theory is changing, becoming more pragmatic and influential, and even becoming a reform agenda, fails, first, to take a long enough historical view and, second, to recognize the need that theoretical ideas serve in giving policy guidance to the ideological complex. The ideas they abstract from contemporary Soviet writings include the needs for regularization and decentralization of decision making and administration, for better coordination of bureaucracies, for improved planning, for the adaptation of institutions to greater information flow, and for more scientific-technical personnel and better use of expertise.[55] (A sixth need, for computerization of production and management, concerns specific means of processing information rather than general restructuring of authority relations.) In this generalized form there is nothing essentially new about such ideas. Theorists in the Soviet Union have always called for rationalized decision making and administration by improving the flow of high-quality information to the central political leadership, improving the coordination of administrative branches, streamlining planning, deploying expertise more effectively, and making the decision process systematic. Reconciling centralism with adequate vertical and horizontal information flows has always preoccupied Soviet theorists. The planning debates of 1920–21 very largely revolved around these issues, for example.[56]

What the theorists of "ideological modernization" miss is the essentially conservative nature of the conceptual adornments hung on doctrine in the Brezhnev era, including the ideas of mass participation, "complexity," "system management," the "scientific-technical revolution," and "developed socialism." However reformist they might superficially have appeared, they were no more than rationalizations for a political outlook hostile to competition or conflict among social interests. They represented reformulations of the old conservative principle that the state reflects a monolithic and solidaristic social interest. In part these ideas reflect the antipolitical, technocratic impulse in Soviet thought, which seeks to escape the dilemma of political choice by reducing politics to administration. More practically, of course, Brezhnev-era theory reflected the political needs of a leadership coalition fearful of jeopardizing its stability through divisive confrontations. The brief Chernenko interlude debased theory still further, driving ideology into its most defensive and conservative period in decades.[57] As a result, the gathering force of near-universal repugnance in society against the intellectual sterility of the Brezhnev line in the early and mid 1980s was joined with a less unanimous but still widespread reaction against its conservatism to produce the extraordinary opening to reform instituted under Gorbachev.

Characteristic of phases of reformism—the 1920s, the late 1950s and early 1960s, and the present—is that the desire to relax excessive central controls in order to stimulate economic growth is reinforced by a loosening of ideological controls over intellectual life, social science, and culture. Reformism always shares the premise, stated baldly in the address by Alexander Yakovlev which was quoted in the Preface, that "bureaucratism requires dogmatism and vice versa."[58] Eloquently dismissing the "pseudotheoretical worship" of outmoded doctrines that characterized social science in the past, Yakovlev demands restoring "the Leninist conception of social practice as the criterion for the quality of theoretical knowledge" in the interests of pragmatism, morality, and the productivity of scholarship.[59] Yakovlev invariably counterposes democratization to the oppressive power of bureaucrats, and he links democratization with radical, market-oriented economic reform: democratization requires an awakened and enlightened expression of healthy economic interests, and economic reform will stimulate democratization.[60] His formulations are reminiscent of the tentative, contradictory gropings toward pluralism that the reformers in Czechoslovakia articulated in the April 1968 Action Program.

Like them, Yakovlev and other reform spokesmen seem to be moving toward a vision of society in which decisions are made not by an arbitrary, impersonal regulator, but through the interplay of competitive interests. Yet except for brief off-hand comments by Gorbachev that restructuring is leading toward "a socialist pluralism,"[61] pluralism itself is rejected, leaving the political essence of the reform philosophy in a somewhat confused and incoherent state, defined more by its intolerance of the former intellectual and political stagnation than by a clear conception of an alternative system. Certainly Yakovlev and like-minded figures have vigorously denounced the view that society under socialism is free of conflict.[62] In a major speech condensed in *Kommunist* in May 1987, the most important statement to date of the current reform movement, Yakovlev expressed scathing criticism of the deadening complacency of social theory in the Brezhnev period, which he regarded as essentially a continuation of Stalinist thought. In its time, he asserted, dogmatism had helped to discredit such essential fields as cybernetics, genetics, economic modeling, and social forecasting. It had "absolutized" the concept of state property and central administration of economic relations. It had closed off "enclaves" of theory to critical, original thought. Only through *glasnost'*, he insisted, can society now break down the monopoly on truth held by clerks.

Moreover, Yakovlev introduced a radical departure from the conventional picture of the struggle between the two opposing world systems, socialism and imperialism, emphasizing that mankind is one, and has common interests and values, particularly in averting ecological catastrophe. Indeed, the very premise that man must "conquer" nature, he asserted, echoing radical environmentalists in the West, undermines mankind's capacity for self-regeneration. His revisionism also extended to international security problems, where he insisted on the principle of "sufficiency" rather than deterrence and superiority. Little wonder that Tatiana Zaslavskaia, one of the most important theorists of economic and social reform, called this "a revolutionary lecture, a pure pleasure to listen to."[63] Even the version printed by *Kommunist* suggests how fundamentally the new leadership is challenging doctrines previously held sacrosanct, as well as the bureaucratic stranglehold over truth that the ideological apparatus possesses.[64] To a degree unprecedented at least since Khrushchev's time and perhaps since the 1920s, the central party leadership is seeking to replace the truth of authority with the authority of truth.

Nonetheless, even the greening of Soviet thought under Gorbachev is not a step toward renouncing ideological authority altogether. Reformist leaders have, if anything, even greater need of fixed reference points to justify their policies. Under Gorbachev, the image of Lenin—especially the Lenin of the New Economic Policy—is constantly invoked. Elements of doctrine associated with the world revolutionary struggle and with the "class" approach to politics have been sharply deemphasized. But older themes linking national pride and power with the potential of socialism have been given new emphasis and programmatic content. Gorbachev has even permitted a certain amount of utopianism in ideological work, particularly in laying out economic targets for the year 2000.[65] The Gorbachev regime is making full use of the system of ideological controls to publicize its policy goals: "restructuring," "modernization," "intensification," "glasnost'," "democratization," "acceleration of scientific-technological progress," "radical reform of the economic management mechanism," and so on. Certainly in many respects, Gorbachev's regime has demonstrated far greater imagination and technical sophistication in its use of the "mighty complex" it inherited than its predecessors.[66] But it is no less dependent upon it.

Chernenko once asserted that "our whole system of ideological work must act like a well-tempered orchestra, where every instrument has its voice and plays its part, and harmony is achieved by skillful conducting."[67] Under Gorbachev the orchestra has begun performing in a new key. If in an ideocratic system the conservative's dilemma is that fundamentalism quickly degenerates into ineffectual, self-referential dogmas, the reformer's is that his antiauthoritarianism subverts the authority of those who set the new line. Nevertheless, so long as ideology and power remain dependent upon one another for their realization, the political system will be unable to dispense with its elaborate machinery for developing and propagating Marxism-Leninism.

2 AKTIV AND APPARAT

THE IDEOLOGY SECTOR OF THE CPSU

In this chapter I examine the organization of the party's ideological work, first describing the specialized branch of the party in which responsibility for ideology is vested, then discussing the multiform settings of what is called mass-political work, that is, the many forms of direct person-to-person agitation in which speakers address public audiences on political matters. After an outline of the structure of these institutions, the remainder of the chapter will consider the recruitment of the ideological activists—the great auxiliary body of spare-time speakers and organizers who actually carry out the bulk of the mass-political work. In chapter 3 the perspective shifts to the ways in which these activists are equipped with doctrine through the party's adult political education system. In this chapter the emphasis is on the relationship between the *aktiv* and the relatively small cadre of staff officials in party committees who comprise the party's apparatus *(apparat)* for ideological control over communications.

The seat of administrative control over ideological work, the ideological sector of the party is specialized and distinct from other kinds of party work, such as economic oversight and personnel work. Its main duties concern oversight of the mass media and coordination of propaganda and agitation. It also has secondary responsibility for many other types of communication and action, including school curricula, the fine arts, recreation, youth work, public organizations, and scientific research. Successful party ideological work therefore demands a balance between day-to-day managerial tasks in agitation and propaganda and the monitoring of ideological trends in society generally. In practice this balance is achieved by vesting ideological responsibility in specialized departments of party committees and through the party presence in other institutions. In addition, party control is complemented by the KGB, charged with suppression of ideological dissent, and, in the armed forces, by the Main Political Administration.

In ideology, as in other sectors, keeping spans of control short and manageable facilitates effective supervision by the party staff over the professionals and activists who extend party control over other institutions. Party work is broken into a pyramid of territorial jurisdictions, and in each, responsible officials maintain a network of horizontal and vertical links with other organizations. Horizontal ties link the party committee with institutions of the same hierarchical rank; vertical ties link officials at two successive rungs. So, for example, an obkom's ties to the oblispolkom, the oblast newspaper, the oblast council of trade unions, and the like are horizontal, whereas the obkom's supervisory contacts with the subordinate raikom and gorkom bodies are vertical. Organizational parallelism between the party and bodies such as the trade unions and Komsomol eases the task of monitoring ideological work. The remarkable symmetry of organizational structure in social life helps conserve party resources. Nonetheless, the drive for tighter control through "complex" planning of ideological work, which reached its height in the late 1970s, clearly attests to the difficulty that ideological managers experience in coordinating the many channels of mass work and political communications.

The content of party ideological control varies with the level of party organization. At the central level, ideological specialists are concerned primarily with coordinating the work of lower party organizations and of the many all-union bodies working in ideologically related fields. At lower levels, a larger proportion of the work is taken up with organizing mass-political work and party education. At both levels, party control is strained by the proliferation of social organizations. Labor collectives abound in study groups, trade union bodies, youth groups, and voluntary societies of every description. A medium-sized enterprise alone might contain as many as sixty or seventy public organizations concerned in one way or another with mass-political work. One surveyed enterprise employing fifteen thousand persons held, on average, about five hundred workers' meetings a month in its various shops and departments.[1] At this level the key to party control is to break the primary party organization (PPO) itself into more localized units—shop committees—which are in turn divided into party groups. In this way, the basic pattern of keeping horizontal ties to a minimum and relying on indirect control through the delegation of authority over ideological work to vertically subordinate party units is preserved. Similarly, the clustering of all-union ideological institutions in Moscow and the fact that ideological policy is set there requires special organizational adaptations at the center. These I now examine more closely.

The Central Level

Vertical ties connect the Central Committee of the CPSU with fifty-five oblast and krai party committees in the Russian Republic and with the fourteen central committees in the national republics, and many more all-union state and public organizations are horizontally subordinate to it. These include approximately thirty central-level newspapers, hundreds of magazines, the Telegraphic Agency of the Soviet Union (TASS), the Chief Administration for the Protection of State Secrets in the Press (Glavlit, the censorship agency), the State Television and Radio Committee, the State Publishing Committee, the State Cinema Committee, the USSR Ministry of Culture, the central boards of the trade unions of the creative intelligentsia, Komsomol, the Main Political Administration, the Central Trade Union Council, the Council on Religious Affairs, the Academy of Social Sciences, the Institute of Marxism-Leninism, the educational ministries, and a variety of avocational groups such as the Book Lovers' Society and the Rodina Society. In most cases the Central Committee apparatus extends its influence over the ideological activity of these organizations indirectly, via their parent bodies and internal party organizations. Even so, the size of the full-time apparatus in the Central Committee responsible for ideology is strikingly small.

According to one estimate, the Propaganda Department, which performs the greatest share of ideological supervision over these institutions, employs only about fifty full-time staff officials, who are backed up by another thirty-five nonstaff (off-budget) officials. The department itself is divided into functional sections, one for the press, one for lectures, one for book publishing, and so on.[2] Parallel to the Propaganda Department are several departments with ideologically related duties: the Culture Department, the General Department, the Science and Educational Institutions Department, and (briefly) the International Information Department. The Main Political Administration combines the status of a Central Committee department with that of a subdivision of the Ministry of Defense, while the departments related to foreign policy (International Department, Cadres Abroad Department, and Liaison with Ruling Parties Department) have important ideological responsibilities. The Propaganda Department, though, is the one most directly concerned with supervising the ideological sector of lower party committees and the mass media; it also oversees the selection and training of personnel for nomenklatura posts in ideology.[3]

Although several of the central ideological institutions enjoy immense prestige, their authority individually is offset by their very number. At lower ranks of the territorial pyramid, newspaper editors and equivalent officials form part of the local power elite. This point may be illustrated by comparing the status of the editor in chief of *Pravda* with that of his counterparts in lower jurisdictions. *Pravda*'s editorship ranks highest among all media jobs; traditionally it carries with it the chairmanship of the Journalists' Union and a good deal of prestige. Yet not since December 1929, when Bukharin was forced to quit both his Politburo seat and the editorship of *Pravda*, has the editor of that newspaper been a voting member of the Politburo, whereas many newspaper editors at lower levels are members of their corresponding party bureaus. (Viktor Afanas'ev, *Pravda*'s editor since 1976, does, however, attend most Politburo and Secretariat meetings, and several other chief editors of central media organizations reportedly do so as well.[4]) An important consequence of this hub-and-spoke arrangement, whereby activists and media professionals radiate the party's influence into society, is that, for members of both elites, transfer to party ideological work at the same administrative level is an upward step. For example, M. V. Zimianin, until 1986 a Central Committee secretary charged with supervision of the Propaganda Department and ideological functions of other departments, gave up the editorship of *Pravda* when he became a Central Committee secretary in 1976. Dmitri Shepilov received the same promotion in July 1955. (The intervening editors of *Pravda*, Pavel Satiukov and A. M. Rumiantsev, suffered reverses in their political fortunes and did not achieve the same promotions.) The prospect of career advancement by communications activists and professionals through service in the ideological sector of the party apparatus helps consolidate the sense of shared elite status among them and to block the formation of a corporate fourth-estate consciousness that might lead to demands for greater autonomy for the media.

The concentration of all-union media organizations at the center explains the existence there of one more layer of political oversight than is found at lower levels. The normal pattern has been for one Central Committee secretary who is also a member of the Politburo to assume general responsibility for ideological matters. Under him, another secretary without Politburo membership oversees the heads of the Propaganda Department and others concerned with ideology, who in turn manage the professional staff of the Central Committee apparatus. In contrast, in lower party branches, the agitation-propaganda department is normally supervised by one secretary specializing in ideological affairs. Since 1986, however, a much looser, and more ambiguous, pattern of relations among the top officials responsible for ideology has prevailed.

Illustrating the flux in the general ideological strategy of the central party leadership since the late Brezhnev years is the high turnover in the position of chief of the Propaganda Department since 1977. Between 1976 and 1986, four were named. From 1977 to 1982, Evgenii M. Tiazhel'nikov, formerly an instructor of Marxist-Leninist doctrine and head of Komsomol for a decade, headed the department. Then, in one of Andropov's first high-level personnel changes as general secretary, Tiazhel'nikov was replaced by Boris I. Stukalin in December 1982. Stukalin had been a journalist and worked on *Pravda* under M. V. Zimianin; his appointment in 1985 to the post of ambassador to Hungary was a demotion connected with the shake-up in ideological policy instigated by Gorbachev. In July 1985, Aleksandr N. Yakovlev (formerly director of the Institute of World Economics and International Relations) was named to head the department. Like his predecessors in the post, Yakovlev had served in the ideological sector, having been first deputy chief of the Propaganda Department from 1965 to 1973. In that capacity he wrote an important article assailing the Russian neonationalists, who had recently gained an outlet in the Komsomol newspaper *Molodaia gvardiia* and other publications.[5] At the time of the Twenty-seventh Party Congress in February 1986, Yakovlev was elevated to the rank of Central Committee secretary and Iurii Skliarov became head of the Propaganda Department.[6]

While the Propaganda Department is the single most important unit of the Central Committee apparatus overseeing ideological work, at least six other departments have important ideology-related duties: the Culture, Science and Educational Institution, International, Cadres Abroad, Ruling Parties, and General departments. The Main Political Administration of the armed forces has equivalent status. (Under Gorbachev, two other related departments, both formed in 1978, International Information and Letters, have been dissolved.) Parallel to these departments are two academic establishments: the Institute of Marxism-Leninism, responsible for doctrinal scholarship, and the Academy of Social Sciences, which now incorporates the Higher Party School. These bodies in turn oversee affiliates at lower levels: the Institute of Marxism-Leninism guides branches in each national republic, and the Academy of Social Sciences oversees fifteen republic-level and interoblast Higher Party Schools in addition to a network of institutes for raising qualifications. The Propaganda Department coordinates the ideological work of these units in addition to supervising the mass media and oral indoctrination systems and directing the agitation-propaganda departments of lower party branches.

For most of the post-Stalin era, Mikhail Suslov occupied the position of senior ideology secretary, shaping the office through his long tenure and great prestige. Under Suslov the quasi-specialized nature of party ideological work reached its broadest application and perhaps greatest influence.[7] At the time of his death in January 1982, Suslov had served as Central Committee secretary for nearly thirty-five years and a Politburo (or Presidium) member for thirty. In his tenure both as secretary and as Politburo member, he therefore outranked all his colleagues including Brezhnev. Reportedly, he refused to assume the party leadership upon Khrushchev's fall, an act of self-abnegation that, together with his reputation for modesty and austerity in his personal life, gave him immense prestige within the party oligarchy.[8]

In the Gorbachev era, Egor Ligachev has emerged as Suslov's heir, at least in terms of breadth of responsibility and seniority. On the other hand, Alexander Yakovlev has attained vastly more influence in the leadership over ideology and foreign policy than Mikhail Zimyanin ever had under Suslov, and is gradually replacing Ligachev as the "second secretary."[9]

Like Gorbachev, Ligachev has worked in both the party and Komsomol. Under Khrushchev he was deputy head of the agitation-propaganda department of the RSFSR before becoming the first secretary of the Tomsk obkom in 1965. In 1982 he took over the Organizational-Party Work Department of the Central Committee, and thus supervised the party nomenklatura system. At the December 1983 plenum—a time when Gorbachev was effectively carrying out Andropov's initiatives—Ligachev became a Central Committee secretary, an appointment that probably rewarded or cemented ties between the two. Then, at the April 1985 plenum, Ligachev was elevated to Politburo membership, evidently retaining general oversight of cadre selection while taking over responsibility for ideology (and being relieved of the Organizational-Party Work Department at the same time). His new status was demonstrated by his address to the graduates of the Academy of Social Sciences, flagship of the party education system, on 28 June 1985.[10] His report on organizational-party work at a Central Committee meeting on 26 July 1985 also encompassed ideological tasks.[11] On the other hand, Gorbachev has played an active part in ideology, repeatedly addressing, for example, the heads of major media organizations at conferences at the Central Committee.[12]

Meantime, without any apparent change in Ligachev's brief, Alexander Yakovlev has risen to a position from which he is setting general ideological policy, suggesting either an unresolved political contest between Yakovlev and Ligachev (a supposition supported by the marked differences between Yakovlev's radical revisionism and Ligachev's moderate conservatism) or a novel division of labor between them. Certainly Yakovlev's rise has been extraordinary. Less than a year after being named Central Committee secretary, he was elevated to candidate Politburo membership in January 1987, and to full membership status in June 1987. His statements on general ideological policy led issues both of *Kommunist* and *Partiinaia zhizn'* in May. His standing was indicated further by his inclusion in Gorbachev's party at the 1985, 1986, and 1987 summit meetings between President Reagan and General Secretary Gorbachev. During Gorbachev's stay in Washington in December 1987, for example, it is more than likely that it fell to Yakovlev to compose the numerous statements Gorbachev delivered to the press and to the various groups with whom he met. The scope of his responsibilities, which include both domestic and foreign policy, and the originality of his formulations, suggest that Yakovlev, rather than Ligachev, has become the active figure setting the general line in ideology.

The overlap between ideological and substantive policy issues means that other Central Committee departments besides the Propaganda Department routinely send directives to media organizations about coverage of their respective areas of responsibility. Functional departments provide specialized background information and guidance, often with the aim of generating favorable publicity for their branches.[13] In addition, the Propaganda Department holds periodic joint meetings with representatives of the branch departments to discuss the bearing of substantive policy on ideological work. An example is the economic education system, a spin-off of the party political schooling system that aims at improving understanding of economic policy on the part of managers. The Propaganda Department held a conference in September 1984 that brought deputy ministers and chairmen of state committees, the chairmen of the economic education councils of the union republics, and heads of media and ideological institutions together to discuss the economic education system.[14] Although Soviet sources do not provide any direct evidence on the point, it is clear that day-to-day advice to central media editors about their coverage is provided by the Propaganda Department.

The lines of control that converge in the Propaganda Department, the ideology secretary, and the "Suslov secretary" thus extend over a sizable network of specialized bureaucracies for theory, communications, and indoctrination. Altogether, Roy Medvedev estimates that at least one million persons work professionally in the areas of ideology and the social sciences.[15] Their reach is further extended into society by the efforts of a corps of around eleven million ideological activists, who serve as spare-time communicators and organizers. Before discussing the ideological aktiv, however, let us examine the ideological sector of the party below the central level.

Intermediate Levels

At lower levels of the party, the organizational structure of ideological work is simpler although similar in essential details to that of the center. Between the all-union and primary branches of party organization stand 14 union republic, 157 province, 10 circuit, 879 city, 641 urban district and 2,891 rural district committees (data as of 1 January 1984). At the lowest rung on the administrative ladder, which includes the party committees of rural and urban districts and some small cities, oversight of the primary party organizations (PPOs) in workplaces is the predominant form of party activity. At the next level up, a provincial party committee might oversee 25 or 30 rural district committees and 12 or more city committees in addition to the horizontally subordinate institutions. In each territorial committee, one secretary oversees ideological work, in that capacity supervising the department of agitation and propaganda. Although party committees vary to some degree in their organizational makeup, all committees have agitprop departments, just as all have departments for organizational-party work.[16] The departments do not have an elaborate structure: each has a head, at least one deputy head, section heads, a small reference staff, and one or more instructors. Staff officials are, however, backed up by a pool of nonstaff assistants comprising a "reserve nomenklatura."

The instructors are the department's legworkers. To them falls the task of liaison between the party committee and the organizations it supervises. Each instructor is assigned *(za nim zakrepleny)* so many lower party organizations to monitor. The form of contact is less that of direct line control than of clarifying, advising, listening, problem solving, message carrying, and general administrative support. These functions are expressed in the Russian verb used for such liaison, *kurirovat'*. Instructors are also often assigned functional duties, such as press and broadcasting, science and education, or youth, sports, or preinduction training. An instructor in an urban district in Kazan reported that his functional tasks included the mentorship movement (*nastavnichestvo*, a formalized practice of assisting new workers to acquire good work habits by assigning them a "big brother" from among the trusted, experienced members of the work force), crime prevention, mass-political work, the socialist "emulation" campaigns (that is, the sponsored competitions between units for the highest output or for other goals), and "propaganda of leading experience" (that is, dissemination of information about the methods used by successful enterprises to improve productivity). He explained that without extensive reliance on activists, he would be swamped.[17]

A valuable recent portrait of the work of party instructors conveys the message that the old definition of the instructor's task—to see to the implementation of party decisions—must now be broadened by adding to it responsibility for assistance in problem solving and goal attainment through direct involvement and assistance to lower party organizations.[18] The book's case studies make it clear, however, that instructors cannot successfully accomplish all that they are expected to do without resorting to established short-cuts and thus shortchanging the lower party organizations they are supposed to assist.

The instructors' administrative overload is one reason ideological work becomes routinized to the point of ossification. Despite numerous pleas from higher levels to make real conviction and real improvement of production the criteria of effective ideological work, both instructors and the PPOs they oversee find it far more satisfactory to assess ideological work in terms of stable and predictable procedures, especially those that can be measured quantitatively. Best of all are plans, where categories and numbers of measures to be taken can be recorded, approved, and checked off as they are fulfilled; so, until around 1981, when quantitative indicators fell into disfavor, party organizations demonstrated the vigor of their ideological work by reporting figures on attendance at meetings, enrollment in theory courses, activists recruited, lectures read, and campaign themes covered. These, in turn, were readily aggregated and reported up the chain of party command as indicators of the success of party work.

The flow of "paper rain" these routines generate is remarkable. On average, the agitation-propaganda department of an obkom sends down to its subordinate committees about one order, instruction, directive, or decree per day, a rate that party authorities recognize to be absurd and counterproductive.[19] By far the greatest part of the instructors' work is taken up with the purely administrative side of ideological supervision: gathering and summarizing the quantitative indices of performances that subordinates submit, receiving and issuing instructions, preparing reports and reference materials for the use of superiors, and attending meetings.[20] Clearly the weak link in the system of formal party control over ideological life, the instructor's role as the interface between the lowest level of territorial party organization and the primary organizations of the party would be impossible were there not other means for developing and sustaining internalized political control over communicators.

Specialization in ideological work inevitably entails bureaucratization. Whether performed on a "public," nonstaff basis, or as a function of a government or public organization, communication and indoctrination follow clearly delineated lines of responsibility. In the workplace, agitation groups or agitation collectives are headed by leaders through whom the party officials in charge of mass-political work can issue instructions and monitor feedback. Likewise, each media organization vests final responsibility in its chief editor, who is backed up by the editorial board (redaktsiia). The editor maintains close working ties with both the secretary of the corresponding party committee for ideological matters and, to a lesser extent, with the first secretary (the editor normally seems to rank somewhere between them). Some localities also sponsor a "house of political enlightenment" to serve as a base for the political education system and to maintain offices, reference facilities, and support staff of research assistants. This institution falls under the jurisdiction of the agitprop department as well.

The decline of ideological vitality in the society has tended to obscure awareness of the centrality of ideological work among the party's regular duties. One survey that analyzed the issues discussed by the bureaus of city and district party committees over a two-and-one-half year period determined that ideological work represented the single largest category; another sizable proportion consisted of questions of education and oversight of mass organizations. Together, these three accounted for one-third of all matters considered by the party committees, as is shown in table 1.

In no other area of party work is the disproportion between the importance of the subject and the number of staff officials handling it so great as in the ideological sector. Whereas over one-third of the matters dealt with by the surveyed bureaus concerned indoctrination and communications, the ideological staff comprised perhaps one-fifth of the total staff employed by the CPSU as a whole.

To estimate the number of officials in the agitprop departments of territorial party committees, it is possible to extrapolate from some fragmentary figures in the Soviet literature. It was reported that in Rostov oblast in 1976 there were approximately 400 staff officials employed in agitation-propaganda departments in party committees at various levels. In the slightly smaller Dnepropetrovsk oblast of the Ukraine, there were 360 staff ideological officials at the various levels of the party hierarchy.[21] Cheliabinsk, with a roughly similar population, employs 430 staff officials for ideology.[22] These figures suggest a certain range for the number of paid ideology staff for each level of party

TABLE 1   Issues Raised at Meetings of Bureau of City and District Party Committees, Cheliabinsk Province, 1971–1973

	Number	Percent
Ideology[a]	912	19.0
Education	265	5.5
Direction of mass organizations	444	9.2
Organizational-party work	829	17.0
Production, construction, transportation	251	5.2
Agriculture	566	11.8
Other	1,536	32.0
Total	4,803	99.7

Source: M. Nenashev, Ratsional'naia organizatsiia ideologicheskoi raboty (Moscow: Sovetskaia Rossiia, 1976), p. 60.
Note: Discrepancies in the reporting of the survey suggest that these figures be used only as broad indicators.
a. The ideology category includes mass agitation work and political education.

organization. In Rostov province there are some 78 lower territorial units with party committees (that is, rural and urban districts and cities). In Cheliabinsk province there are 55, in Dnepropetrovsk, 57. A first step is therefore possible if one estimates the number of officials per party committee. A 1976 report indicated that in Krasnodar krai each raikom employs 4–5 staff ideology officials.[23] A department head, 1 or 2 deputies heading sectors, and 1 or 2 instructors suffice. In addition, it was noted that the rural districts in the province employ 49 instructors among them. Since Krasnodar krai had (as of 1983) 44 rural raions, our estimate of 1 or, at most, 2 instructors per raion is plausible. City committees have somewhat larger full-time agitprop departments; it was reported that the Shakhty city committee of Rostov oblast in 1982 had 7 staff members.[24] As far as higher levels of the party apparatus are concerned, it is known that the agitation-propaganda department of the Ukrainian Central Committee employs 40 staff officials. Finally, for the employees of the all-union Central Committee Propaganda Department, "A. Pravdin," it will be recalled, gives a figure of 48–51 responsible staff positions.[25] Certainly this figure tallies with the others cited.

If one interpolates the per unit estimates into the known breakdowns of territorial subdivisions of Rostov, Cheliabinsk, and Dnepropetrovsk provinces and compares the total obtained against the known totals, the estimates are within range but not exact. (For Rostov the expected range is 378–456 as against the given figure of 400. For Dnepropetrovsk, though, the expected total is 285–342 whereas the given total is 360. And for Cheliabinsk the expected figure is 329–391 whereas the total is 430.) Evidently, therefore, some territorial committees employ more (or fewer) than the norm. Very likely the reason for this has to do with the number of PPOs that the district and city committees supervise. Perhaps the party rules permit so many full-time staff to be hired per number of PPOs or per number of party members in the work force. If total population represents a rough surrogate for these figures, then one would expect some correspondence between population and staff size, and indeed such is the case. In Rostov oblast, the population is about 4 million as compared to the 400 staff officials (a ratio of 10,000:1). In Dnepopetrovsk oblast the ratio applies rather well: 3.67 million population as compared to 360 staff officials. But in Cheliabinsk oblast, with a population of 3.46 million, the ideology staff is unexpectedly large, at 430 officials.

Using the per capita and per unit methods as alternative methods of extrapolating a total figure for ideological staff throughout the CPSU yields very similar results (see table 2). The population in 1982 was approximately 270 million; the 10,000:1 ratio suggests 27,000 staff workers in ideology. The upper range obtained by the per unit method yields roughly the same number.

To this total should be added another 4,500 or so full-time secretaries specializing in ideological work. If these figures reflect the approximate size of the ideological sector within the party, then it is possible to estimate the proportion of total party apparatus made up by this group. In Vologda oblast, the 32 city and district party committees employed 255 instructors in 1983, or about 8 per unit. Moscow's 32 district committees employed about 800 instructors, or 25 each—which is probably the upper limit. The city party committee in Dzhambul employed 23 instructors; the city and district committees in Kustanai oblast, 192. Further evidence on the total size of the party staff is provided by the figure of 20–25 given in a *Partiinaia zhizn'* article for the average size of party staffs in the city and district committee organizations of Kaluga province.[26] If the normal district

TABLE 2   Estimated Party Ideology Staff, 1982

Level of Party Organization	No. of Units in USSR	Average No. of Officials per Unit	Total
City district	631	4–5	2,524–3,155
Rural district	2,855	4–5	11,420–14,275
City	874	7–8	6,118–6,992
Province (oblast, krai, and okrug)[a]	168	10	1,680
Republic	14	40	560
All-union	1	50	50
Total			22,352–26,712

Source: Compiled by the author.
a. Also includes Moscow and Kiev, the city party committees of which have the status of oblast committees.

party committee employs 7–8 instructors, and the ideological department 1 or 2, and the ratios of higher-level staff officials remain constant, then nationally the ideological sector comprises no more than
15–25 percent of the party apparatus.

Though neither the 1:10,000 benchmark ratio of staff officials to
population nor the per unit extrapolation method yields a perfect
estimate of the total number of ideology staff, they do yield convergent
results. It is reasonable to suppose that some formula taking into
account the size of the population or work force, or the number of PPOs
to be overseen, or all of these, is used by the party in determining how
many staff positions are authorized for any given party organization.
Since it is a point both of doctrinal pride and of fiscal control to restrict
the growth of the party apparatus as much as possible, the small size of
the ideological sector of the party is doubtless a product of the most
deliberate policy controls. Indeed, strong evidence indicates that it is
precisely because of strict budget limits that unpaid staff positions are
created to complement the regular staff. Philip Stewart found that the
recruitment of such nonstaff or volunteer instructors in Stalingrad
oblast in the late 1950s was, in fact, a response to the mandated
reduction in the paid staff of party committees that took place between
1956 and 1958.[27] Brezhnev may have brought about further reductions,
because he boasted at the Twenty-fourth Party Congress (1971) that,
whereas the party's membership had doubled in the previous fourteen
years, the "staff of the party apparatus had been reduced by over
20%."[28] If we had full access to the data, we would probably find that,
as the number of full-time staff fell or remained constant, the growing
complexity of ideological work as an administrative responsibility of
the party prompted an increasing reliance on the aktiv.

"A. Pravdin" said that the 50 or so paid staff officials in the Central
Committee apparatus were backed up by another 35 nonstaff officials.
Similarly, in Dnepropetrovsk province, the 360 paid staff officials were
supplemented by another 200 nonstaff officials. These individuals are
named by the city and district committees and are regarded as a pool of
potential replacements for paid staff. When a job falling under the
nomenklatura opens up, such as that of head of an agitation-
propaganda department or staff instructor, the back-up instructors,
who have been trained and groomed for these positions, are available

for appointment. The party maintains files on them, monitors their performance, and treats them as a second line of staff officials.[29]

Recruitment of the unpaid backstoppers to become party officials, a practice found in all departments of party committees, has become highly institutionalized in recent years. Harasymiw believes that, after a protracted period of dormancy, the reserve nomenklatura system was revived in the late 1960s and has become so formal a part of the regular system for managing nomenklatura appointments that the reserve is usually formalized in a list of potential appointees called the *uchetnaia nomenklatura*.[30] The reserve nomenklatura is treated as a traineeship as much as a form of public service; indeed, this quality of preparation for eventual promotion is probably what distinguishes inclusion in the reserve nomenklature from ordinary unpaid administrative duties. Those added to the reserve list are assigned to internships on party committees, where they back up staff instructors and are expected to attend political school, all the while, presumably, being paid by their place of work.[31]

Since turnover is very high among party instructors, committees are acutely aware of the need for trained and qualified replacements. As a result, many committees strive to keep 2 or 3 reserve cadres on hand for every nomenklatura position. Some, however, fail to have even an average of 1 backup per staff position. A recent *Pravda* editorial chided a raikom in Tadzhikistan for keeping only 30 persons available for 422 executive positions in the district. Harasymiw estimates that there are 1–2 persons eligible for every regular position in the nomenklatura of party organizations.[32] The recruitment of a reserve pool of candidates for advancement to party staff positions from the larger network of party activists makes a virtue out of necessity; it helps party officials escape the burdensome restrictions of budget limits by hiring, in effect, off-line staff personnel, who in turn acquire specialized on-the-job training for party administration work.

The implications of this practice for ideological work are quite significant. First, it means that a sizable proportion of those who perform spare-time duties for the party and who accordingly demonstrate the party's mass character are, in function and no doubt outlook as well, closer to the full-time party officials whom they will replace than to the members of the work force where they are nominally employed. If Harasymiw's figure of 1–2 reserve cadres for every staff position is accurate (and the figures cited above for the ideological sector suggest that it may be high), then the estimated number of 27,000 ideology officials would have to be doubled or tripled to give a rough measure of the true size of the party ideological apparatus.

If one examines the recruitment of reserve cadres into staff positions over time, an even more striking pattern of integration between party staff and other institutions becomes apparent. Moves by activists into junior positions in the party apparatus, followed after two or three years by a transfer to a staff position in a party, government, or other organization are common, particularly for younger personnel. This observation is supported by the data on turnover among instructors. Experience as a party instructor seems to be equivalent to an expected tour of duty, for ticket-punching purposes, in a high-pressure, low-prestige post, the bottom rung of the local party nomenklatura. A major reason for high turnover rates is that instructors are themselves treated as a primary pool of eligible candidates for recruitment to executive positions in the party nomenklatura. For example, in one raikom in Belorussia over a three-year period, eleven staff members of the apparatus, almost 50 percent, were moved into executive positions in party, soviet, and economic organizations. A secretary of the Kazakh party organization even calls instructors the main pool of candidates for advancement to executive posts.[33] However, rates of turnover are frequently too high to suit party officials, a fact that suggests that the undesirable nature of the job is also a factor. In Moscow, for example, fewer than one-half of the instructors of raikoms have worked in their jobs for more than three years (at the level of the city committee, the figure is about one-half). As a result of the attempt by Moscow's city committee to stabilize the rates, turnover is slowly declining.

A consequence of high turnover is youthful staffs. Over 60 percent of Moscow's instructors are thirty-five years old and younger; lower-level committees have even younger staffs. In Vologda province, almost 70 percent of the instructors are under forty. They tend to have had experience in party or Komsomol work before service as instructor, however. In Moscow 60 percent of the instructors have served as secretaries of their primary and shop organizations and been members of committees and bureaus of lower party organizations. The number that had been under "reserve" control must therefore have been high. But many then seek to improve their lot. The head of the organiza-

tional-party work department of the Buriat obkom reports having seen
the staff of instructors in his department undergo complete turnover
three times in the last five years.[34]

Turnover among activists and staff members tends to reinforce
career specialization rather than undermine it. Specialization in
ideological work begins in the PPO, where the deputy secretary normally takes responsibility for coordinating the many channels of
intraworkplace indoctrination, working through a group of activist
employees who take on functions of agitation, propaganda, political
information, and other types of communication and political work.
Outside the party, the ideology career track includes managerial work
in the mass media, the Komsomol, and the culture and education
organs of local government.[35] Careful analysis of career patterns of
members of obkom bureaus led Joel Moses to conclude:

> Closed and patterned careers are even the more predictable lot of
> ideological specialists. On obkom bureaux the ideological
> specialists can be defined by those interchangeably assigned to be
> obkom ideology secretary, editor of the regional newspaper, or first
> secretary of the regional Komsomol. Prior to their bureau election,
> the careers of ideological specialists are already set by their promi-
> nence in positions normally associated with implementing vari-
> ous facets of ideological policy: director of regional publishing,
> movies, cultural departments or deputy chairman for education-
> culture in the oblispolkom; head of the obkom propaganda-
> agitation or science-educational institutions department; urban or
> regional Komsomol secretary; or party secretary for a borough in
> which strategic scientific-cultural institutes and many cultural
> intelligentsia reside. Reassigned from a region, ideological
> specialists reasonably can expect to find themselves only in posi-
> tions for which their career specialization allegedly prepares
> them: secretary in the union-republic Komsomol, minister of
> publishing affairs, deputy editor of an All-Union newspaper, or
> department head of propaganda in the All-Union Central Com-
> mittee.[36]

My own study of appointments to media organizations between 1974
and 1986 indicates that 36 percent of all those appointed as chief

executives over that thirteen-year period had had experience at some point as staff members of party committees. For 1986, this figure was 56 percent.

Specialization in the ideological area of party work, as John Armstrong pointed out in his 1959 study of party administrators, is cultivated by intense training in doctrinal theory and the burden of responsibility for a distinct and central sphere of party work. Armstrong found evidence that indoctrination specialists formed a relatively closed group, with a sense of vocational solidarity that was reinforced by the tendency for line officials (in charge of production, for example) to look down upon "men of the word."[37] Career mobility across institutional lines shows a pattern in a common area of responsibility that helps cement a shared vocational outlook as well as awareness of belonging to the larger membership of the political elite.

So, though at any given time the number of full-time officials employed by territorial party committees in ideological work is small, this fact alone can be misleading. The party staff is backed up by an equally large pool of reserve cadres sharing a common political orientation. Further, high circulation across occupational lines within ideological work tends to consolidate ties between party officials, activists, and executives in the media, education, culture, and youth work by creating a common career background. These factors tend to make ideology a distinct and identifiable branch of party work extending into a broad range of related institutions.

In the end, of course, the point of ideological work is its impact on society. Since the greatest share of direct personal contact with rank-and-file citizens is conducted by workplace activists, it is time to turn to the primary level of the system.

The Primary Level

In the more than two million labor collectives of the USSR, responsibility for coordinating ideological work is vested in the PPOs and their constituent elements, shop committees and party groups. The deputy PPO secretary takes charge of organizing it and works through the heads of the groups performing the main forms of indoctrination and communication: agitation, political information, lectures, reports, and political education or propaganda. Together, these and other forms of ideological work addressed to general audiences comprise mass-political work. Some links in the propaganda system, since they are targeted at activists and officials, lie outside mass-political work, and some mass-political work reaches the population at places of residence. The "center of gravity," however, as party writers put it, of mass-political work is the workplace, and current party policy calls for intensifying the attention given to it as the main focus.[38]

The many forms that mass-political work takes today stem initially from agitation. Historically, the distinguishing elements of agitation's content were emotionality, simplicity, and orientation to action. Though not all agitation was or is oral, the personal influence of the agitator and direct interaction beween speaker and audience have always been crucial features of the setting. As party ideological work developed, the informational component of agitation gained ground at the expense of pure exhortation and led to the institution of new types of mass-political work. The term *agitation* today applies to short, pointed addresses delivered in person by activists in the workplace or residential neighborhood. Extraordinary efforts are made to organize agitation in the remotest work sites, even among the groups of workers flown in to the Tiumen oil and gas fields.[39]

A defining feature of agitation is the small size of the audience. Nearly one-half of the agitators polled in one survey worked with groups of eleven to twenty-five persons, the commonest range.[40] Agitators are usually drawn from the work force of the enterprise where they conduct their agitation in order to reinforce their political message with their personal authority. Indeed, though many agitators are not party members, nearly all hold positions of influence within their workplaces. A study of agitators in a Dnepropetrovsk industrial association found that they were primarily shop foremen, brigade leaders, and other "middle-rung leaders" *(rukovoditeli srednego zvena)*, of whom three-quarters were party members.[41] Residential agitation, conducted at "agitation points" in apartment complexes, tends to be more sporadic and clusters most frequently at times of elections to the soviets.[42] In the workplaces, agitation usually centers on production themes, such as socialist emulation campaigns.

In the Brezhnev period another form of face-to-face communication, called political information, arose.[43] Agitation can be carried out by an individual who lacks any political expertise and whose educational level is little higher than that of the audience. The concrete and hortatory character of the message does not require knowledge in depth or theoretical sophistication. Political information was developed to provide similar audiences with speakers who had had special training to give informative talks and to respond to questions about political affairs more knowledgeably and confidently. A recent definition notes that political information "especially covers facts, events, and phenomena of the political aspect of social life—relations among classes, nations, states. It includes economic and social events that have political significance."[44] Like agitation sessions, political information talks tend to be short (fifteen to twenty minutes, thirty at most) and to occur at the end of the work day, although in some enterprises they may be offered at the start of a shift, during it, or during the lunch break. Some party committees combine political information talks with social evenings.[45] Since the party divides political information into four branches—national policy, international affairs, the economy, and culture—many party committees work out a schedule whereby speakers specializing in each branch rotate visits, often on a one-talk-per-week basis or once every two weeks.[46] A survey conducted in the late 1960s found that nearly one-half of the political information talks concerned international affairs, and about one-quarter concerned domestic policy.[47]

The political information speaker is given guidance by the party committee of the enterprise or the local agitation-propaganda department. Houses of political enlightenment help prepare reference aids and lecture notes. I once came across an example of such a lecture aid, a mimeographed document of about thirty pages entitled "The Current Moment (Material to aid reporters, lecturers, and political information specialists)" and prepared by the house of political enlightenment of the Leningrad provincial and city party committees. It offers a review of current domestic and international developments for the month of May 1974. It offers speakers both facts and ways of presenting them. Speakers using the material can choose portions for elaboration. Each piece of information is related to a larger pattern of events, the driving force of which is the continuous progress of socialism and national liberation in the face of opposing imperialist and reactionary forces. Individual data are selected that are consistent with the underlying principles, but in themselves, many are relatively accurate and objective, if often piquant and anecdotal. The material illustrates the interest that can attach to political information as an alternative channel of information to the print and broadcast media because, after a stylized tribute to Lenin and the regime at the beginning, it offers relatively fuller and more objective information than can normally be found in less ephemeral media, and it gives listeners the chance to ply the speaker with questions afterward.

Another primary form of political work is the "report," designed for occasions such as "unified political days," "open letter days," and "Lenin Fridays." The common element in reports is the use of ranking party, government, trade union, managerial, and other officials as speakers. Normally each participating official is assigned a particular site, and all speak on a single predetermined theme. In Saratov oblast, for example, on one such day, 8,000 speakers addressed a total of 600,000 people (nearly one-quarter of the population of the province).[48] In many areas the unified political day has become a regular monthly event.

Employment of executives and specialists to speak is intended to lend the information additional credibility, and the selection of a single topic reinforces the impact of particular ideological campaigns. It also reduces the thematic variation and unintended leakage that might occur otherwise if so many speakers addressed so many different audiences on a variety of topics. These talks help foster the impression of contact between rulers and masses, and they serve as another channel of feedback for the party authorities. After each report, speakers summarize the questions that were asked, forwarding the results to the agitation-propaganda department. The staff compares a number of such summaries, and the analysis is then transmitted to appropriate government agencies and higher party offices.[49] Study of the feedback is a useful gauge of the temper of the people in different workplaces and communities; low morale in one enterprise is likely to stand out more clearly when all audiences throughout the jurisdiction have been exposed to the same information on the same topic. It is understandable, therefore, that the party has encouraged the development of the report form.

Similar in structure is the open letter day sponsored by newspapers and television stations. In preparation for it, a media organization solicits questions and comments from the public. It then calls upon officials from party, government, and other organizations to respond to the readers' queries at a large open meeting. The sponsoring organization publicizes the meeting in advance and follows up afterward on the questions raised and answers given. A newspaper may carry a series of subsequent articles to ensure that official promises are kept.[50] For example, in two Estonian cities where open letter days were held, the impending event was heavily publicized by the press. The sponsoring newspapers set up suggestion boxes in many locations, inviting citizens to submit complaints, questions, and suggestions on issues such as local services, cultural amenities, and public order. Then, on the appointed day, a large open meeting of the city party committee was held, at which the first secretary of the *gorkom* analyzed the content of the responses received. Afterward the party sent bulletins summarizing the information on particular topics to the appropriate organizations.[51]

Party organizations vary in the degree to which they impose formal organization on the practice of reports. Some gather speakers into "reporters' groups" and even break these down by topical specialty. One oblast, for example, has 1,700 groups of speakers at the disposal of the local party committees, offering 11,000 speakers in all. In the course of one year, they gave 17,000 addresses to 1.2 million persons, on such topics as "the Leninist path to communism" and "the Twenty-fifth Party Congress."[52] In Penza province all heads of departments of party committees and many local government officials, trade union officials, and other figures are numbered as reporters for one or another party committee. This means that once a month, when the oblast holds a unified political day, all go out and speak.[53] A smaller number of them (around 8,000) were recruited to serve as political information specialists, a fact that suggests both that this is a more restrictive category and that it calls for somewhat more preparation. In Saratov oblast, one raion committee has about 40 reporters on its rolls. It divides them into four groups, each headed by a secretary of the party committee or a government official. The party committee maintains a chart showing how many speeches each group has made, and it uses the group to monitor the questions and responses received from the audiences.[54]

Related to reports are the lectures offered under the auspices of the Znanie (Knowledge) Society, which is equivalent to a nationwide speakers' bureau. Znanie began as a body of volunteer speakers recruited to conduct atheistic propaganda by opposing religious belief with scientific knowledge. Today atheism is only one of the categories of lectures given by Znanie speakers; a large variety of popular scientific as well as directly political themes are covered. One of every nine or ten talks concerns laws; this is considered one of the more popular categories of lectures.[55] The society's activity extends beyond lectures to publishing: it puts out some 150 million copies annually of books, magazines, and brochures.

The reported numbers of lectures given are impressive but subject to inflated reporting. Some 100,000 lectures are given annually in Pskov oblast. On average, 7.3 million lectures are given every year in the Ukraine.[56] Probably 25–26 million lectures are given annually in the Soviet Union as a whole.[57]

Like all forms of mass-political work, lectures assume highly standardized formats. Those treating social and political themes tend to have a normative style, somewhat like a newspaper editorial, giving a general assessment of a particular issue followed by a turn to critical particulars signaled by the famous semantic transition odnako ("however"). The negative factual material then gives way to an upbeat conclusion about prospects for the future. The typical length for a lecture is an hour, after which the speaker answers questions from the floor. The team surveying ideological work and communications in Taganrog in the late 1960s found a characteristic pattern of combining positive and negative treatment of subject matter. Virtually all references to the United States and other capitalist states were negative (nine out of ten evaluative and factual statements were unfavorable) whereas nearly all references to the USSR overall were positive (87 percent). Yet when the lecturers dealt with matters concerning the locality of their audiences, the factual material was likely to be negative, and on questions of private life and the family, the material was overwhelmingly negative (92 percent). This is because lectures treat social problems, such as alcoholism and the stubborn resilience of religious faith.[58]

Most organized lectures fall under the Znanie Society's aegis while forming part of the corresponding party committee's ideological plan. (The proportion is suggested by the fact that in Cheliabinsk oblast in 1976, 300,000 lectures were given, of which 280,000 were organized under the Znanie Society.)[59] The Znanie Society enrolls about 3 million members, of whom over 50 percent are party members. However, one survey found that only 33 percent of the members actually gave lectures. Another survey found that a small minority of the total enrolled membership of the Znanie Society—about 14 or 15 percent —gave 50 percent of all lectures.[60] Unionwide, this would mean that a highly active lecturer gives about 30 lectures per year, or about one every twelve days. Like other types of public activity, particularly those in the ideological field, lecturing is a good deal less widely distributed than reported participation figures would indicate. However, lecturers do receive a nominal fee for their efforts, which may spur participation.

Attendance is also very unevenly distributed among the population. Many citizens attend lectures frequently, but others never attend at all. A survey in Cheliabinsk oblast of 2,000 persons found 20.5 percent who had not attended a lecture in the past year, 24 percent who attended one or two, 46.7 percent who had attended for three to ten, and 9.6 percent who attended over ten lectures. The researchers sought to learn the reasons for nonattendance. Of those who had not attended, 43.5 percent explained that none were available.[61] In contrast to forms such as agitation, political information, and reports, lectures achieve lower coverage of the population, principally because most are held outside the workplace. The desire to saturate the environment with a mutually reinforcing system of information and persuasion is one reason the party lays such stress on capturing the labor collective for ideological work.

THE IDEOLOGICAL AKTIV

Although it has now leveled off and even dropped slightly, the number of ideological activists expanded dramatically in the 1950s, 1960s, and 1970s. At the close of the Stalin era, there were perhaps 2.5–3.5 million ideological activists. Through the 1950s and 1960s, this aktiv grew at an average annual rate of 3.5–4.5 percent, reaching around 7–8 million by

1970. Through the 1970s the nominal expansion continued at a rate of 4–5 percent on average per year before leveling off around 1981. Most recently, a 1985 report by M. F. Nenashev indicates that there are around 11 million ideological activists altogether: 2.2 million propagandists, around 3.7 million agitators, 1.8 million political information speakers, more than 3 million Znanie Society lecturers, and 300,000 reporters.[62]

Of course the number of regular speakers is far smaller, because of the tendency on the part of local party committee to inflate reports of participation in ideological work. Some list every pep talk by a manager to the workers as a lecture. Many individuals listed as activists perform multiple tasks and so may be counted twice in these totals; far more, perhaps in excess of one-third, are purely nominal participants. A survey, for example, of the Cheliabinsk Tractor Association found that one-third of those employees listed as having social assignments did not, in fact, carry them out.[63] If, then, as is reported, leading work collectives boast that 10 percent of the labor force perform spare-time ideological assignments, the average figure throughout the country must be closer to 8 percent, and regular participants may number fewer than half that.[64]

In fact, the decline in reported totals of ideological activists after 1982 must be attributed to a decision made at the highest levels of the party leadership to end the growth of the ideological aktiv and to end the substitution of quantitative for qualitative criteria for evaluating mass-political work. An allusion to such a decision is made by the ideological secretary of a Leningrad raikom, who wrote that, after the 1981 Central Committee resolution on improving the party education system, the raikom passed along instructions to PPO secretaries and enterprise heads to cease their efforts to expand the number of listeners enrolled in the political education system (they were told in particular to end the recruitment of nonmembers of the party), and instead to improve the quality of instruction. As a result some 7,000 persons. most of them pensioners, were dropped from the party education system.[65] At the beginning of the 1980s, the new watchword became "better fewer, but better." Pravda ceased carrying proud reports of growing numbers of speakers and listeners; quantitative data are hardly reported at all. Gorbachev's leadership has strongly continued the new retrenchment. The last sentence of a *Pravda* editorial in September 1985 read, "And, in organizing, directing, and developing [ideological work], it is necessary to proceed from the fact that the basic indicator of the effectiveness of upbringing efforts is not at all the number of measures conducted but the actual influence on the consciousness and mood of Soviet people, on their position in life."[66] It is well to remember, though, that retrenchment phases in the past have been followed by new phases of expansion.

Although the figures on ideological activism are hardly exact, their precise magnitude is far less important than two undeniable observations about them. First, however ritualistic this activity is, and regardless of the actual significance either speakers or listeners attach to it, it is carried out on a very large scale: it involves a very sizable proportion of the adult population as activists and virtually all as audience. Second, the growth in the size of the aktiv, however much it is discounted for padding, came about by coopting a large number of members of the country's social and political elites to ideological work. As a result, at higher rungs on the ladder of social and political responsibility, individuals are more likely to take part in some form of ideological work: levels of sociopolitical status are closely correlated with incidence of public activism, and at higher levels of sociopolitical status, activism is likelier to take the form of ideological work. It is also the case, however, that the larger the number of social assignments an individual takes on, the likelier it is that some are nominal; a corollary finding is that the larger the number of activists recorded by a particular party organization, the greater the probability that many of them are fictitious.[67]

Soviet surveys report characteristic rates of participation in public activity as around 40–60 percent for all people employed in the industrial sector (rates vary widely from enterprise to enterprise), 60–80 percent for managerial and technical staff, and 80–nearly 100 percent for the top echelon of the intelligentsia. A survey in one city, for example, found that about 50 percent of the population employed in service occupations had social assignments, as did about 66 percent of the managerial, technical, and administrative staff of enterprises and institutions, and over 80 percent of the intelligentsia.[68] A survey of Dnepropetrovsk found that 61 percent of the work force in industrial enterprises had public work assignments: 80 percent of the ITRs and 55 percent of the manual workers participated. Among the workers, 66 percent of highly skilled workers as against 41 percent of low-skill workers did public work. Among specialists, 39 percent performed ideological assignments, as against 28 percent of highly skilled workers, 13.5 percent of moderately skilled workers, and 10 percent of low-skill workers.[69] A study of coal mining in Rostov province found that participation rates rise monotonically with levels of job skill and occupational responsibility, with education, and with earnings. (These factors are of course intercorrelated.) For example, the likelihood that an individual earning less than 100 rubles per month was taking part in public activity was five times less than that of an individual earning 250–300 rubles per month. The average low-skill worker spent 1 hour 13 minutes per week on public work in 1976; a skilled worker 2 hours 47 minutes; a highly skilled worker 3 hours 17 minutes; and a member of the engineering-technical staff 3 hours 44 minutes.[70]

A survey of two scientific research institutes in Moscow found that only 1.4 percent of the scientists had no social assignment and, of those with assignments, over 20 percent were propagandists. In some regions, all heads of institutions serve as propagandists. A survey of Vologda province found that 90 percent of the executive, engineering-technical, and specialist staff were enrolled in some form of ideological work, many, for example, by becoming reporters.[71] Since the aim of political days and like events is to turn out local officials to address the public directly, it is not surprising that virtually all high-status individuals are called upon at one time or another to deliver a report. Among ordinary ITRs participation rates in ideological work usually fall between 30 and 40 percent.[72]

The overlap between the sociopolitical elite and the ideological *aktiv* suggests that the stratification of status corresponds to the hierarchy of forms of political work. The type of ideological effort demanding the greatest theoretical competence is political education, so it is logical that executives and specialists dominate the corps of propagandists. M. V. Zimiamin reported that in 1984, 33 percent of the country's propagandists were ranking economic managers. Of the 31,500 propagandists active in Belorussia in 1975, 12,000 were economic specialists; 8,300 were scientists and academics; 7,200 were heads of

enterprises and institutions; and 1,700 were party and Komsomol officials. In Penza province, 70 percent of the propagandists are "executives, engineering-technical personnel, and specialists."[73] It seems reasonable to estimate that as many as 75 percent of the more than 2
million propagandists are managers, engineers, technicians, and other
specialists in government, economic, research, educational, and other
establishments; and that 50 percent or more of the individuals in these
categories carry out some form of ideological work.[74]

If senior managers, scholars, and specialists predominate among
propagandists, middle-rung specialists and supervisors frequently become political information speakers. Party members comprise a higher
proportion of political information speakers than of agitators (70 percent for political information speakers, 60 percent for agitators).[75]
Fewer blue-collar workers serve as political information speakers than
as agitators. In Amur oblast 70 percent of the political information
speakers are managers and specialists, whereas the agitation groups are
mainly composed of leading workers and middle-level managers from
enterprises and farms. A survey of Dnepropetrovsk oblast in 1979 found
that most political information speakers were managerial and technical personnel, whereas the proportion of agitators who were workers
had risen in the late 1970s by about 10 percent to just over 50 percent.[76]
The proportions of agitators and political information speakers who
were party members had risen by a similar percentage, a figure that
suggests that most of the newly recruited worker-agitators were drawn
from among party members.

Social status is a strong determinant of the likelihood that an individual will serve as an ideological activist, but so too, independently, is
party membership. To be sure, party membership rates are, as the
research of Harasymiw and others has shown, correlated with social
status, since the party is concerned to recruit individuals in positions of
prestige and influence, those in controlling positions in society and
particularly those in vital branches, and those with highest levels of
education.[77] But membership rates are also affected by recruitment
principles having to do with the desired intake of women, national
minorities, workers, and other social categories representative of the
general population. Some of these counteract the tendency for the
party to recruit most heavily from among high-status groups.

Harasymiw observes that higher social status is the motor of recruitment into the party: manual workers in higher skill brackets and white-collar employees in higher-status occupations are likelier to become members. Education is also a strong determinant of selection. But the party's policy of maintaining a high intake of blue-collar workers, combined with the rapid growth of the most highly educated strata in society, may lead to what Harasymiw calls a problem of underrepresentation of the intelligentsia.[78] Party membership, therefore, since it is not a perfect mirror of the ladder of status and power in society, and specifically because of the requirement that each party member assume one or more spare-time social obligations, partly undercuts the correlation between social status and ideological activism.

Thus the rapid postwar growth of the specialist segment of the labor force, and within it, of the ITR stratum, explains most of the expansion of the ideological aktiv over the same period. Soviet data indicate that although the growth of the industrial labor force slowed by the end of the 1970s, the ITRs were the fastest-growing segment, rising from 8.3 percent in 1950 to 14 percent in 1982.[79] As table 3 shows, total employment in the state sector of the economy grew less than three and one half times between 1941 and 1983, while the number of specialists in the economy grew around thirteen times and the increase of the ITR stratum was over eighteen-fold.

The cooptation of engineers, managers, and other specialists into the ideological aktiv is therefore best explained by a combination of push and pull factors, to use Harasymiw's terms. Their recruitment was the object of a concerted effort by the party, which also drew them into the party as members at rates faster than they were being added to the labor force despite the much slower growth of party membership itself. Although many members take on assignments outside the ideological sphere, this fact is offset by the recruitment of nonparty skilled workers and lower technical personnel as agitators and political information officers. Both the trends in party recruitment and the expansion of the ideological aktiv reflect the party's interest in ensuring that as many as possible of the executives and specialists in each enterprise help extend its influence over the micro-milieu of the labor collective.

Administrative Service

Party management of mass-political work demands an extensive machinery for planning and coordination as well as for information gathering and processing, much of it performed by nonstaff activists who often are formed into groups overseen by an ideological commission. The commission is the usual overarching body in an enterprise or territorial jurisdiction linking the many activist groups conducting political work. The ideological commission of a large factory in Minsk oversees the reference group, the sociological survey group, a body planning coordination and control, the section for culture and sports, the section for the prevention of crime and alcohol abuse, the group overseeing mass participation in management, the group overseeing mass-political work, the "05 Service" (a dictating machine used as a suggestion box), a group of ideological consultants, and a group respon-

TABLE 3   Growth of Labor Force (in millions and indexed to 1941)

	1941	1960	1970	1980	1983
All workers and employees (*sluzhashchie*)[a]	33.9 (100)	62.0 (183)	90.2 (266)	112.5 (332)	116.0 (342)
Specialists[b]	2.4 (100)	8.8 (367)	16.8 (700)	28.6 (1192)	31.6 (1317)
Specialists[c]	—	7.9	14.8	—	—
ITRs[d]	0.77 (100)	—	7.8 (1013)	—	14.1 (1831)

a. Excludes collective farmers. Employees include clerical, service and office workers, including specialists. Sources: *Narodnoe khoziaistvo SSSR 1922–1982* (Moscow: Finansy i statistika, 1982), pp. 399–401; *Narodnoe khoziaistvo SSSR v 1984* (Moscow: Finansy i statistika, 1985), pp. 409–11. Figures in 1941 column actually refer to 1940.
b. Specialists are those with specialized secondary or higher education working as specialists in the economy. Sources: *Narodnoe khoziaistvo SSSR 1922–1982*, p. 407; 1983 figure taken from V. I. Ivanov et al., eds., *Razvitie sotsial'noi struktury obshchestva v SSSR: Aktual'nye problemy sotsiologicheskikh issledovanii* (Moscow: Nauka, 1985), pp. 109–10.
c. A somewhat smaller estimate of the number of specialists actually employed as specialists is provided by M. N. Rutkevich and F. P. Filippov, *Sotsial'naia structura razvitogo sotsialisticheskogo obshchestva v SSSR* (Moscow: Nauka, 1976), p. 32.
d. Refers to engineering-technical personnel, including agricultural technicians and veterinarians. Sources: for 1941 and 1970, Rutkevich and Filippov, *Sotsial'naia structura*, p. 87; for 1983, Ivanov, *Razvitie sotsial'noi struktury*, pp. 109–10.

sible for analyzing the results of ideological work. Each of these forms a governing council, and each council supervises an aktiv.[80]

An ideological commission of a territorial party committee might be still more elaborate. A Tadzhik raikom commission, for example, draws together a number of existing activities. The heads of the various groups are staff ideology officials of the party, but the members take part on a spare-time basis. (Most members, however, are also members of the raion party committee, a fact that suggests the high degree of overlap between the "elective party aktiv" and the "ideological aktiv.") The commission oversees five councils, each of which is divided into sections. One council, headed by the director of the district veterinary institute, supervises political education; another prepares notes and reference materials for speakers; another organizes lectures. One council is responsible for sports and military-patriotic education and is headed by a war veteran (and reserve officer) who also doubles as party secretary of the local sports society. The deputy chairman of the sports council is an instructor from the agitprop department of the raikom. The ideology secretary of the raikom chairs the full commission; his deputy is the head of the agitprop department. Thus the party staff, local activists, and local notables form an interlocking directorate for political work.[81]

Although no single blueprint for assembling ideological commissions exists, accounts suggest several regularities in the functional areas covered, the method of formation, and the close relationship between aktiv and apparat in their makeup. The functional areas, which generally include political education, mass-political work, labor education, youth work (stressing fitness, military skills, and patriotism linked to military heroism), and, particularly in multinational regions, "international" education (in the Soviet context, this refers to promotion of harmony among the Soviet nationalities). These themes in turn correspond to the major clusters of activist political work in the workplaces. To a large extent, the ideological commission connects the many organizations operating in a particular territory or workplace, giving each one's efforts a specific mission in the overall scheme.

By the same token, the use of ideological commissions to integrate more closely already existing forms of ideological work raises the familiar problem of paper organizations—schemes that aim at formalizing control and coordination but in fact either become dead letters or generate greater disorganization because of the greater burden of managerial work needed for the new structure. This problem becomes still more acute because of the reliance on an already overloaded aktiv of ITRs, managers, trade union and Komsomol activists, and leading workers. The more complex the nominal structure of an ideological commission, the likelier it is that its actual activity is sporadic or fictitious and that actual administration of activist political work is performed by the instructors of the local party organization. An instructor in Kazan commented, for example, that his colleagues frequently complained that ideological commissions were purely fictional and did no work; he himself, however, found that he could rely on his local network of activists.[82] His experience is likely to be the exception proving the rule. When the new retrenchment phase began in the early 1980s, party literature acknowledged that the elaborate schemes for "ideological plans" and "ideological commissions" tended to be purely pro forma devices, mechanically joining many separate branches of political work in a grand common framework. It was pointed out that such forms facilitated the use of quantitative performance measures, but, in the new spirit of pragmatism, they are considered somewhat primitive.[83]

Most party committees maintain reference offices, usually as interdepartmental sectors serving the agitation-propaganda department as well as other departments. According to "A. Pravdin," the Central Committee Secretariat established an information sector in 1966 to support both the Science and Educational Institutes and Propaganda departments. It collected information from lower party branches such as the results of polls measuring the impact of ideological work. It was weakened in 1971–72, however, evidently as part of the party's conservative turn in ideological policy.[84] The scale of nonstaff assistance in reference offices is suggested by the fact that even the Central Committee's Information Sector employed only three to five staff officials. In province and district committees it is common for the information office to be headed by a staff instructor but run by unpaid officials and activists.[85]

Information offices gather and file notes pertinent to the themes emphasized in ideological work as well as data about lower party committees, territorial units, and particular enterprises. They assemble the reports from activists and lower party branches about the various meetings, seminars, lectures, and other activities that have been held. Often the information office also processes and analyzes the letters sent by citizens to the party committee. In some areas "methods councils" and "offices of political enlightenment," run by activists, perform reference work for the use of the political education system.[86] Connected to information offices in many party committees are opinion polling services, nearly always using amateur sociologists. Many enterprises maintain such offices, as do about 100 territorial party committees and about 400 ministries and agencies of government. (Another 1983 estimate is that 540 party organizations have units for sociological research.)[87] In addition to probing popular and expert opinion on such subjects as labor turnover, familiarity with current party policies, and attitudes about crime, drinking, and other problems, the surveyors often draw up profiles ("passports") of a given enterprise or community. The breakdowns of occupation, age, party status, and such data are intended to help party speakers tailor their addresses more closely to their audiences.

Still, although information from below may help in adapting political work to the characteristics of particular workplaces and towns, the thematic content of indoctrination is determined largely by political priorities set from above and embodied in thematic plans of ideological work. Planning in communications and indoctrination, as in production, facilitates bureaucratic control over the use of resources, and it is imposed on all types of ideological work—mass-political work, party education, and the mass media. In the PPO, plans enable the deputy PPO secretaries to impose uniformity and coherence on mass-political work; these telescope in turn into the ideological plans devised by each territorial party committee, which also incorporate thematic plans by media organizations. Through planning, the party strives to avoid undue repetition, fragmentation, or lapses in the presentation of political information; it maintains thematic balance over time and across audiences. Planning allows the party to target special content for particular audiences, to respond to fresh directives from above, and to emphasize or ignore local issues. Plans summarize the work to be performed over a target period, enabling higher authorities to comment on, amend, reject, or approve the proposals. Through planning, the party restricts unwanted variation in the content of political communication.

Ideological planning became a widespread practice in the Brezhnev era as organized ideological work grew in volume and variety and demanded greater attention to control and coordination. For example, the Leningrad party obkom began drafting ideological plans in 1967, in conjunction with the observance of the fiftieth anniversary of the October Revolution.[88] In keeping with the preoccupation in the Brezhnev era with organizational complexity, *complex planning* became a watchword in party literature in the late 1970s, resulting in elaborate paper structures intended to coordinate the many institutions carrying out some type of mass-political work. The concept of complex planning recognized that ideological work needed to serve multiple goals simultaneously with multiple segments of the public, as opposed to the kind of blanket or saturation effect achieved when all other interests are subordinated to one overriding priority, as in a phase of high mobilization. In a complex plan, each affected organization fits its particular responsibilities into the common framework. The party committee lists the areas of ideological work it will emphasize during the plan period, adjusting these to the priorities set down by higher-level officials. Every party committee is expected to maintain a plan, and each such plan must cover the work of the agencies in the committee's immediate jurisdiction. Only the party group, the most elemental and informal of party structures, is exempt from the requirement of planning, but even so, the group leader is encouraged to maintain informal plans or diaries.[89]

Party committees draw up plans of ideological work both for short periods—usually a month at a time—and for longer ones. In the case of PPOs, the long-term plan is normally for a year; at higher levels, such as city and district committees, it may run for two, three, or even five years. The short-term plan, called a current or running plan, lays out the particular themes that should be emphasized in all forms of communication in the coming period. The longer-term plan, called a perspective plan, lays out the broader directions of work that correspond to major national campaigns and policies, such as a party congress or a major anniversary. The plans are relatively comprehensive, even in

PPOs. Here the plan will normally state the content of such routine and frequent measures as agitation sessions as well as the activity of the trade union, people's control, and Komsomol organizations in the enterprise, the enterprise newspaper, the posters hung on the walls, the meetings, political education classes, lectures, reports, conferences, and discussions that will be held.

Different organizations divide the areas of planned ideological work differently. Most plans, however, have five or six sections, covering topics such as Marxist-Leninist indoctrination, counterpropaganda (that is, propaganda specifically designed to counteract the influence of Western ideology), labor education, military-patriotic education, international education, and atheism; and enrichment topics such as moral, physical, environmental, and aesthetic education.

Plans lend a stable structure not only to the organization but also to the content of communication. They lay out the goals and symbols to which current information is linked. Some of the headings under which information falls are permanent, such as the image of Lenin, World War II, and the October Revolution. Often, though, these and other themes are invoked for policy campaigns of limited duration. As new policy themes are introduced and old ones dropped or deemphasized, the plan is modified. As in any system of dogma, particulars are used to reveal aspects of universals. The fluid and changing are instantiations of the fixed and enduring. Planning helps the party monopolize the right of drawing broader generalizations from individual instances, and, contrariwise, of breaking down general principles into specific lessons for actions. Complex planning means keeping many themes active at once.[90]

Pathologies of Control

Planning the content of communication, while it helps maintain bureaucratic control over the flow of information, nonetheless entails serious drawbacks. On the positive side, the campaign form allows the leadership to focus the attention of the public and officials on new policy objectives. Shortly after the conclusion of the intense campaign surrounding the fortieth anniversary of victory over Germany, several of Gorbachev's initiatives dominated the spotlight of official publicity:

the broad-gauged campaign to accelerate scientific-technical progress, the counterpropaganda offensive against the West, the campaign against alcoholism and drunkenness, and the drives to improve the educational system, raise productivity, and improve consumer goods and services. Among these, the industrial modernization policy takes priority and has widened into a general campaign for the "restructuring" of society by eliminating sloth and inertia. The effect of the campaign form that planned communications inevitably take is self-limiting, though. Frequently the media accompany discussions of the themes of modernization and progress with a warning against "campaignism" (kampanieishchina), the pro forma repetition of current policy watchwords. The inability to escape campaignism so long as ideological work is subject to planning is doubtless deeply frustrating to a leadership such as Gorbachev's, which is seeking to redirect ideological work itself—without, of course, abandoning the existing administrative structure of control.

Campaignism results from the tendency for each policy campaign to die away as it is superseded by new policy initiatives. The succession of campaigns gives each a seasonal and temporary quality, regardless of the intentions of the political leaders. Planning can ensure that any given policy theme is kept before the public, but it cannot prevent the routinized treatment that campaign themes receive.

For symbols and ideas with long half-lives, their use becomes ritualized—repeated so long and often that they become hollow and meaningless, and they retain their significance only by common agreement to keep up pretenses. Virtually all public communication in the USSR is ritualized at least to some degree, as is of course a certain portion of public life in Western democracies as well, as Walter Bagehot recognized in distinguishing the "dignified" from the "effective" roles of the British Parliament. The problem is to inject freshness and credibility into the deployment of essential normative reference points. Moreover, many ideological officials complacently prefer the comfort of existing routines to the risks of novel methods. Constant public reaffirmation of the founding myths and conventional pieties seems to satisfy many interests without provoking much public opposition.

Ceremony attends most public meetings. Like other forms of mass-political work, meetings are planned through the party's ideological sector and are therefore readily susceptible to ritualization. Some are intended to be ceremonies; others display a face of spontaneity. Public ceremonies combine several basic elements: an assembly of the "masses," a program, and a collective act of affirmation and rededication.[91] At the workplace, where, it will be recalled, even a moderately sized enterprise might hold about five hundred meetings each month, a meeting runs according to the following routine: administrative business, five to six minutes; main report, twenty minutes; prepared responses ("debate" or *preniia*), thirty minutes; discussion by the floor and adoption of a resolution, four to five minutes. No more than four to six people normally take part in the debate. The resolution, with or without amendment, is generally adopted unanimously or by a majority.[92] Although on occasion meetings open into unplanned exchanges between audience and speaker after the formal presentation is over, allowing listeners to raise difficult questions, the popular response to most meetings, not surprisingly, is boredom and indifference.[93]

The deputy PPO secretary in a factory recently described how she organized a meeting of the workers to observe the one hundred tenth anniversary of Lenin's birth.[94] She took her cue from a Central Committee resolution recommending such meetings as an appropriate way of celebrating the event and urging that the meetings be linked to discussions of tasks currently facing the society. The PPO bureau formed a special commission to prepare for the meeting; the commission included representatives of the enterprise party committee, its bureau, secretaries from some of the shop committees in the plant, longtime party members, representatives of management, and leading workers. Overall responsibility for the meeting was assigned to the deputy PPO secretary for ideological work. No doubt following well-trodden paths, she made the necessary preparations. In order to create a mood of anticipation beforehand, she organized a contest in the factory for the best visual display. She had special lapel pins (*znachki*) made and distributed. The secretary of the PPO was to deliver an address at the meeting. Copies of his speech would be distributed in advance, and various people in the factory were assigned to raise appropriate questions after it. She saw to it that the resolution to be adopted at the meeting was prepared in advance. The proceedings would conclude with the singing of the "Internationale." Planning extended to all aspects of the meeting—publicity, purpose, contents, audience response. It included the cooperation of the enterprise trade union branch and Komsomol organization. Moreover, it called for accompanying measures, including a *subbotnik*, field trips for the youth, special lectures, meetings of young workers and old-timers, special articles in the factory newspaper, and posters.[95]

Under Gorbachev, some effort is being made to reduce the elements of ritualization in ideological work. One instrument is emphasis on the 1983 law on labor collectives, full use of which, press articles assert, would cut down on the forces of inertia, indiscipline, and secretiveness that impede social progress. One article pointed out that workers' meetings could play a much greater role but that at present they are often conducted "formally, for the sake of a check mark [*galochki radi*, that is, in order to check off the accomplishment of a measure on a list], are often full of ceremony [*byvaiut polny paradnosti*], and because of this are sometimes almost useless." About a rural district where party life had been ritualized for years, a *Pravda* article entitled "A Fresh Wind" recounted the recent triumph of frank and self-critical public communication over pretense, window dressing, vanity, irresponsibility, and empty rhetoric. Formerly, party meetings were conducted "limply, according to a pre-set model, without sharp criticism or self-criticism" and "according to the old clichés." But after the promise by the new general secretary of a "struggle against any manifestations of doing things for show, empty chatter, conceit, and irresponsibility," things changed, and "a new working day has dawned."[96]

In addition, Gorbachev has used the occasion of political meetings himself to draw attention to his policy goals through unplanned interventions into meetings. (Of course, so far Gorbachev has not gone so far as to deliver a major unplanned assault on his predecessors, as Khrushchev did in 1956.) The cost of spontaneity, though, is the personalization of ideological authority, which brings risks when personal loyalties to the leader erode. For example, at the conference of Stakhanovites convened by the Central Committee in September 1985, the familiar notes of personal allegiance were sounded by more than one of the speakers interrupted by Gorbachev. A master of an oil and gas drilling association in Tiumen expressed his personal appreciation to Gorbachev. "The workers are grateful to you, Mikhail Sergeevich, for having sharpened attention to these important problems when you were in Tiumen. . . . We are in your debt, Mikhail Sergeevich; we will not lag behind."[97]

Ritualism and campaignism are likely to bedevil any political use of the instruments of communication where the outcome of discussion is planned in advance. They are inevitable organizational responses to pressures from superior levels for evidence of satisfactory performance in the ideological sphere. So long as planning is the key method for coordinating the activities of all who play a role in the ideological process—leaders, activists, masses—and for ensuring that the content of each message conforms to more general political guidelines, ossification of the channels will inevitably result.

Whatever the formal mechanisms of control and coordination, party management of the work of the ideological aktiv requires close contact between the territorial party officials and the aktiv administering political work. Essential to this contact is frequent consultation between the PPO secretaries and the local party staff and between the PPO secretaries and their deputy secretaries, the shop committee secretaries, and the group organizers. Typically the secretaries and department heads of lower party committees hold weekly or monthly briefings for the PPO secretaries in their jurisdictions, who in turn guide the activist administrators in the workplaces. The deputy PPO secretaries might also have regular meetings with the raikom staff.[98] When a special campaign is being planned, raikom officials may convene the administrative aktiv to discuss the overall purpose of the campaign and to instruct activists about the area of responsibility of each.[99] At regular or irregular intervals, officials from higher organizations visit workplaces and meet with the ideological aktiv. Alternatively, the ideological aktiv of a district or city, or even province or republic, may assemble for a major conference. In Moscow the city party committee holds an annual conference for the PPO secretaries.[100]

Occasionally an all-union meeting of ideological activists takes place. The 1979 ideology resolution led to two follow-up conferences of unionwide scale. Six months after the resolution was promulgated, a two-day conference in Moscow brought together secretaries and agitation-propaganda department heads from party organizations down to the district level to hear addresses by officials from the Central Committee Secretariat as well as by government officials, scholars, media heads, writers, and other prominent figures. Mikhail Suslov himself addressed them, discussing how the ideology resolution affected them and elaborating on the demands it made. During their stay, the officials toured factories, farms, and research institutes and heard a special concert in the Kremlin.[101] How much substantive information can have been conveyed at such a conclave remains a question, but the exalted nature of the occasion itself must have impressed on participants a sense of the gravity of their mission and reinforced the consciousness of their common calling. Similarly, provincewide or citywide meetings of the ideological aktiv, particularly of activist adminstrators and group heads, must help instill identification with their party vocation.

It is the short, dense ties at the interface between the bottom rung of the territorial hierarchy and the ideological aktiv in the enterprises that provide the regular substantive guidance that grass-roots activists need to perform their duties. These ties also enable them to channel back to the apparat their impression of the public temper, sources of grievance and satisfaction, and other kinds of information based on comments and questions raised in workplace meetings. Perhaps most important, they maintain the sense of common purpose between the aktiv and the apparat. If the vertical ties connecting officials and activists on different rungs of the party ladder foster the sense of specialization in ideological work, horizontal links delegating political responsibility to the social elite serve the strategy of cooptation of prestige and authority generated in society for the political needs of the party. Cultivation of a common language of power and responsibility helps weaken demands for institutional or professional autonomy. The strategy requires, however, a careful balancing of cooptation of the elite with opportunity and equality for the masses. It has been difficult for the party to strike the right balance between the concentration of political authority in the ideological aktiv and the activation of the larger public. Success depends on the party's ability to reconcile elite solidarity with the need to build popular support.

3 POLITICAL EDUCATION

THE DOCTRINAL BASIS OF PROPAGANDA

An ideology requires a system for propagating itself, as N. B. Bikkenin observes. "Ideology and propaganda should be viewed as an organic unity and not in isolation. Ideology determines the content and type of propaganda, and propaganda gives ideology a concrete social mechanism for its reproduction on a mass scale and a means of functioning."[1]

In Soviet society not only does "communist upbringing" play a major part in mass-political work, in the schools, and in youth groups but—and this is the topic of the present chapter—theoretical instruction is a major instrument in training, activating, and integrating the social and political elite. Marxist-Leninist doctrine provides the theoretical core of an elaborately differentiated system of study circles, courses, lectures, discussions, and seminars in which some 65 million persons—close to half the employed population—are at least nominally enrolled.

Since both content and structure of political education are shaped by official conceptions of ideological theory, it is to be expected that over time, political education, like other forms of ideological work, has oscillated between theoretical and practical orientations. Roughly every twenty years the old dispute over the relevance of theory to practice arises anew. In the late 1970s and early 1980s, as was noted earlier, the relationship of ideology to propaganda became central again in speeches by the leadership and in resolutions. In addition, in the

71

major 1979 ideology resolution, the June 1983 Central Committee plenum, Gorbachev's address on ideology in December 1984, and subsequent party pronouncements, a substantial effort has been made to revitalize propaganda.

Since the 1960s, however, such change in the forms and content of political education as has occurred has been manifested in relatively minor reorganizations that have tended to increase the complexity but not the effectiveness of the system. Several reasons account for the difficulty in achieving reform. Although determining the main thematic lines of party propaganda is a function of the central party leaders and theorists, in its administration the political education system is relatively loose and decentralized: most of its components are organized by the PPOs of workplaces, supplemented by parallel classes run by the party's mass auxiliaries, the Komsomol and the trade unions. As a result there is a good deal of diversity in form and structure. Most units operate as study-discussion circles of fairly small size: a good-sized factory might boast fifty or one hundred such groups. In the higher tiers, particularly those designed for senior officials, instruction is organized on a territorial basis. To a large extent, teachers, referred to as propagandists, are recruited from the senior specialist and administrative stratum of the collective in which they work. Like mass-political work, then, political education relies to a large extent on mobilizing existing social ties among peers in the work collective, both the horizontal relations of comradeship and internal lines of authority. More than is the case with the more topical types of oral ideological work—agitation, political information, reports, and lectures—however, political education has become differentiated occupationally. As a result, listeners in a particular group usually share similar vocational or avocational duties as well as social rank.

A major step in the diversification of the system by vocational specialization was the reestablishment in 1971 of a hierarchy of economic education courses to parallel the party system and the Komsomol and trade union networks (an economic education system had been created first in 1956 but reached major proportions only following the 1971 decree). At the same time the Academy of Social Sciences created a division for continuing education of cadres, called the Institute for Raising Qualifications of Leading Party and Soviet Cadres, which runs a series of courses through the Higher Party Schools. Still another such creation was the formation of two sets of courses for different sections of the party aktiv in 1981: "schools for the economic aktiv" and "schools for the ideological aktiv." Expansion of the party school system has increased the number of courses taught. Acknowledging that the proliferation of courses has grown excessive, M. V. Zimianin, the Central Committee secretary in charge of ideological work from 1976 to 1986, observed early in 1985 that the 130 subjects currently being taught through the party education system could not be adequately serviced with teaching materials and qualified instructors.[2] It is harder to reduce than to expand the scope of political education, however, since at any given time the range of issues needing to be kept in public consciousness through courses and schools in the system is quite broad, even though the themes themselves tend to be general enough to accommodate discussion of new policies. Content therefore changes incrementally, with shifts in general orientation heralded more in the accompanying speeches and articles of party leaders than in drastic reforms.

Still, the accumulation of minor reorganizations and the drift of expansion have produced a system in many ways different from that inherited by Khrushchev or even Brezhnev. Little remains of the older supposition of the Stalin era that there is a single body of knowledge representing the core of Marxism-Leninism, as was summarized, for example, by Stalin's "Fundamentals of Leninism." Today, instead, doctrine comprises several branches of learning; among these, perhaps the most general is "scientific communism." (A small but telling step in this respect was the 1981 decision to begin phasing out the old "schools of the fundamentals of Marxism-Leninism," formerly the main workhorse of party education, by establishing new "schools of scientific communism".) Other branches include political economy, Marxist-Leninist philosophy, and scientific atheism. These in turn lend intellectual shape to a larger number of applied subjects, including the study of economic management, international relations, methods of ideological work, and government and administration. Although the general organization of political education can still be traced to the three-tier hierarchy (elementary, intermediate, and advanced, each corresponding to the equivalent level of general education) set up by the decree of August 1956 on ideological work,[3] in fact the system has outgrown this framework. Today it is assumed that the near universal attainment of secondary education has acquainted all new party members with elementary political learning. The 1981 decree demanded the formation of new "schools of young communists" as the appropriate primary unit for new members.[4] Perhaps another sign of the breakdown of the doctrine as a codified entity was the sad result of a contest run in 1981 by the Academy of Social Sciences and the Institute of Marxism-Leninism of the Central Committee and the Politizdat publishing house for textbooks in the fields of Marxist-Leninist philosophy, political economy, scientific communism, and scientific atheism. Only thirty-six manuscripts were received. None was deemed worthy of a first prize in any field. No second prize was awarded in the fields of Marxist-Leninist philosophy, political economy, or scientific atheism. Indeed, in the last field, no prize at all was awarded.[5]

Instead, the overt task of political education has evolved in the direction of linking the functional duties of members of the elite and activists with current party policies, using party documents and ceremonial observances as the principal vehicle of instruction. In part, this emphasis reflects the trend of development of the 1965–80 period, in which the de facto policy was to maximize participation in the system through the establishment of units tailored to a wide array of functional roles and increased enrollments. By the end of the 1970s, however, a coalition of party conservatives and modernizers expressed sharp displeasure with the stagnation that had beset political education and called for a major program of revitalization aimed at reversing the widening gap between word and deed by making all channels of communication and socialization into efficient agencies inculcating communist consciousness. The deaths of Suslov and Chernenko (January 1982 and March 1985, respectively) brought this transitional phase to a close. Under Gorbachev the pragmatic direction that political education has taken reflects a new phase of the ongoing struggle over the appropriate balance of theory and practice in the content taught. To a striking degree, Gorbachev has revived Khrushchev's sharp critique of hollow and self-referential theory and his emphasis on economic performance as the only measure of value for political education.[6]

For example, a *Pravda* article in August 1985 on political education divided the impending 1985–86 academic year into two parts separated by the Twenty-seventh Party Congress. Before the congress, the party, Komsomol, economic, and mass-political educational systems would be based on materials from the April 1985 Central Committee plenum, the June 1985 Central Committee conference on accelerating scientific-technical progress, the new edition of the party program, the proposed revisions to the party by-laws, and the economic program for 1986–90 and to the year 2000. After the congress, lessons would incorporate the materials from the congress. The specific themes enumerated in the article suggest the new preoccupation with making political education serve economic goals.

The new academic year would begin with the topic "All possibilities and reserves—into the successful fulfillment of the 1985 plan and socialist obligations, a worthy greeting of the Twenty-seventh Party Congress." The basic point of this lesson was to inculcate a sense of the importance of socialist competition, familiarity with the new plan target figures, and identification of underutilized human and material resources ("reserves").

Until the congress, schools of the fundamentals of Marxism-Leninism, schools of scientific communism, and theoretical and methods seminars (these being the predominant forms of party education now) were to study "the acceleration of socioeconomic progress, an urgent task for the party and the whole people, . . . current problems of the qualitative transformation of the material-technical base of society, . . . the party's course in improving the political system of society, strengthening order, organization, and discipline and confirming a sober way of life," and "the consolidation of world peace and the strengthening of the positions of socialism in the world arena." Listeners in those units of the schools of scientific communism organized for teachers should continue to study the school reform and add themes dealing with computer education and scientific-technical progress. Since many branches of the economy were scheduled to go over to the new management system (the reorganizations introduced in Andropov's initially limited economic "experiment"), schools and courses dealing with economic subjects were to organize lessons on "From the experiment to a new system of economy."[7]

The tone and spirit of the Gorbachev-era changes in orientation of the system are also reflected in comments made by Egor Ligachev, the Central Committee secretary in charge of organizational-party work and ideology, in an address to the graduates of the Academy of Social Sciences in June 1985. Observing that the graduation was occurring at a critical time, when the mood of the population had been uplifted by the party's new optimism and the beginning of the attempt to eliminate the negative tendencies previously besetting the economy, he stressed the priority of action—of deeds over words.[8] In a report to second secretaries and heads of organizational-party work departments in July 1985, he expressed similar impatience with the current state of ideological work, charging that the party was often "too much distracted by mass, sometimes for-show indicators" and had not done enough to carry out the program of the June 1985 Central Committee conference and the December 1984 ideology conference (both of which emphasized that the only proper criterion for evaluating and justifying ideological work was its contribution to economic productivity). It was essential, he insisted, to involve economic managers, who are able not only to discuss problems but also to solve them.[9] A similar emphasis on practical impact has been expressed in *Pravda* editorials since Gorbachev came to power. Summarizing the results of the 1984–85 academic year, a *Pravda* editorial in June 1985 praised those courses that had given participants ways of tying their studies with the current policy problems of improving scientific-technical progress, efficiency, and quality, pointing out that everything must be tied to the chief task, accelerating scientific-technical progress. Interestingly, Marxism-Leninism received mention only in the first and last sentences; much of the editorial was a criticism of still prevalent habits of "formalism."[10] Shortly before the beginning of the following year (the general school year begins on 1 September, the party educational year on 1 October), an editorial in September 1985 admonished readers that the measure of propaganda's effectiveness is not the number of listeners reached or lectures read, but its effect on actual attitudes and behavior.[11]

The curriculum since 1985, emphasizing themes central to Gorbachev's policy program, such as mobilization of reserves, acceleration of technological modernization, the temperance campaign, and economic reform, might be contrasted to the guiding themes of the curriculum in the Brezhnev period, when much of the study was occupied with observances of the fiftieth and sixtieth anniversaries of the October Revolution, the one hundredth and one hundred tenth anniversaries of Lenin's birth, the fiftieth anniversary of the Soviet Union, and the materials produced by the Twenty-third, Twenty-fourth, and Twenty-fifth Party Congresses.[12] That a covert struggle over the shape and direction of political education occurred in 1984 and 1985, with Gorbachev the sponsor of a group of impatient modernizers seeking to make political education an instrument of pressure for improving productivity, may be inferred from the critical tenor of the remarks of Ligachev, Gorbachev, and others, and the defensive tone of statements by Zimianin and others.

For example, M. V. Zimianin, the longtime "under" secretary for ideology, defended theory in his address at the December 1984 conference on improving ideological work, noting (somewhat gratuitously, one might think) that he fully agreed with the position expressed by Gorbachev in the keynote speech at the conference about the need for better social science. As Chernenko did in the June 1983 plenum speech, calling upon managers and specialists to take part wholeheartedly in ideological work and not to relegate it to the ideological sector, Zimianin criticized "certain economic and even party leaders" who lacked "a taste for theory" and underrated the importance of scientific research.[13]

The alternation between phases of theoretical and practical emphasis has characterized political education from the inception of the regime, if not, indeed, from the earliest days of the Bolshevik movement. Until the late 1930s party education served both to raise the overall political consciousness of society and to train a cadre of agitators and organizers who could carry the party word out into the masses. Particularly in the first decade or so, party education in effect compensated for the limited availability of secondary education, offering the equivalent of a general secondary education to many cadres. (Its role as a surrogate for general education continues today, though usually at the tertiary or postgraduate level. All district and city party ideology secretaries today, for example, have higher educations, but one-third of these degrees have been granted by party educational institutions.[14]) At Lenin's demand, theoretical education in doctrine was also incorporated into the occupational education that cadres received following a Sovnarkom decree of 1920.[15]

Emphasis on basic political literacy sacrificed theoretical depth. Beginning in 1937–38, at the height of the decimation of the old Bolshevik cohort and after the enormous expansion of the state bureaucracy, Stalin decreed a turn to elitism and doctrinal orthodoxy. A decree of 1938 made this change explicit and condemned the former stress on political education at the expense of training for the "higher Soviet, party and non-party intelligentsia, consisting of yesterday's workers and peasants."[16] At the same time the decree made it clear that ideological education would be reconstructed from its near destruction by the great purge on the basis of different levels of study of the *Short Course on the History of the All-Union Communist Party (bolsheviks).* At the mass level, doctrinal study was dominated by the simple, basic tenets that the *Short Course* propounded. Higher-level cadres would study it in conjunction with works of Marx, Engels, Lenin, and Stalin; however, Stalin also took a further step in downgrading Lenin's theoretical legacy in favor of the codified, dogmatic, and, above all, Stalinized version of doctrine, mastered at different levels of theoretical proficiency by masses and cadres. The cult of Lenin had already been largely replaced by that of Stalin by 1933. Now, in 1938, a secret decree was passed essentially banning Lenin scholarship, ostensibly because the tendency in ideological work had been to counterpose Marx to Lenin.[17] During Khrushchev's fight to make political education practical and, in particular, oriented toward economic productivity, he and his supporters attacked the *Short Course* for being too theoretical and detached from life. It would, however, be more accurate to call the *Short Course* profoundly antitheoretical in its hostility to abstraction and its dogmatic insistence on obedience to authority. To be sure, in its neglect of economic issues and its antagonism to empiricism, it of course offered the party little assistance in posing policy choices. As an argument for the infallibility of the party as led by Stalin, though, it served its purpose. To quote Leonard Schapiro, "As a means of propaganda it could scarcely have been excelled. It became the basis for the training of a generation of communists who, while little tempted to think for themselves, need never be at a loss for the official answer to every problem."[18]

The ostensible tension between theory and practice is in fact a proxy for the deeper problem inherent in reforming a system of dogma. *Theory* became the surrogate term for *dogmatism*. Replacing "theory" with empiricism, pragmatism, and instrumentalism ultimately affected the claimed ideological basis for authority in politics. De-Stalinization revived the problem of generating and justifying the party's political authority in the absence of the dictator. The claim that Marxism-Leninism (or scientific communism) is at once revelation *and* discovery, empirical *and* deductive, reflects the party's inability to accept the consequences for its power of rejecting either alternative. Dogmatism produces fettered thinking, instrumental motives, deception, and private rebellion; but it sustains unified power. The impartiality and independence of inquiry that result as dogmatism breaks down have the effect of weakening the structure of authority regardless of the actual content of the belief system that is disintegrating. It is not so much the bearing of specific beliefs upon specific policies that makes ideology essential to an ideocratic polity as it is the need to justify the supposed unity of truth and power.

For this reason, Khrushchev's efforts to de-Stalinize both the content and focus of party education had major political consequences, which have still not been resolved. Khrushchev sought to infuse new spirit in the symbols of Soviet power, such as the name of the party, the image of Lenin, the prospect of communism, and the epochal struggle between socialism and capitalism. For the intelligentsia, Khrushchev's tolerance of honesty and other ethical themes in the arts restored a measure of credibility to doctrine. For much of the population, Khrushchev identified party doctrine with rapid increases in popular well-being and the successes of Soviet science and technology. He attacked the scholasticism of ideological training under Stalin by claiming that it "divorced ideological work from production": improved training in technology was to be the new rationale and content of party ideological work.[19] These changes of course were aimed at undermining the base of support that Khrushchev's opponents found in the defense of tradition. Likewise, the populist and mobilizing features of Khrushchev's policies, including the drive to maximize ideological influence on the population by opening party education to the nonparty masses, aimed at both weakening entrenched Stalinists and stimulating system performance. The major decree on political education of January 1960, which demanded that ideology contribute immediately to the needs of production and urged widening of enrollments, however, also preserved the three-tier system and the sanctity of the doctrinal core. As Jonathan Harris shows, it reflected a compromise between Khrushchev and his conservative opponents, headed by Mikhail Suslov.[20]

Among Khrushchev's reforms in propaganda, the promise that the doctrine would be vindicated by extraordinary improvements in system performance had the most serious consequences by exposing the ideological authority of the party and especially its leaders to disillusionment and ridicule. The changes in political education instituted by Khrushchev's successors aimed at undoing the damage; of these, the sharp reduction in enrollments was most visible, but the doctrinal retrenchment was still more significant. Let us first examine the general trends in enrollments. Under the stimulus of the August 1956 and January 1960 decrees, particularly the latter, the exposure of the populace to party education skyrocketed. Then followed the cutback in 1966–67, after which, however, enrollments crept back up before leveling off in 1981. Enrollments (in millions) were as follows:[21]

1957–58	6.2
1958–59	6.7
1961–62	22.5
1964–65	36.0 (of whom 25.0 were nonparty)
1966–67	13.5 (of whom 9.6 were party)
1976–77	20.8 (of whom 12.4 were party)
1980–81	22.6
1985–86	21.2

Supplementing party education were the Komsomol and economic education systems, the latter of which expanded rapidly in the 1970s. Unfortunately, economic education is not clearly distinguished from the other forms of political education, particularly since economic subjects are often taught through the party, Komsomol, and trade union schools. Thus, for example, the official report, "CPSU in Figures," supplies the following breakdown for enrollments (in millions) in the economic education system in 1970–71 and 1976–77.[22]

	1970–71	1976–77
Party and Komsomol schools	5.8	6.4
Schools of communist labor	2.5	9.9
Economic schools	4.1	11.6
People's universities	1.4	1.1
Institutes, educational establishments, and other general schools for raising qualifications	—	5.0
Total	13.8	35.0

Slightly different figures (also in millions) were provided in the 1981 and 1986 reports.[23]

	1976–76	1980–81	1985–86
Party study	18.7	22.6	21.2
Komsomol study	7.1	8.7	10.3
Economic education	31.0	38.0	38.6
Total	56.8	69.3	70.1

The aggregate figures that are supplied in party writings reflect the fuzziness of categories and counting rules. Although the totals reported here claim 70 million listeners, in his address to the December 1984 ideology conference, M. V. Zimianin referred to 65 million people in political and economic study; the *Pravda* editorial of August 1985 claimed only 60 million in political and economic study.[24] Either figure would indicate that enrollments have leveled off since the beginning of the 1980s.

A more direct confirmation of the new policy of retrenchment in 1981 may be gleaned from the report from the ideological secretary of a district party organization in Leningrad. Evidently in response to instruction from higher levels, the raikom met with PPO secretaries and enterprise heads after the 1981 Central Committee resolution on party education and advised them to cease their efforts to expand the number of listeners in the political education system (particularly through recruiting nonmembers of the party). There followed an overall reduction in the number of enrollments by nearly 10 percent (7,000 persons, out of a total for 1980 of 86,800 in the political and economic education systems), most of those dropped being retired persons.[25] From this one may infer that an internal party directive accompanying the 1981 decree that reorganized political education called for a modest trimming and stabilization of the system but not a radical reduction.

Of greater interest, however, than the boom-bust cycles in enrollment has been the effort to fill the theoretical void left by Khrushchev's adamant emphasis on the practical and his vain attempt to prove the validity of doctrine by identifying it with dramatic achievements in science, technology, and consumer well-being. The third party program went very far to link doctrine with the fulfillment of the economic promises contained in the program and accompanying propaganda, such as the claim that, over the next two decades, the country's national income would quadruple, permitting the solution of the housing problem and the introduction of free goods and services in many consumer sectors.[26] The revival of speculation about the nature of communist society opened the door to a variety of utopian projections for the future.[27] The very description of the ideological character of the state changed with the introduction of the idea of the "all-people's state." There followed a reaction that took the form of retreating from such concrete promises and timetables and introducing a new conception of the stage at which Soviet society found itself on its long road to communism: developed socialism.[28] The view that having achieving the stage of developed socialism, the Soviet Union would remain there for an indefinite period, perfecting it by small steps rather than leaping soon to the next stage, was expressed clearly enough in Brezhnev's report to the Supreme Soviet when the new Constitution was ratified.

> The stage of the perfection of socialism *on its own basis*, the stage of mature, developed socialist society, is a necessary element of the social transformation and *constitutes a relatively long period of development* on the path from capitalism to communism. Moreover, knowledge and utilization of all the possibilities of developed socialism *is at the same time a transition to the construction of communism.* The future does not lie beyond the limits of the present. The future is rooted in the present, and, by accomplishing the tasks of today—of the socialist present—*we are gradually entering tomorrow*—the communist future.[29]

Brezhnev warned against excessive expectations not only by insisting on the protracted nature of the current stage, but, perhaps even more importantly, by underscoring the continuity between present and future by suggesting that the future is no more than the slow accumulation of minor improvements over the present. The new concept was a rationalization for a conception of much slower social change than was foreseen in Khrushchev-era propaganda. In turn, while downplaying Brezhnev-era theoretical innovations, Gorbachev, in his address at the Twenty-seventh Party Congress, asserted that theory cannot be reduced to a "collection of frozen schemes and recipes" and criticized the previous leadership for inertia and decay.[30]

As I argued in chapter 1, changes in the ideological line concern politics as much as policy. Much as the antidogmatic and pragmatic orientation promoted by Khrushchev and his supporters sought both to weaken the power of the remaining Stalinists and to make propaganda a tool of some substantive value in revitalizing society, so Gorbachev's ideological campaign targets both the holdovers of the Brezhnev period and the inertia in policy they represent. Like Khrushchev, Gorbachev seems to be shifting doctrine from a deductive logic of validation, represented, for example, by the invention of a new notional stage of development, to a positivistic logic of observable progress. The truth of Marxism-Leninism is to be borne out in the achievement of accelerated modernization, which will require the effective use of propaganda to activate "the human factor." The problem for Gorbachev is the same as that faced by Khrushchev, therefore. The benefit gained from endorsing popular scorn for a petrified doctrine has only limited returns, and the doctrine itself cannot be discarded as a theoretical basis for propaganda without opening the public realm to other ideologies, any of which would inevitably attack the party's monopoly. Ideological work must therefore be linked to future payoffs, and, to have any inspirational value, these need to be impressive. The pragmatist in an ideocratic polity ends by becoming a utopian.

FORGING THE POLITICAL ELITE

To make ideological doctrine the common heritage of all members of the political elite—those in administrative posts in the party, government, army, public institutions, mass media, and so on, cultural and technical specialists, and opinion leaders in settings down to the immediate work group—has been the avowed goal of political education since the civil war. Peter Kenez has recently described how intense the commitment of the early Soviet regime was to the creation of a system of political education that would provide cadres in the new society with appropriate tools of thought and language. A three-tiered hierarchy quickly sprang up in the first years after the October Revolution. By 1922–23, ten communist universities had been founded, by 1928, nineteen. These institutions trained cadres for senior positions in party work; for cadres in intermediate levels there were "soviet-party schools," which in turn offered courses at two levels. By October 1921 some 50,000 students were enrolled in these, before the system underwent one of its first retrenchments and enrollment fell to 20,000 by the end of 1922. As has repeatedly happened, though, enrollments slowly rose again after the cutback and reached 45,000 by the end of the 1920s. Finally, at the bottom of the ladder there were "political grammar schools" intended to give every party member some exposure to the rudiments of doctrine. The party succeeded in extending the reach of this system very widely during the first Soviet decade: by 1927 nearly three in ten party members had trained in an elementary political school.[31]

It was stressed in chapter 2 that the manager or specialist in an economic or cultural organization is usually at the same time an activist on behalf of the party or government, extending party influence through the discharge of daily responsibilities and, still more directly, through spare-time party assignments such as mass-political work and elected offices in party, Komsomol, soviet, and trade union organizations. Political education complements the intertwining of leadership across organizations horizontally and between levels of organization vertically by supplying members of the elite with a common ideological framework and focusing their attention on a common set of policy tasks. In this way it forms another channel of direction and feedback tying the social elite with political professionals. By all accounts, the inculcation of actual conviction is simply a nominal goal. By the same token, one should not too quickly dismiss the propaganda system's importance in providing a universal *façon de parler* for all public occasions.

Although often sharply discrepant on other points, the testimony of Soviet émigré scholars and other longtime observers of Soviet society is nearly unanimous in commenting on the pervasiveness of behavioral bilingualism—a phenomenon defined by Yuri Glazov, for example, as "that mode of behaviour in accordance with which a member of a given society, while more or less soberly understanding the essence of what is going on around him, conducts himself with absolute conformism on the official level, whereas in a narrow circle of friends or among his own family members he expresses well-considered or even extremist viewpoints which refute the basic principles of the official world outlook. . . . By language we assume a culture, a mode of behaviour."[32] Vladimir Shlapentokh has advanced the notion of two levels of mentality: one "mythological"—the absorption of official ideology, governing verbal behavior; and the other "pragmatic," regulating material behavior. In the latter area, Shlapentokh asserts, Soviet people behave with such widespread disregard for official norms that they are sliding "into an abyss of complete demoralization." In Shlapentokh's view, the only official value that has achieved much real internalization is patriotism.[33]

On the basis of the observed compartmentalization of public and private behavior, many observers argue that the actual, but not nominal goal of propaganda is not to persuade but to provide cadres and activists with the necessary languge of political discourse, the ideological cues and reference points through which party power and policies may be justified. Michael Voslensky writes, for example:

Nowadays nomenklaturist propaganda does not even take the trouble to try to make people believe what it says. Its aim is a different one, namely to make Soviet citizens understand that they must use a definite phraseology. This terminological constraint imposed on the population in general and intellectuals in particular has the following peculiarities: In the first place, Soviet propaganda no longer makes any serious attempt to persuade its readers or hearers of the correctness of its assertions and slogans, but confines itself to repeating them tirelessly with a view to engraving them in everyone's mind. Secondly, nomenklatura propaganda is inseparably connected with terror. If anyone dares to cast doubt on a propagandist claim or actually to deny it, the nomenklatura does not try to reason with or instruct him, but punishes him.[34]

Similarly, Alexander Zinoviev argues of the crucial role played by the ideological apparatus that it "teaches and compels people in certain situations which are vitally important in the life of society, to think, speak and behave alike and in a way desired by their rulers. . . . People's acceptance of ideology is expressed by the fact that they will act as society demands."[35] If the testimony provided by the émigrés is accurate, then it is not understanding or belief that the propaganda system aspires to achieve in its audience but the standardization of public discourse. One might add only that the same observation has been made about propaganda in earlier periods of Soviet history.

For example, Peter Kenez recently surveyed the effects of political education on party activists of the 1920s, who, according to one survey, were acquainted with the "patristic" writings of Marx and Lenin hardly at all, knew the doctrine largely through press references and speeches but were avid readers of the local press and *Pravda*. For them, Kenez concluded, political schools "with their catechism-like method transmitted a way of thinking, which assumed that there was one and only one correct answer to any question. The schools taught a language in which Party activists were expected to express themselves" and thus helped develop "the particular Soviet-type political discourse." Similarly, referring to Stalin-era indoctrination, Leonard Schapiro wrote, "No one understood better than Stalin that the true object of propaganda is neither to convince nor even to persuade, but to produce a uniform pattern of public utterance in which the first trace of unorthodox thought immediately reveals itself as a jarring dissonance."[36]

If the actual goals of party ideological specialists can only be inferred, only slightly more accessible to observation are the effects of political education. Reviewing a large body of recent Soviet surveys about the effectiveness of party propaganda, Stephen White has agreed that ideological work has only limited effectiveness in inculcating values and beliefs not already established in the political culture; and, like émigré scholars he also calls attention to the phenomenon of "dualism": use of the official phraseology while privately retaining a contrary system of values. White has, however, imputed several other intermediate goals of propaganda short of persuasion, among them the engagement of party activists in common tasks, facilitating exposure of the actual political beliefs of citizens, and, possibly, contributing to economic performance.[37] These are of a general nature, though. The interlocking structure of the systems of political education and social authority, in particular the disproportionate incidence of participation by elite groups, suggests two more specific goals of propaganda: focusing the attention of administrators and specialists on current policy goals and, as a second-order benefit, building a sense of solidarity on the part of elite groups to which a share of political responsibility has been allotted. These can, however, be argued only tentatively and on the basis of a closer look at the actual organization of propaganda.

With the adaptation of political education to elites in a variety of institutional sectors, the old three-rung division of political study by level of theoretical depth has become largely vestigial, having been overtaken by vocational differentiation and by the general advancement of the public's educational attainments. This is particularly so in the case of the primary political schools, which now account for no more than 5 percent of the enrollments in political education. Twenty years ago they accounted for about 42 percent of all listeners; ten years ago, about 11 percent.[38] Their role has been taken over by schools of young communists for new party members and by the continuing reliance on mass propaganda run by the Komsomol and trade unions. Komsomol education, like other forms of political education, expanded rapidly from the late 1960s to the early 1980s.[39]

1966–67	3.2 million
1970–71	6.2 million
1976–77	7.1 million
1980–81	8.7 million
1985–86	10.3 million

Mass propaganda, generally organized through the trade unions, offers rudimentary political instruction with an applied bent. For example, "schools of communist labor," introduced in 1962 as an alternative to party schooling, emphasize themes such as a "communist attitude to labor," linking them with practical problems of production.[40] Similarly, some 44,000 "people's universities" survive from the same period, currently enrolling some 14 million listeners.[41]

Although people's universities are mainly intended to offer elementary knowledge, they are becoming more specialized. Rising educational attainments of the population have changed their character. They have a large contingent of youth (half are under thirty) and therefore often enroll individuals with complete secondary or even higher degrees; 39 percent have at least some tertiary education. In many cases special courses are designed for activists of various specialties, including nonstaff correspondents for the media, lecturers, or members of people's control committees. In other cases courses are specialized by topic, such as atheism, economics, and technology.[42]

The 1971 decree that reorganized political education instituted a new three-tier system of economic education parallel to the party schools. Production-oriented courses in the existing people's universities and schools of communist labor were designated the bottom level of the new hierarchy. At the intermediate and advanced levels courses in economics and management were set up intended for specialists and administrators.[43] After the Twenty-sixth Party Congress in 1981, a new Academy of the National Economy was formed to crown the system, in parallel to the Academy of Social Sciences, which guides party education.

As intermediate-level party and economic schools increasingly take over the bulk of political instruction, they have become more functionally differentiated. Formerly, "schools of the fundamentals of Marxism-Leninism" were the bulwark of party education both for communists and for nonparty activists who are not in, but may aspire toward, administrative posts. These cover party history, philosophy, political economy, and other branches of doctrinal learning. They will continue to exist—though it will be assumed that listeners will already have a secondary education—but are to be supplemented by "schools of scientific communism," which are to be more closely concerned with current events and national policy. To give a standard course in such basic matters as the party by-laws, the party program, and the outlines of party organization for candidate members and newly admitted party members, schools of young communists were given encouragement by the 1981 Central Committee decree.[44] Some lower territorial and enterprise party organizations had already been running such schools, but it was reported that, under the influence of the decree, by the spring of 1982 they had been organized "everywhere" and enrolled some 76,000 persons.[45]

The tendency toward functional specialization is most pronounced at the top tier of education. Here the schools for activists have bifurcated into schools for the party-economic aktiv and schools for the ideological aktiv. The latter are aimed at serving the very considerable body of activist-organizers in the ideological sector, including deputy PPO secretaries, heads of agitation groups, heads of media and cultural organizations, propagandists, and the staff in political education offices, houses, clubs, and similar institutions. So highly differentiated has the schooling system become that separate courses are sometimes offered for each of these categories. How the schools for ideological aktiv are organized in a highly industrialized province was outlined by the ideology secretary of Donetsk oblast in a 1982 article. The oblast has 60 city and district party organizations with thousands of deputy PPO secretaries for ideology and a similar number of editors of wall newspapers. There are another 200,000 propagandists, political information speakers, agitators, lecturers, and other activists.[46] All city and district party committees, and almost two dozen of the larger enterprise party organizations, sponsor schools for the ideological aktiv. Choice of a head of each school is dependent upon approval by the local territorial party committee and apparently is subject to review by the obkom. Classes are held one Saturday per month, six hours each session, eight sessions per year.[47]

The schools for the economic aktiv have a similar vocational bent. Intended for managers, they cover economic and social issues, methods of administration, and current economic policy. Here apparently the challenge is to keep the sessions from being turned entirely over to discussion of day-to-day problems at the expense of doctrinal theory.[48]

Two other categories of higher party education have been carried over from the past, universities of Marxism-Leninism, the most important task of which traditionally has been and continues to be the training of propagandists, and "theory-methods seminars." The latter, though not a new form (they were first organized in the 1930s) have been emphasized lately as the appropriate vehicle of instruction for the growing scientific-technical and cultural intelligentsia, and they have expanded rapidly in enrollment.[49] A study of the much surveyed scientific personnel of the Oktiabrskii raion of Moscow found that 70–90 percent of the researchers were enrolled in some form of political education, and of these, 50 percent were listed as taking theory-methods seminars. They had multiplied rapidly: in the mid 1970s the raion had only 68 such units, but five years later it reported 175. But the same survey found that sizable proportions (30 percent in one institute, 15 percent in the other) claimed to be studying independently while enrolled in theoretical seminars and were not in fact studying at all.[50] If these were the reported figures, how much higher is the actual incidence of fictitious participation?

The same survey found that enrollment in political education is much higher among scientific personnel than is party membership: in the sample of 2,000 researchers in scientific-research institutes, with an average age of thirty-three, party membership was just under 20 percent, Komsomol membership just over 20 percent, whereas enrollment in political education, as noted, reached 70–90 percent. There was wide variation in the rating of effectiveness given to different forms of study; universities of Marxism-Leninism were rated about 30 percentage points higher than Komsomol study on the question of how interesting respondents found them (76.1 percent to 46.4 percent). The function of political education in supplying listeners with information about current foreign and domestic policy was most highly valued; effectiveness in teaching party history, social analysis, and canons of doctrine was rated lower. The respondents did not show particularly high regard for the qualities of the instructors. Asked how fully (on a scale of "fully," "not fully," "weakly," and "hard to say") the propagandists manifested the qualities of methodological preparation, general culture, adherence to principle, ability to persuade, and knowledge of life, approximately 50 percent or more of the respondents answered either "weakly" or "hard to say." Only on the issue of theoretical preparation was there a more favorable rating: 34.1 percent "fully" and 22.1 percent "not fully." Still, 11.3 percent said "weakly," and 22.5 percent found it "hard to say." The relatively poor ratings may reflect the more critical attitudes of members of the scientific elite, as well as a greater willingness to answer honestly.[51]

Theory-methods seminars combine independent study (nominally, at least) with seminar discussions of scholarly problems. (In some cases, seminars are conducted as theory-methods seminars; in others, theory is taught separately from methods.) A seminar might comprise a group of scholars from the same faculty or division of a research or educational establishment and remain together for a period of several years. In a factory there might be twenty or thirty theoretical seminars running concurrently.[52] A portrait in *Pravda* of a highly regarded propagandist in the Ukraine will suggest something of the qualities admired by the authorities. Platon Grigorievich Kostiuk, a member of the Academy of Sciences and director of the Institute of Physiology of the Ukrainian Academy of Sciences, is considered one of the best propagandists in the Ukraine; his seminars attract top scholars. Seminar topics include "the essence of the qualitative distinction between living and physico-chemical processes" and "the unity of analysis and the synthesis of knowledge of living matter." Perhaps another clue to Kostiuk's popularity is suggested by the comment that he often discusses his travels abroad, presenting slides and films he has taken, to which, *Pravda* writes, "people always listen attentively."[53]

One final segment of the propaganda system remains to be discussed. For political professionals, there is a small pyramid of party courses at the peak of which is the Academy of Social Sciences, which trains several hundred party officials per year (from the Soviet Union as well as other socialist countries) through basic, advanced, and correspondence courses. It also oversees the rest of the propaganda system, a responsibility it shares with the Institute of Marxism-Leninism. Next below it come fifteen higher party schools attached to the union republics; these graduate about six thousand persons per year. A parallel component of the Academy of Social Sciences is the Institute for Raising the Qualifications of Leading Party and Soviet Cadres, which in turn oversees equivalent courses administered by lesser party schools. These provide continuing education to party and government officials and heads of media and cultural institutions. Around 50,000 officials take these courses each year.[54]

Dissatisfied with the effectiveness of cadre training, the Gorbachev leadership has undertaken yet another reorganization of the structure and curriculum of political education. Georgii P. Razumovskii, since 1986 the Central Committee secretary responsible for personnel matters, has outlined the goals of the new policy. More top party officials are to study; enrollments in higher party schools are to double, and in their correspondence divisions to triple. Younger cadres, who make up the great majority of the party's officials, will now be required to enroll in higher party schools. Instead of taking a single one-month refresher course once every five years, the new requirement for ranking officials will be to take two shorter (2–3 weeks) courses twice over five years.[55]

A major Central Committee resolution published in 1987 enumerates several related changes in the total system of political and economic education. Ministries are to direct economic education in their branches, under the supervision of the Central Committee and lower party committees. New forms of mass economic education in the workplaces are to be instituted, including "quality circles." The new economic thinking is to be inculcated everywhere. The journal *Political Self-Education* is to be renamed *Political Education* and to appear eighteen instead of twelve times per year. Universities of Marxism-Leninism are to be merged with the houses of political enlightenment and their personnel retrained. The courses "acceleration of the socioeconomic development of the country is the strategic line of the party" and "intensification of production" are to continue.[56]

The changes are modest indeed. As always when the line changes, the textbooks are to be rewritten. Administrative duties are to be dispersed here, combined there. The age threshold for enrollment in the highest tier of the system is being lowered as a result of the general rise in educational attainments. The goal of universal and regular exposure of cadres to party education is reaffirmed: indeed, the principle of "voluntariness," according to the new resolution, will only apply to the choice of "forms and courses" of study. In short, despite the leadership's call for a "radical restructuring" of political education, it is making only superficial adjustments in the curriculum and structure of the system.[57]

Seen in longer-term perspective, then, the current emphasis on increasing the exposure of all ranking cadres to continuous doctrinal training will probably result in the same pressures for expansion of participation that occurred in the 1970s, when, for example, in the Ukraine, the reported number of listeners in the party education system rose 150 percent over the course of the decade.[58] In 1979, the ideology secretary of the Moscow city committee claimed that 92 percent of all employed city residents were engaged in political study.[59] Admittedly, Moscow is unusual for the large number of high-ranking officials living there. Although no other region has boasted such high participation figures, most of the localities described in the party press were reporting enrollments of well over 50 percent of the employed population: 66 percent of the work force in Estonia were said to be in political and economic study in 1981; among miners in Rostov oblast, 72 percent of highly skilled workers and 51 percent of low- and medium-skilled workers were reported as being engaged in economic education in 1980; at an association in the Urals, all ITRs and 90 percent of the workers were reported as having passed introductory economic education courses in 1979.[60] Enough has been said, of course, to indicate that these figures must not be taken too literally.

One difference between the current period and the 1970s, however, is that the pressure to incorporate managers and specialists from outside the nomenklatura into ideological work as teachers and students may have abated. Through the 1970s the greatest gains in enrollment in political education were achieved by intensive efforts to recruit from these groups. This trend also helps explain the rapid increase in the numbers of listeners enrolled in the tertiary tier of the political education system. In the Ukraine, for example, by the end of the 1970s, two-thirds of all listeners were enrolled in the highest level of propaganda; in Moscow, one-half.[61] Comparable developments occurred at the all-union level. The figures below show enrollments in party schools in millions:

	1966–67	1976–77
Primary	5.2	2.4
Intermediate	3.0	8.0
Higher	5.3	10.4
Total	13.5	20.8

These totals include 9.6 million party members and candidates in 1966–67, 12.4 million 1976–77.[62] In the earlier period, therefore, about 70 percent of enrollments were accounted for by party members, but after the swelling of the system in the early 1970s, only 60 percent were party members. Meantime, even larger proportions of nonmembers were enrolled in economic education. Also note that the proportion enrolled in the top level of political education had risen from 40 percent to 50 percent. This trend continued through the remainder of the decade.

The new policy reaffirms, however, the practice of requiring all nomenklatura officials of a certain rank to take courses in higher party schools.[63] Indeed, the importance of inculcating support for Gorbachev's restructuring program and the desire to rebuild the reserve nomenklatura with young cadres sympathetic to the new line lend urgency to this task. It will therefore be difficult to avoid the same preoccupation with achieving high enrollment rates for their own sake that was prevalent in the 1970s. A secretary in Arkhangel'sk obkom wrote in 1976, for example, that the obkom was attempting to provide a higher party education for all staff officials on party committees able to take leave, and all managers and specialists of economic enterprises.[64] The head of the agitation-propaganda department of the Kazakh Central Committee stated that the party was especially concerned to give a grounding in ideological theory to the republic's "leading cadres, especially those entering the nomenklatura of party committees."[65] In Belorussia in 1976, 41 percent of those enrolled in the republic's sixteen universities of Marxism-Leninism were nomenklatura officials.[66] A report from Gur'ev oblast' of Kazakhstan in the same year indicated that around 30 percent of the nomenklatura officials of the province were currently enrolled in upper-level party schools, and another 23 percent had already obtained party educations.[67]

The three-way correlation between social or political rank, performance of activist political duties, and regular exposure to courses in political theory is thus likely to continue under Gorbachev. Those who hold high status in political and social institutions are still obliged to study political doctrine, while a precondition of attaining such status is the completion of lower level party education courses. A *Pravda* article cited the case of an unskilled worker who first entered Komsomol study circles when she began working at a particular factory and who then went on to study in a school of the fundamentals of Marxism-Leninism. She was thereupon admitted to the party and was later elected a member of the city party committee and subsequently of the oblast party committee. Similarly, a second secretary of a gorkom attended a university of Marxism-Leninism, was promoted to first secretary, and eventually became a teacher at the university himself.[68] The suggestions is that having studied in the party education system is part of the "good record" the individual demonstrates as a candidate for higher positions, which in turn lead to the assumption of further spare-time duty. In this sense primary and intermediate levels of political education are funnels into nomenklatura positions; incumbency in these in turn carries the expectation, if not the requirement, that the individual enter an appropriate unit of the vocationally specialized propaganda system at the top level.

In turn, those taking political education courses are urged to assume social assignments as part of their program; a 1978 survey of 5000 persons in twenty regional and republican party organizations found that over 80 percent of those taking political education courses had permanent social assignments. (On the other hand, only 20 percent were carrying them out satisfactorily.)[69] Many take on assignments as propagandists at lower levels of the political education system. In Leningrad, 97 percent of the propagandists are economic specialists, scientists, or senior executives.[70] In the Ukraine, one-third of the propagandists are heads of workplaces, and 90 percent have higher educational degrees.[71]

Does the saturation of the elite with political education indicate that the Soviet system is being transformed by the rationalizing effects of education, as some argue?[72] To be sure, the rise in nominal qualifications of officials can be documented. Secretary Zimianin noted that almost half of the ideological secretaries and heads of agitation-propaganda departments in republican and regional party organizations had candidate or doctoral degrees. Moreover, all raikom and gorkom ideology secretaries have higher educational degrees. On the other hand, one-third of these are degrees granted through the party education system, where academic standards are notoriously slack.[73] It would be unwise to ascribe much significance to the education received through these channels. First, as I have noted, the individual decision to enroll is generally motivated by instrumental reasons, either compliance with pressure from above or a calculation of career benefits, particularly through an advanced degree. Second, learning is formalistic, with the trappings rather than the substance of scholar-ship.[74] Third, the near-universal exposure of the nomenklatura stratum to political education is motivated above all by the party's need to supply all members (and prospective members) of the elite with a common language of power and privilege, a uniform means of treating political information across regions, institutional sectors, and social strata. Propaganda of the official doctrine serves as an indispens-able means of helping to preserve political integration among the social elite.

4 PLANNING THE NEWS

THE MASS MEDIA: SATURATION, SEGMENTATION, CENTRALISM

Chapters 4, 5, and 6 discuss the flow of communication through the print and broadcast media. Ideological controls are particularly interesting in the case of the mass media, since they are enforced from both outside and within media organizations. Relations between media and party organizations are diverse and multifaceted: they are influenced both by the particular mixture of objectives, mandates, and constraints that party officials impose on ideological work in their jurisdiction and by the balance of political power between given party and media organizations. Moreover, the *glasnost'* policy has changed media operations in fundamental ways.

The three chapters address three aspects of the media. This chapter surveys the Soviet media system overall and compares it with the more decentralized media system of the United States. It also looks at the processing of information by the media: where they obtain their raw material and how they use it. Chapter 5 analyzes party relations with media organizations and identifies the factors that reinforce party oversight and those that contribute to media independence. Chapter 6 concerns the journalists themselves and particularly the political and occupational influences on their trade.

Throughout, I will place the media in dynamic perspective, recognizing that time has affected the Soviet media system unevenly. In the post–World War II period, the number and reach of media channels have grown rapidly; but the degree to which they are the principal structure for selecting, processing, and disseminating information in society has grown far less. Their political independence continues to be undercut by three factors that will be discussed in this chapter: the segmentation of constituencies, the deeply entrenched tradition of populism, and the media's dependence on centrally controlled sources of news and guidance. The combined effect of these factors enables the party apparatus to go far to secure one of its principal ambitions with respect to the mass media: to act as an extension of the party apparatus itself. But the close integration of the mass media with the party's ideological staff undermines the effectiveness of the former in the other roles they are assigned—persuaders, problem solvers, and the party's scourges of the bureaucracy.

Since I am concerned foremost with political news and opinion, I shall deal primarily with newspapers and broadcasting. The two are organized differently. Newspapers, of which there are approximately eight thousand in the country, are published under a wide array of institutional auspices, whereas television and radio are always organs of government subdivisions (except for in-house radio stations in large enterprises) and fall under the jurisdiction of appropriate units of the government broadcast agency. However, it is unwise to make too much of the administrative differences. As a book published under the auspices of the Central Committee's Higher Party School and Academy of Social Sciences expressed it, "television, radio, and newspapers all have one 'publisher'—the party of the working class, the director of the whole cause of communist construction." The same author adds that generally, the same forms used by the party for guiding the press are used for television as well, so that a unified system of state direction exists for all media.[1]

In 1970, after considerable evolution in administrative structure, television and radio were placed under a separate, joint agency, the State Television and Radio Committee (Gosteleradio) a union-republican state committee overseeing analogous state committees under the councils of ministers of the union republics and departments of provincial governments. Local television and radio departments are therefore triply subordinate: not just to the higher state television and radio committee, but also to the corresponding government executive body (council of ministers or soviet executive committee), and to the corresponding party committee.[2] In addition, as will be discussed below, all media content with certain exceptions is subject to prior approval by authorized representatives of the censorship agency, Glavlit. Supervision over all forms of media is, with varying degrees of complexity, exercised by multiple overlapping channels of authority.

In the end, it is of course the party's ideology sector that is responsible for the political content of all media. The recent replacement of the longtime head of Gosteleradio, S. G. Lapin (appointed in 1970, when the present structure was adopted), serves as a case in point. Addressing a report-and-election meeting of the communists in Gosteleradio in November 1985, Gorbachev's ideology secretary, Egor Ligachev, delivered a tough and critical speech. He preceded it with what *Pravda* termed a "frank, concerned conversation" with senior staff members of the main editorial boards, in which he voiced serious dissatisfaction with the work of Gosteleradio. In his address he told the party meeting that, after reaching a certain level of quality, Gosteleradio had grown complacent. "Your chief task can be formulated in the most condensed form as follows: our television and radio must be entirely and fully political television and political radio. Of course, we are not talking about uttering political slogans in every broadcast. The question is different. All television and radio programs must be subordinate to one goal—propaganda, exposition, and implementation of party policy. They must be class oriented in essence."[3] Remarkably enough, Lapin had the audacity to oppose Ligachev, reportedly telling employees that it was not necessary to follow every word of Ligachev's advice, specifically that pertaining to the need for political content in every broadcast. He was replaced on 15 December 1985.[4]

Dominating the system of mass media are the central media: about thirty central newspapers, Central Radio, and Central Television. The central press's dominance may be gauged by, among other things, the fact that it accounts for about one-half of all copies of all newspapers published in the country annually.[5] The press runs of just the 8 largest central papers (see table 4) account for about one-third of the total one-time press run of all Soviet newspapers.[6] The one-time printing of all newspapers in the Soviet Union provides an average of sixty-six copies of newspapers for every one hundred persons (a ratio that varies

238979

TABLE 4   Comparative U.S. and Soviet Media Output

	United States	USSR
Number of newspapers		
All types	9,100	8,273
Dailies	1,688	194 (1981)
Total circulation of newspapers[a]	63.0 million	179.0 million
Circulation of 8 largest newpapers[b]	9.0 million	67.3 million
As percentage of total	14.3 (1985)	37.6
Number of periodicals	11,000	5,300
Number of radio stations	9,871	170 (1975)
Number of TV stations	1,220	120
Percentage of households with TV sets	98.0	85.0
Number of radio sets	489.0 million	70.0 million[c]
Number of journalists and editors[d]	191,000	100,000

Sources: Broadcasting and Cablecasting Yearbook 1986 (Washington, D.C.: Broadcasting Publications, 1985), p. A-2; U.S. Department of Labor, Bureau of Labor Statistics, Occupational Outlook Handbook, 1986–87 (Washington, D.C.: U.S. GPO, April 1986), p. 216; Editor and Publisher International Yearbook, 1955 (New York: Editor and Publisher, 1985), n.p.; IMS/Ayer Directory of Publications Fort Washington, Pa.: IMS Press, 1985, p. viii; B. A. Miasoedov, Strana chitaet, slushaet, smotrit: statisticheskii obzor (Moscow: Finansy i statistika, 1982), pp. 52–54; P. S. Gurevich and V. N. Ruzhnikov, Sovetskoe radioveshchanie: stranitsy istorii (Moscow: Iskusstvo, 1976).

Note: Soviet data are for 1983 and U.S. data for 1984–85 unless otherwise indicated.

a. U.S. figure reflects average daily, including Sunday, net circulation. Soviet figure reflects total one-time press run of all newspapers.

b. U.S. figure is 1985 average daily weekday circulation. The newspapers (with circulation in millions) are: Wall Street Journal 1.96, USA Today 1.4, New York Daily News 1.3, Los Angeles Times 1.0, New York Post 0.93, New York Times 0.93, Chicago Tribune 0.78, Washington Post 0.73; Trud 14.0, Pravda 10.2, Komsomol'skaia Pravda 9.8, Pionerskaia Pravda 9.7, Sel'skaia zhizn' 9.5, Izvestiia 6.2, Sovetskii sport 4.6, Sovetskaia Rossiia 3.3.

c. In addition, there are 75 million wired reception points throughout the USSR.

d. U.S. figure reflects the number of writers and editors, a category used by U.S. Census Bureau for all writers, editors, press agents, and similar personnel working in newspapers, magazines, television, radio, news agencies, corporations, government organizations, and the like. The Soviet figure is an estimate of total professional staff.

widely by republic, attaining a high of eighty-six in the Russian Republic, a low of thirty-one in Uzbekistan).[7] Original production of media
matter is dwarfed by the enormous system for reproducing and trans-
mitting it. Fewer than one-quarter of Soviet newspapers appear daily,
and the vast majority are no more than four to six pages long.

Even more than the press, broadcasting is organized in such a way as
to distribute a relatively concentrated, standardized, and centralized
set of messages over a vast territory rather than to encourage circulation of locally generated information and opinion. More than five
hundred cities and settlements receive three radio programs, aided in
large part by the renewed development of cable transmission to ensure
that Program One of Central Radio, and Maiak (or its republican
equivalent), plus a local station, are received everywhere.[8] Although
centralization of broadcasting is by no means so stringent as it was, for
example, during World War II (when news, war bulletins, and the daily
Pravda editorial had to be broadcast on every radio station in the
country, making local stations, in effect, outlets for the one program
operated by Central Radio), Central Radio's programming continues to
dominate over local. Central Radio runs ten programs altogether, four
of which repeat its Program One at different times for remoter regions.[9]
A 1985 decree jointly issued by the party and the government calls for
the continued upgrading of radio's technical base and the further penetration of cities and countryside, and it sets a goal of serving all cities
and settlements, as well as many rural areas, with three-program
broadcasting.[10] The decree reaffirms the philosophy that the broadcasts of Central Radio should be received everywhere in the country.

The same dominance of central programming may be observed in
the structure of television. Although the stringent centralist philosophy of broadcasting in the postwar years relaxed during the post-Stalin
period, the boom in locally produced television during the late 1950s
provoked still another centralist reaction in the 1960s. During the late
1950s and the 1960s, many towns built their own studios, and Moscow
television added new channels. In both cases, resources were spread
thin, and the quality (particularly, it seems, the ideological quality) of
programming suffered. Gradually, local studios were taken over by
Gosteleradio (from the more technically oriented jurisdiction of the
Ministry of Communications), ensuring closer central supervision

over programming. In the case of the expansion of Moscow television, it was decided by the party that the new, fourth channel was leaching resources from the important First Program; as a result, original programming for the Fourth Program was curtailed, and the channel was assigned to rebroadcast good cultural programming from the other channels.[11] At the same time a network of retransmission stations was built in order to relay signals from Moscow. One by one, Moscow's programs have been upgraded to all-union status: in 1962 a party decree made an all-union program out of Moscow's First Program; in 1982 Moscow's Second Program became the second all-union program, and eventually Moscow's Third Program, specializing in educational and scientific programs, will become a third all-union program. Currently the audience for the First Program is about 87 percent (240 million) of the entire population; the audience for the Second Program at present is only slightly over half that, 127 million, but growing rapidly.[12] In addition, the major news show on Central Television, "Vremia," is now watched by an average of 150 million persons; some 80–90 million watch the internationally oriented news broadcast "Segodnia v mire." (By comparison, 120 million people watched the 1986 Super Bowl in the United States.) Serials and films capture up to 100 million.[13] The distribution of television signals from Moscow throughout the country has occupied a very high priority, to judge from the government's willingness to fund the creation of increasingly sophisticated satellite and ground station transmission systems, including, most recently, the Ekran series, which allows smaller and remote communities to pick up central signals by community satellite dish antennae. At present, Central Television broadcasts in eleven programs, four of which rebroadcast Program One to Central Asia, Kazakhstan, Siberia, and the far northern and far eastern USSR at convenient local times.[14] Given the distances involved and the sparseness of population in much of the country, raising the percentage of the population reached beyond the present figure of just over 90 percent is a remarkable and expensive undertaking.

Centralization of programming enables the broadcasts of Central Television to dominate but not to monopolize television. All the republican capitals and many major cities have studios that produce their own programs. Viewers in Alma-Ata (Kazakhstan), for example, choose among five different channels: two from Moscow broadcasting in Russian; the local Alma-Ata station alternating Kazakh-language programming with Russian; and the Frunze (Kirgizia) station, broadcasting in Russian and Kirgiz for about six hours each evening. In addition, three evenings a week, a special channel called Alatau broadcasts in Kazakh and Uighur.[15]

The final indication of the high priority given to saturation of the society with the mass media is the rapid growth in the production of radio and television receivers. From 1950 to 1960 the number of radio receivers in use rose from 3.6 million to 27.8 million, and doubled again by 1980. Figures for 1983 indicate that there are 70 million receivers in operation, and in addition, 75 million wired reception points. Production of television sets has risen at a still faster pace: from 4.8 million in use in 1960 to 34.8 million in 1970, to 75 million in 1980, and to 85 million in 1983, of which 15 million are color sets.[16] Of every 100 families, on average, 85 possessed television sets in 1980; even by the late 1970s, a survey in Leningrad found that over 95 percent of the households owned television sets, and nearly 10 percent had two. Annual production now exceeds 7.5 million.[17]

In short, the Soviet communications system is distinctive, by comparison, for example, to that of the United States, in the allocation of its resources among the tasks of production, supervision, and distribution. A small cadre of professional editors and journalists runs a large number of print and broadcast outlets for an enormous number of media consumers, under the supervision of a small cadre of full-time party and government officials. Among these media outlets, those of all-union scope predominate in volume of issues printed and hours broadcast within the entire media system and are available, in effect, to everyone everywhere.

Another aspect of centralism is the preeminence of the party daily *Pravda* over the other central organs. Its editor (in 1988, Viktor G. Afanas'ev) is a full member of the CPSU Central Committee, an honor shared (in 1986) among media heads only with the chairman of Gosteleradio, the chief editor of *Literaturnaia gazeta,* and the editor of the party theoretical journal, *Kommunist;* and he is, by tradition, the chairman of the Journalists' Union. *Pravda* is considered the most authoritative source of policy guidance among the media and is, in addition, held up as a model of a well-produced newspaper. Recall that it was pointed out in chapter 2 that the editor of *Pravda* has not held Politburo membership since Bukharin's fall in 1929; however, heads of several top newspapers including *Pravda* attend Secretariat meetings regularly, and Afanas'ev attends each weekly meeting of the party Politburo.[18]

Although the central organizations continue to dominate the total media system, diversification—in the sense of the creation of additional media outlets corresponding to particular territorial-administrative units, audience segments, or agencies—has also characterized the development of the communications media since the revolution. In certain periods of Soviet rule, each connected with a major expansion in the territorial or social penetration of state power, media have proliferated quite dramatically. An examination of the founding dates of 492 central, republican, and provincial newspapers indicates that there have been several periods and years in which a particularly large number of papers were established, among them the First Five-year Plan period, the post–World War II years, and the late 1950s. Since then relatively few new papers have been founded.[19]

A similar story emerges when the number of new publications is compared to average press runs. Over time, the number of new newspapers above the institutional level has grown far less dramatically than the average press runs per newspaper. At 8,273, the total number of newspapers published in the USSR in 1983 differs little from the totals of 7,831 in 1950 or 7,936 in 1978. A burst of enthusiasm for setting up collective farm newspapers in the Khrushchev period caused a temporary increase in the total, which then slid back to the 8,000 level after Khrushchev's fall. Total one-time print runs rose dramatically in the 1950s and 1960s before stabilizing around 1975, as table 5 indicates.

The principle that there be media addressed to each major segment of society, to each occupation, and to each territorial-administrative unit, has been carried out faithfully. Apart from the rule that every jurisdiction of government have a corresponding newspaper, the segment of the population singled out for most attention is youth, a fact that reflects the importance of the socialization mission the media are assigned. Komsomol puts out nearly 250 youth and children's newspapers and magazines (about 160 newspapers and 90 magazines); each union republic, krai, and oblast publishes a Komsomol newspaper. Komsomol also operates its own publishing house, Molodaia gvardiia.[20] Occupational and other demographic segments are far less heavily supplied. The All-union Central Council of Trade Unions publishes the newspaper with the largest print run of any at the present time, Trud, which puts out nearly 20 million copies six days a week and has an estimated readership of 50 million. Its importance as a voice of and for blue-collar workers was emphasized in a resolution of the party Central Committee of 3 September 1982 that, undoubtedly reflecting the influence of the Solidarity period in Poland, sharply criticized the newspaper for slack performance.[21] Besides Trud, the trade unions publish another 9 newspapers and 27 magazines. Other vocational and avocational groups are served by periodicals, of which there are some 5,300 altogether.[22]

The literature on the Soviet media has tended to stress its hierarchical organization but to underemphasize the complementary aspect of compartmentalization, meaning the segregation of audiences. One manifestation of this principle is the limitation of newspaper and periodical subscription by territorial and nationality jurisdiction. One may subscribe freely to central level publications anywhere, but most lower-level publications may only be sent to subscribers within the

TABLE 5   Soviet Newspaper Production, Selected Years

	Number of Newspapers	Total One-time Press Run (millions)	Average One-time Press Run (thousands)
1940	8,806	38.36	4.4
1950	7,831	35.96	4.6
1960	9,544	68.56	7.2
1970	8,694	140.72	16.2
1975	7,985	168.03	21.0
1980	8,088	176.22	21.8
1983	8,273	178.84	21.6

Sources: Pechat' SSSR v 1981 godu (Moscow: Statistika, 1982), p. 113; Ezhegodnik (1983) of the Bol'shaia sovetskaia entsiklopediia (Moscow: Sovetskaia entsiklopediia, 1983), p. 92.

jurisdictional unit to which they are attached; this policy not only facilitates the penetration of the major Moscow media, but also favors Russian-language publications at the expense of other national languages. In addition, a policy introduced in 1975 and relaxed slightly in the early 1980s explicitly mandated a reduction in the circulation of non-Russian publications in the national republics while continuing to encourage increases in the circulation of the central press.[23] The affiliation of most media organizations with a particular territorial jurisdiction, through which they serve as the voice of the government, party, Komsomol, or trade unions for that area, eases the party's supervision of the flow of information and opinion within each administrative subdivision. The pattern of dominance of the center and isolation of local media organizations from one another is one of the crucial and enduring structures maintaining party power in the Soviet system.[24]

In practice, therefore, there is an all-union public served by a relatively small number of all-union information media; then there are localized and segmented groups, many of them with distinct ethnic, linguistic, cultural, or religious characteristics. In addition to the thirty all-union-level newspapers, there are, roughly speaking, ten newspapers on average for each union republic, about two for each province-level unit (oblast, krai, or okrug), and one for each city, city district, and rural district. Finally, nearly 4,000 enterprises, organizations, and farms issue their own papers.[25] Local production of television and radio is much less widespread: there are around 170 program-producing radio stations in Soviet cities and about 120 television stations.

The practice of dividing party from government publications, exemplified in the division of labor between *Pravda,* organ of the CPSU Central Committee, and *Izvestiia,* organ of the Supreme Soviet, is not typical at levels below the center, where a single newspaper usually is the joint organ of the jurisdiction's party committee and soviet. Most administrative guidance for such newspapers is supplied by the agitation-propaganda department of the local party committee, particularly its press sector, and by the party secretaries of the committee. In many cases, the editor is a member of the bureau of the corresponding party committee and in nearly all cases belongs to the party committee.

Soviet citizens residing in a large city may receive an urban district paper, the city paper, the oblast paper, one or more republican papers, and any of two and a half dozen central papers; they may tune into three or more local radio stations, of which two are Program One from Moscow and Maiak; they may also watch two, three, or more television channels, including First Program from Moscow, a republican channel, and perhaps a local city station. The Soviet citizen does not live in a media-starved world, but, as I shall point out in chapter 7, information hunger is nonetheless acute.[26]

SOURCES OF MATERIAL

The news media rely on three principal sources of raw copy: the news agencies, their own reporters, and outside contributors. The far heavier dependence of Soviet media, particularly newspapers, upon contributions from the public and the proportionately higher usage of dispatches from the news agencies help explain the smaller number of editors and reporters employed in the Soviet as compared with the U.S. media system. At the Sixth Congress of Journalists in March 1987, it was reported that the Soviet Journalists' union had over 85,000 members and that the total number of working journalists was 100,000.[27] Over the previous five years the number of union members rose by 10,000, but the total number of journalists stayed approximately constant.[28] Of these 85,000, around 13,000 are registered in the Moscow branch of the Journalists' Union. In the United States, the Census Bureau estimates that some 191,000 persons made their living as "writers and editors" in 1985.[29] In addition to being more dominated by central-level media, then, the Soviet media system also has a smaller establishment of full-time personnel, provided, that is, that one excludes the censorship apparatus from the count.[30]

A general characteristic of news media in any society is the requirement that they reduce the limitless stream of experience to a set of reports appearing at regular intervals. Media organizations apply standard procedures of selection and processing to maximize their control over the conversion of incoming information into reportable stories. Decisions about the stationing of correspondents, the significance of particular events, the amount of time or space to be given each item, and many other issues make news organizations gatekeepers regardless of the structure of ownership and control imposed on them from without. Soviet news media are distinct from Western media, however, in their use of internal planning, not just of the next issue or broadcast but of those falling within longer plan periods, of which the most usual are quarterly, yearly, and quinquennial.

Planning of coverage by theme allows a media organization to satisfy higher-level demands for illumination of particular topics and issues with specified levels of intensity: from total darkness to spotlight brightness. The party organization under whose supervision a media organ falls, in turn, uses the organ's plan as a part of its own plan for fulfilling ideological obligations devolving from above. At the same time, planning is one tool by which the media organization, above all its editor, exercises administrative control over the organization, shaping the raw copy received from the wire services, reporters, and the volunteer contributions and letters. Planning minimizes randomness, variation, and flux in the stream of events to which the media respond, and it maximizes predictability, order, and control.

However, it would be unwise to overemphasize the principle of planning in explaining the stylistic qualities of Soviet news products. After all, organizational routine more than editorial judgment accounts for the devotion of U.S. news organizations to such automatic news sources as press conferences and the hitherings and thitherings of celebrities.[31] Likewise, the practice of editorial planning does not explain the selection and treatment of material in the Soviet media on a day-to-day basis any better than the directives issued by Gosplan can explain managerial behavior at the plant level.[32] Among other factors, simple convention—such as the reliance on stock photographic images of fresh-faced milkmaids and bemedaled war veterans conversing with grandsons—weighs heavily on Soviet media. The weakness of Soviet writers for unadulterated corn, the ingratiating tone of the "family friend" that they adopt, the predilection for vague and windy rhetoric coupled with a "Tolstoyan" eye for the telling detail—these and many other literary affectations should sooner be ascribed to journalistic convention than to ideology. Day in and day out, Soviet editors and journalists adapt incoming material according to standard criteria; but to a greater extent than in the United States, these are affected by ideological considerations. Thematic planning is one manifestation of the editor's need to regulate the flow of information, but it is also a necessary means for integrating news media into the larger political environment.

The degree to which a particular media organ relies on one or another of its sources of material—staff reportage, wire service dispatches, or outside contributions—varies with its position in the media hierarchy. Those lowest in rank—positioned *v gushche mass* ("in the midst of the masses") as Soviet jargon would put it—draw most extensively on the material submitted from the public. Those in the upper ranks use their own correspondents most heavily. Those in the middle ranks, the city and provincial levels, balance the three sources. At all levels, however, TASS occupies a commanding position. Overall, between one-third and one-half of all newspaper space is given over to material from TASS and its republican branches. For all-union and republican papers, with their own strings of staff and nonstaff correspondents, the proportion is somewhat lower, perhaps one-fifth to one-third.[33]

TASS is the principal news service for the Soviet media. It operates as an integrated network of news-gathering and news-producing offices organized both at the all-union level and in each republic. Outside the Russian Republic, its branches are named for the republic (for example, in Estonia, ETA, for Estonian Telegraph Agency). In the Russian Republic it maintains over 70 correspondents' posts. Although TASS provides a large number of services, its most important function for Soviet news organizations is as a source of what Soviet journalists call protocol, or official, information, such as communiqués, government press releases, or texts of decrees. In this sense, TASS enjoys the status of being the most authoritative medium of information about official matters. However, it is far from being only a spokesman of the party and government, although for most Soviet media organs, as for Western media, this is how it is normally used. TASS is a formidable organization, comparable in scale of operations to the largest capitalist news agencies. It employs on the order of 500 reporters in the Soviet Union and still others in 126 foreign countries. It manages a network of teletype machines linking 300 cities. In addition to its own staff correspondents, TASS maintains contact with a loose network of volunteer correspondents.

The strong principle dividing "inside" from "outside" sources is manifest in the division of labor between the chief editorial board for domestic information *(glavnaia redaktsiia soiuznoi informatsii)* and that for foreign information *(glavnaia redaktsiia inostrannoi informatsii).* The foreign news board is subdivided by area of the world and processes all information received from its bureaus abroad. The domestic news board oversees four thematic editorial boards, including separate ones for industry and agriculture. TASS also has a chief board for photography, which supervises several hundred staff photographers.

TASS's daily output is estimated at over 2.5 million words. It provides dispatches, by teletype or mail, to 20,000 subscribers, including half the newspapers in the country (generally speaking, institutional papers do not subscribe to TASS), all radio and television stations, and another 300 foreign subscribers. The republic branches of TASS prepare special bulletins on republic-level affairs for use by district and city newspapers in the republic. Some of these are in the national languages. TASS also offers scaled-down and less expensive services to smaller media organizations, although even these are sometimes too expensive for the smallest newspapers.[34]

The great bulk of TASS's subscribers are not in fact media organs but party and government agencies. Here the principle of segmentation and hierarchy is refined to a high degree: it offers a variety of services for particular economic branches, occupations, regions, age brackets, and other categories. TASS has been supplementing its "hard news" dispatches with surveys, statistical summaries, and even some investigative reporting. It issues a daily bulletin for foreign subscribers in Moscow with economic and commercial information. For high officials it also provides the famous "colored TASS" bulletins—the white or "service" TASS and the even more inaccessible red TASS. It also prepares special bundles of material connected with particular ideological campaigns, thus helping media organs and propagandists incorporate campaign themes into their thematic plans.[35]

A study was conducted by Soviet researchers on how TASS planned its coverage of the observances of the fiftieth anniversary of the formation of the Soviet Union. The general theme of the anniversary campaign was that "the formation of the Soviet Union was the deciding factor in the socialist transformation of society, the economic and cultural uplift of all the republics, and the growth in the defensive and international might of the state." This accommodating statement allowed many particular themes to be tied to the general theme of the campaign, and it provided a central focus for all aspects of the anniversary's observance. The campaign ran from March to December 1972. In advance, newspapers sent in orders for material, specifying the number and length of items needed. TASS used these to draw up a plan for the material it would send its subscribers by theme, deadline, and the different needs of subscribers. It determined the major themes that were to be given emphasis in the course of the campaign and the way in which individual stories and events might best illustrate these themes.

Finally, a comprehensive plan of content was drawn up listing the number of items pertaining to the Soviet Union as a whole and the number pertaining to each union republic to be prepared. It listed the number of speeches by leaders to be sent out and the number of articles contributed by leading officials. For example, from among the 116 basic items that would be dispatched, most from the union republics and a few from the center, TASS determined that 39 would be speeches by leading figures from the union republics. Among these there were so many from each social sector—science, culture, labor, agriculture, and the like. It also determined how many items would have to be written by TASS's own reporters and how many would be needed in each genre, such as interview, sketch, reminiscence, and so on. Each month, TASS sent to its subscribers packets of materials, each containing one item on every republic and one on the Soviet Union as a whole. For the agitation-propaganda departments of party committees, TASS made up special pamphlets, coordinated with the general outlines of its coverage, which were used in oral presentations.

TASS monitored both how well its plan was being fulfilled and how extensively its materials were carried in the media. It did modify its plan as the year went on, in some cases because its republic branch agencies did not prepare materials as scheduled or because new items became available and could be added. TASS surveyed a sample of national and republican papers and found that, toward the end of the campaign, the proportion of items used rose; many papers began carrying items that TASS had sent out much earlier. An article by the first secretary of the Uzbek party, Sharaf Rashidov, released on 4 April, was carried by 79 papers by 10 September, 84 by 10 October, and 103 by 10 November. TASS found similar effects with other specific items. Although it did not make a special study of the use of its materials by lower-level newspapers, it found some evidence that district and city papers relied more heavily on them than did provincial and republican papers.[36]

Why did usage rates rise in the course of the campaign? Since editors were not compelled directly to carry TASS's items, the incentive to do so was inherent in the political and economic environment of the media organizations. The requirement that local media conduct the campaign with like intensity and over the same time span as central media imposed a need for a stream of material suitable for the fulfillment of the paper's own plan. When the supply of locally generated copy ran thin, TASS materials represented a steady source of entirely appropriate matter. The political environment demands compliance with the ideological requirements of the party; editors accordingly experience a constant hunger for material reflecting the given themes, with proper balance among nationalities, regions, and branches. TASS satisfied this need.

The other central news agency supplying material to Soviet media organizations is Novosti Press Agency, or APN, founded in 1961. APN differs from TASS, first, in that it fulfills a major foreign propaganda mission and, second, in that it provides foreign and domestic subscribers with "softer" news and features. Although details are unclear, it is reasonably certain that APN inherited the assignment for producing foreign propaganda that the Sovinformburo, first created in the early days of Germany's attack on the USSR in 1941 to coordinate the reporting of war news at home and abroad, had previously carried out.[37] However APN is formally the joint creation of four public organizations, the Journalists' Union, the Writers' Union, the Znanie Society, and the Society of Soviet Leagues of Friendship with Foreign Countries, and was created to back up TASS as a source of material on Soviet life more broadly. Charged with fostering friendship and goodwill among peoples, it prepares features, interviews, and stories—some 50,000 items yearly—that present a sympathetic Soviet face to the world. It puts out the newspaper *Moscow News* in several languages including Russian. It is active in book publishing, using its own publishing house as well as others, including some that it apparently creates for the purpose.[38] It publishes over 600 titles a year in 15 million copies. Within the Soviet Union, APN has about 750 subscribers, to whom it sends a daily "international information bulletin." The limited scale of its operations within the country compared to its enormous efforts abroad indicates that its principal role is as a conduit of propaganda to foreign publics.[39]

Although the materials provided by TASS and APN are adapted to some degree to the planning needs of media organs, they are not as useful in that respect as the work produced by staff correspondents, which deals with local problems. Similarly, letters and other contributions from the public mainly reflect individual concerns more than current campaigns (although many are prompted by officially sponsored discussion campaigns). Moreover, editors are under some restrictions with respect to the use of TASS dispatches. According to a report based on experience in the early 1960s, editors may not tamper with the language of TASS materials; they may cut whole paragraphs but not alter the language of any given paragraph.[40] Some news agency material may help editors carry out their thematic plans; occasionally the material sent in by the public or volunteer correspondents do so; but since the plan schedules coverage of foreseeable events, lays out assignments by department and reporter, and specifies the themes that the resulting item will illuminate, the source of copy that the plan most immediately affects is the reportage supplied by a media organ's own staff. According to M. V. Shkondin, *dotsent* of the Department of the Theory and Practice of the Party-Soviet Press at Moscow State University Journalism Faculty, thematic planning is the key to successful relations between editors and writers.[41]

The organization of Soviet news media corresponds to the needs of the planning process. Overseeing the production process is the editor in chief, who works with one or more deputy editors and an editorial board *(redaktsiia)* consisting of heads of the departments into which the organ is divided—industry, agriculture, party life, culture–daily life, letters, and sometimes others. The editor has broad responsibility for the organization and its product, dealing with the party, government, and other authorities, answering their complaints and taking their suggestions. The editor submits the editorial plan to the party bureau for approval and attends meetings and briefings with party and other officials. Because editors' duties lie to such an extent with the paper's contact with external bodies, the editor rarely oversees actual production. Rather, this function is vested with an official who on newspapers is called the "responsible secretary," equivalent to a managing editor on a U.S. paper. The secretary sees to it that the paper is put out: he or she coordinates the work of the departments and sees that they produce according to plan. The secretary oversees content, sharing proofreading duties with the proofreader *(korrektor)* and, in some cases, a "control editor" *(kontrol'nyi redaktor)*.

Staff reporters work for one or another of the departments. Much of their work consists of reporting and writing stories; but much of it also consists of rewriting the submissions received from the public. Often reporters work under quantitative quotas that set minimum numbers of lines to be submitted each week or each month. A survey of district and province newspapers found that journalists on the district newspapers usually were charged with producing 100–200 lines of their own material per issue and an equal amount of rewritten from the items sent in. At the oblast level, it found, the work load was lighter. At a particularly hard-pressed district newspaper in Kursk oblast, the editor required a certain number of lines per month from everyone on the paper; journalists had to submit 3,500 lines, department heads 4,000, the responsible secretary 1,300.[42] Probably departments work under an obligation to provide a certain number of items to each issue as well as a quota governing the minimum number of lines to be contributed.

Recently the magazine *Zhurnalist* ran a story about a district newspaper where each reporter had to submit 15 items *(informatsii)* each month and no fewer than 2,500 lines; material reworked from the public's submissions counted toward the quota. The editor, however, set himself a much lower quota, only 900 lines; and the responsible secretary had to produce only 700 lines a month. Moreover, as is customary, the editor and secretary had the right to write accounts of local party and government ·sessions from the minutes and to count them toward their quotas, while the rest of the staff struggled to meet theirs. When the quota was met, each member of the staff was eligible for a bonus *(gonarar)*, depending on the number of lines submitted in excess of the quota (at some papers, the quality of submissions is also a determinant of the size of the bonus, but this was not the case with the paper in question). Therefore, the editor and secretary usually received 40 or 50 rubles per month from the 150-ruble bonus fund, while the rest of the staff received 5–17 rubles. This created a certain amount of ill will among the staff.[43]

Accounts such as these, together with the analyses of newspaper work published by party officials and communications scholars, suggest that it is not a surfeit of political control, in the form of censorship or intrusive commissars standing over reporters' shoulders, that drives media organizations at the level of day-to-day operations. Rather, the principal motivation is internal to the organization: the concern that there will not be enough of the right sort of copy to fill each issue. It is for this reason that newspapers are advised to keep enough material on hand to fill eight or ten issues.[44] For the same reason, editors assign quotas to reporters and use planning to assign each department and each reporter a certain number of items on particular subjects for each issue. The dependence of the media on other organizations for information in order to be able to fill each issue or broadcast provides an incentive for maintaining close contact with party and government organs quite apart from the general political requirement that they faithfully reflect official policy. This aspect of the behavior of the media, resulting from the internal economy of the media organization, is analogous to the dependence of Western media organizations on stable news sources.

Ideological control over the Soviet media is both internal and external, positive and negative. Where internal controls—the editorial judgments made by writers and editors—are satisfactory, interference from outside by party ideology officials and censors can be reduced correspondingly. The effectiveness of positive controls such as guidelines for editorial plans helps obviate the need to cut and ban. Editors are of course given guidance by the annual index of prohibited topics issued by Glavlit, and more broadly by the policy directives from the party, but most final decisions about the acceptability of the tone, topic, or treatment of particular stories rest with editors rather than with censors.[45] Censorship has evolved, becoming less concerned with political and editorial content than with preserving state secrets.

So effective, indeed, was the party's previous policy of spreading responsibility for keeping the media tractable that under *glasnost'* it has been extremely difficult for the leadership to reverse course. While a few newly appointed editors, such as Sergei Zalygin of *Novyi mir,* Vitalii Korotich of *Ogonek,* Egor Yakovlev of *Moscow News,* and (during the nine months of his tenure) Ivan Frolov of *Kommunist,* have probed the limits of the permissible, the majority of media organs, above all local organizations, have scarcely changed. The contrast between the extraordinary iconoclasm of the boldest of the articles in a few central publications and the tenacity of the old ways at lower levels suggests how great is the discretion given to editors and writers to apply ideological parameters set by the party.

Crisis Management: The Cases of KAL and Chernobyl

Planning in the Soviet environment helps to ensure that the editor will never lack copy of the appropriate quantity and quality. The environment shapes organizational values to its needs. Timeliness of news does not take precedence over suitability in meeting plan and other political criteria, despite critical calls for fresher, more "operative" information. It is more important to keep a supply of usable copy on hand in case reporters fail to fulfill their obligations or censors reject an item than to scoop another news medium. Timeliness simply cannot be a decisive consideration when a media organ must stockpile stories and editorials to meet the plan.[46] The nature of the political environment, particularly the identification of all news media with the state, reinforces other organizational values, such as the importance of authoritativeness and the editor's interest in obtaining party clearance for a sensitive report. Soviet media do not carry "unconfirmed reports": if there is an event, it must be confirmed to be such and its treatment decided upon by competent political authorities before it can be reported by the media. Similarly, prompt reporting of misfortunes requires a political decision that they may be covered at all. When these conditions have been met, then timeliness is desired.

Two dramatic cases demonstrate that, where high-level political decisions must be made about the nature of the story to be reported, timeliness concedes to political considerations. These are the treatment of the shooting down of Korean Air Lines flight 007 on the night of

31 August–1 September 1983 and of the nuclear accident at Chernobyl in April–May 1986. In both cases, media coverage underwent three stages: first, a lag between the event and the official acknowledgment of it; second, a period of transition in deciding the basic angle for covering the story; and third, adoption of a stable approach to the story and its associated themes.

In keeping with normal practice for major international news, TASS issued the first announcement on the KAL affair. Its initial report came several hours after Soviet air defense forces had shot the plane down, and it indicated only that KAL 007 had disappeared without trace. About twenty-four hours after the interception, TASS acknowledged that the airliner had entered Soviet airspace and that Soviet air defense forces had sent fighters aloft, but it still mentioned neither that the plane had been intercepted nor that it had been shot down. Meantime the United States revealed that it had evidence of orders by Soviet ground controllers to the Soviet fighters to shoot the plane down, orders that had been carried out. Still, even in the new TASS statement issued on 3 September, the nature of the incident was obscured: TASS went no further than to indicate that the Soviet planes had fired warning shots with tracer shells and added the falsehood that the KAL plane had ignored these and continued its flight. However, the statement counterattacked by imputing responsibility for the intrusion into its airspace to the U.S. government. This it then softened with an expression of regret over the loss of lives. On 5 September *Pravda* carried a statement by the chief of staff of the air defense forces, not by TASS, which added further detail to the "warning shot" story, continued to accuse the United States of staging a provocation, but failed to acknowledge Soviet responsibility for shooting the intruder down. Finally, after the United States had played tapes at the United Nations that documented that ground controllers ordered Soviet interceptors to shoot the plane down, on 6 September the Soviet delegate to the United Nations read a statement giving the last official position adopted by the Soviet authorities and stating that the flight had been "stopped." This statement marked the adoption of the basic story. The famous press conference held in Moscow on 9 September, at which the chief of the Soviet general staff, Marshal Nikolai Ogarkov, offered a vigorous defense of Soviet actions and was flanked by a first deputy foreign minister and the head of the party Central Committee's International Information Department, added detail but did not modify the Soviet position taken on 6 September.[47]

Several points might be made on the basis of this case. First, the treatment of the facts evidently required a high-level political decision, since Soviet reportage was responding to international expressions of outrage; official statements progressively widened the acknowledged degree of Soviet responsibility. Second, before the final version of the facts was decided—or perhaps even known by those responsible for managing the story—the Soviet Union had counterattacked by charging the United States with moral responsibility for the plane's destruction. The stance was adopted before the story was set. Third, the obvious lack of coordination between the chain of authority responsible for ordering the plane to be shot down and that responsible for handling the public information damaged Soviet credibility, particularly outside the country, but also, according to survey analysis, among the Soviet population, because Western news reports broadcast into the Soviet Union presented an accurate version of the facts before TASS could counter it.[48]

The Chernobyl crisis tested the new Gorbachev leadership's *glasnost'* policy, intended to open to media coverage types of stories and angles that had previously been unacceptable. The explosion that destroyed the nuclear reactor at Chernobyl occurred shortly after 1:00 AM on Saturday, 26 April 1986; the first announcement about it in the Soviet media was a brief TASS dispatch shortly after 5:00 PM on Monday, 28 April, a lag of about sixty-five hours.[49] Later, Soviet sources such as Valentin Falin, chairman of the Novosti Press Agency, and Vladimir Gubarev, *Pravda*'s science editor, acknowledged to Westerners that the USSR should not have waited so long to release the first report about the accident.[50] Forty minutes after the bare-bones TASS announcement—which stated little more than that an accident at the reactor had occurred—a second TASS dispatch carried information about past nuclear accidents in the United States. As in the case of the KAL crisis, the damage control and counterpropaganda effort thus began almost simultaneously with the disclosure of the news of the event. The next morning, Radio Moscow broadcast a comment containing two of the principal political lessons that were subsequently to be repeatedly drawn about the accident: first, that nuclear power would continue to be necessary despite this setback; and second, that if peaceful nuclear reactors present dangers, nuclear weapons and their testing pose vastly greater threats.

Meantime, although attacks on sensationalism in the Western media were stepped up, not until 6 May did the media disclose any information about actual radiation levels in the Soviet Union or beyond. At no time did the media acknowledge the frightening fact that, between 2 and 6 May, radiation emissions from the reactor increased rapidly, from 2 megacuries per day to 8, along with temperatures in the core.[51] Only when the temperatures and radiation emissions stabilized and began dropping off did the authorities feel sufficiently confident to hold a press conference at the Foreign Ministry at which the evacuation of the local population was discussed along with radiation levels and wind directions in general terms. The greater openness about Chernobyl once the greatest danger was past was also reflected in the introduction of human interest themes, particularly related to the bravery and technical skill of those coping with the disaster. The famous "firefighters" story, for example, about the extraordinary efforts to extinguish the blaze atop the reactor, appeared on 7 May. From this point the basic story and its associated themes were established.[52]

That the extreme sensitivity and magnitude of the Chernobyl story prompted close and high-level coordination of the media is indicated by the fact that only a very small number of sources supplied the rest of the Soviet media system with reports from Chernobyl: the teams from TASS, *Pravda*, *Izvestiia*, and Central Television. Local newspapers in European Russia and Central Asia that I read during the three weeks following the accident used TASS's dispatches as well as the official notices from the Council of Ministers. This ensured continuity and consistency in coverage.

Further evidence of the centralized nature of the story's management is provided by the consistent omission or distortion of several points. For example, on 8 May, Kiev radio announced that schools were being closed early and young children sent out of the city; the same news was given by a Kiev official to visiting journalists on 9 May. Yet on that day, *Pravda* carried a comment specifically denying that schools were being closed early and children evacuated from Kiev. Not until 13 May did the central media acknowledge this decision. At no point did the Soviet media disclose the effects of Chernobyl's radiation on the environment of neighboring countries. No data were given that would allow comparison of the scale of the disaster with other nuclear accidents, though the constant reference to past accidents in the West created the impression that Chernobyl was no worse. In fact, as the report to the International Atomic Energy Agency in August stated, "the accident took on catastrophic dimensions."[53] The absence of a containment vessel enclosing the Chernobyl reactor was never mentioned in Soviet reports, nor did Soviet media discuss the sequence of steps in the operation of the reactor that led to the explosion.

Where a crisis overtakes the normal flow of events, these two case studies indicate, mechanisms for high-level management of news coverage ensure an exceptionally uniform line in its treatment by the media. Centralized coordination is facilitated by the dependence of the rest of the media system on the news products of a few media organs that dominate the system: Central TV and Radio, *Pravda*, *Izvestiia*, and TASS.

Planning and Adaptation

Some organizational values in the media stem from the general priority of "production" over "consumption" in society. News stories produced by the industry department, for example, tend to be valued more highly by editors than those produced by the culture and daily life department, as is reflected in the likelihood that a given item will be carried.[54] Likewise, the preferences of the party authorities in coverage are much more salient to media organizations than are the wishes of the public. The survey of provincial and district newspapers to which I have referred found that, at editorial meetings, editorial plans were frequently discussed; the problem of the skill level of the reporting staff came up often; errors that were caught in the paper were sometimes discussed; but the questions and comments of readers were mentioned only rarely.[55] Although in principle, media organizations must cover cost (having since 1965 been placed on a basis of *khozraschet,* or cost accounting), commercial considerations play a far smaller role than they do in the U.S. media. However, neither commerce nor the aim of reaching as large an audience as possible are absent as considerations. Periodically writers condemn the practice of local newspapers of serializing exciting detective stories during the annual subscription renewal season. Selling advertising space may bring a local newspaper as much revenue as subscriptions and sales and be an indispensable source of income.[56] Like clear and lively writing and timeliness of reportage, maximizing audience penetration is one of the working values of media organizations. But, where a trade-off between political acceptability and audience acceptance cannot be avoided, the former takes precedence.

There are other, perhaps less formal, operating rules in media organizations as well. Some of these are norms acquired by experience or a feel for the political climate. The responsible secretary for *Pravda* tried to enumerate some of these. Going over the layout of a new issue, the secretary checks to see whether different regions (and, doubtless, nationalities) are mentioned—that some are not mentioned too often, others not at all. What individuals' names are mentioned—are some named too frequently? Is there an appropriate balance of positive and negative material? What occupations are mentioned?[57] Emigré sources cite another such rule—that there not be too many obviously Jewish names in any one issue.

Planning and the scale of informal working rules help editors give explicit structure to the flow of incoming information. Individual items are examples of larger lessons (though the converse of this principle is also true—that in sensitive matters, general lessons are reduced to the single case in point, with as little generalization as possible) that can be infinitely repeated. Planning does more than apportion responsibility for producing material to individual departments. It sets forth a hierarchy of themes ranked by generality. Some important ideas become the leading themes for the long-term plan (the "perspective" plan), which is usually quarterly in the case of dailies. Special plans for a campaign may be drafted for a period of a year, and the plan for covering a party congress at the all-union level runs for even longer.

In the ideal case, but rarely in practice, the perspective plan "bubbles up" more than it "trickles down." That is, the editor calls on departments, and departments call on reporters, to suggest topics, stories, themes, and emphases for incorporation into the plan. At *Pravda*, where the planning process has often been described in order to set it before other papers as a model, each department proposes a plan for its work in the coming quarter and submits its ideas to the deputy editor in chief and the secretariat for review. Shortly before the beginning of the quarter, the secretariat assembles these proposals into a comprehensive plan, adjusting them to take account of impending campaigns. The editorial board discusses this draft, amends it, and finally approves it (presumably not before further review by officials in the Central Committee's Propaganda Department). The final document, *Pravda*'s secretary has warned, should not be excessively detailed; a few pages should suffice. Too much detail raises the danger that the plan will become inapplicable when actual coverage begins to depart from its projections. A general plan is more readily adjusted to changes and is less likely to lose sight of the principal objectives of the plan period in concentrating on individual themes.[58]

The perspective plan thus responds to current national priorities and relates the broad themes of coverage to the catchphrases and slogans of the period. In order to give substance to these broad categories, the current plan, one of intermediate generality—standing between the perspective plan and the immediacy of day-to-day coverage—is drafted. Here themes are somewhat more concrete and are assigned to particular issues (a current plan may outline a week's content for a daily paper, a month's for a weekly). Items may be assigned to particular correspondents. The current plan also lays out quantitative targets: the number of items and lines from each writer and department. The detailed plan for a given issue of a daily paper is drafted the previous day, so that the responsible secretary on any given day is seeing to the composing of the following day's paper and the production of the current issue.[59]

A standard form in current planning is to relate articles to campaign themes through rubrics, which are headings that identify a slogan or goal that a given article is advancing. The rubric ties a series of articles to an overarching theme, such as "perfecting the economic mechanism" or "accelerating scientific-technical progress." A rubric runs over a period of time, constantly refreshing readers' memories about a central objective and illustrating it with commentary and case studies. Since it is a relatively easy way to keep certain themes before the public with set frequency, the rubric is a very convenient device for meeting editorial plans and is greatly favored by editors. Rubrics are apportioned among departments, each taking on an obligation to provide so many items under each rubric in a given plan period; in turn, departments may apportion particular rubrics to individual reporters in the department. Again, the rubric exemplifies a set of news values, particularly didacticism and repetition, that keep media language dull and cliché ridden. Public language has become "newspaperized," Viktor Shklovsky complained not long before his death, "neutralized, sterilized, standardized, arithmetically averaged language that is intended for everyone in general and no one in particular."[60] Despite the desire for the effects of freshness and spontaneity in reporting, it is thematic control that takes precedence in editorial operations.[61]

The final source of media material is contributions from the public. For several reasons, Soviet media do act, to some degree, as tribunes of the people, as doctrine commands them to be. Dotsent Shkondin, stating that "every organ of the press in our country is a tribune of public opinion," argues that for this reason the media must adopt a "broad" approach to the issues, identifying themselves with the state's interests.[62] Many of the public's contributions are solicited for officially sponsored campaigns, such as the great "discussion" of the draft 1977 Constitution, in which, Brezhnev reported, some 140 million persons had taken part and which resulted in 30,150 letters to *Pravda* alone.[63] Apart from the wish to display the close bonds between party and people, one may identify three substantive reasons why media organizations rely on outside contributions. First, they are needed to meet the constant requirement for original material. Second, Soviet citizens pay visits and write letters in extraordinary numbers—not just to the media, of course, but to the party, government, trade unions, Komsomol, procuracy, and individual public figures as well. Finally, the media are under pressure from the party to publish a certain amount of criticism, and the public's complaints and petitions— "signals," as they are called—are an inexhaustible source of material.

How many letters do people write the media? In 1983, Central Television received about 1.7 million letters, all-union radio over 600,000; Moscow radio, over 170,000. The main central papers each receive on the order of 500,000 letters annually; oblast newspapers commonly receive 30,000–35,000 letters a year.[64] The trade unions received some 2 million letters and oral statements during the Tenth Five-Year Plan period (1976–80); the All-union Central Council alone received 225,000 letters and 60,000 personal visits.[65] The largest volume of such contacts is directed toward the party, and of these the largest number are addressed to local party committees. In 1983, some 3.3 million written and oral communications were received by party organizations below the CPSU Central Committee level; of these, 2.2 million went to city and district committees. In 1971–76, the Central Committee received more than 3 million letters, and its reception office saw more than 100,000 persons; local party organizations received more then 15 million written and oral statements.[66] Undoubtedly Nicholas Lampert is justified in conjecturing that it was the rise in the volume of contacts from the public that motivated the authorities to take several steps in the late 1970s to extend various legal protections to authors of letters and complaints and to systematize their reception and processing in the Central Committee.[67]

The flood of mail the media receive therefore forms only part of the general system of parochial contact—approaching those in authority for redress of personal grievances. Together with party offices, soviet executive committees, trade unions, and other governmental or quasi-governmental bodies, the media (primarily newspapers) are considered public offices capable of assisting individuals with their problems. The greatest share of such contacts concern complaints arising from quotidian problems: missing pension checks, leaky roofs, faulty heating, and the like, and in such cases petitioners commonly turn to numerous offices simultaneously or sequentially.[68] As a result, the volume of material submitted to the media is staggering. One Soviet source claims that nearly 10 percent of the adult population exert some influence on the media, suggesting topics, taking part in inspections, and supplying articles, and that another 6 percent write in with letters and other materials, for a total of perhaps 30 million persons who at some time or other contribute somehow to the media.[69] Inevitably, therefore, the portion of the mail that the media can use is a tiny fraction of that received. The former head of the construction department of a big city newspaper indicated in an interview with a U.S.

scholar that his department processed about one hundred letters *daily*. All but twelve to fifteen were referred to the organization that was the target of the complaint, and a notice was sent to the letter-writer that action had been taken. Of the letters kept, at most one or two might be published.[70]

Some letters not published are used as the basis for investigations by staff reporters. This very labor-intensive procedure helps media avoid the embarrassment of printing crank mail or taking the wrong side in a dispute. It also helps ensure that the facts are presented and interpreted in a way consistent with the paper's political attitude. The need to check into each individual case before a complaint is printed or commented upon is of course another reason so few letters, compared to the proportion received, are used. As a Soviet writer expresses it, once published, a letter becomes part of "public opinion," supported by the authority of the editors, who in turn reflect the authority of the corresponding party and government organizations.[71]

Informal rules govern the use of letters. There are a number of criteria for the selection of suitable case materials; some are journalistic: that they be typical, violate normal expectations, make a good story, or concern a crime.[72] Others concern treatment of critical materials. A media organization does not normally criticize officials and organizations at its own rank, only at lower ranks. Clearly the ground rules for criticism have changed under Gorbachev. Nicholas Lampert concluded that in the 1970s, even in the central press, some territories and organizations remained off limits to criticism.[73] This fact was tacitly confirmed by Egor Ligachev in his speech at the Twenty-seventh Party Congress, when he warned, "All ministries and agencies, including ministries of internal affairs and foreign trade, and any other, and all organizations, whether they be in Moscow, Leningrad, the Ukraine, Kazakhstan, Stavropol, Tomsk, or Sverdlovsk—all must be in the zone of criticism and accessible to party criticism."[74] Since then, of course, harsh public criticism of some province- and republic-level party officials and the "Berkhin case," involving criticism of province-level KGB officials, have given force to Ligachev's pronouncement.

Critical materials are not only used as copy or the basis for copy. They are also subjected to systematic review and analysis for the benefit of party and government authorities. *Pravda* prepares ten or so topical surveys each month and forwards them to departments of the Central Committee or other party and government offices.[75] Emigré sources also report that the KGB uses the mailbags of media organizations both as general indicators of the public temper and as a source of names and addresses of particular complainants. A few papers have gone so far as to computerize the processing of mail.[76]

The letters department is the main point of contact between a media organization and the public; usually it receives editorial mail and routes it to the appropriate department. It also receives visitors, often setting up reception hours to hear visitors' tales and offer counsel (such as where to receive appropriate assistance). Letters departments also organize meetings with readers outside the institution's premises and to follow up on particular requests and complaints. Media organizations make an effort to draw the entire staff into the work of processing readers' letters, but the convenience of delegating it to a specialized department seems to reinforce the remoteness of the public from most journalists. In some cases, at least, it is the largest department in the organization.

Although most audience mail stems from the personal complaints, questions, or comments of the public, about 2–3 percent of it, and more during heated campaigns and discussions, consists of direct responses to items previously published.[77] Campaigns and discussions based on contributions from the public require careful preparation. As much as possible, controllable elements, such as topic, time period, and final resolution, are guided by the editors. Sometimes a discussion follows from an unexpectedly heavy volume of responses to a particular article; in that cáse, the editors decide that it will be useful to air a sampling of the views contained in the letters. In other cases party authorities or editors decide that a discussion should be opened on a particular topic. Good planning, however, requires that the editors judge in advance (from previous mail or intuitive feel) the range of opinion among the public about the subject, in order to plan the lines of argument that will be developed in the course of the campaign. It is also wise, experienced editors have learned, not to raise the public's hopes too high about what the discussion can achieve or how many letters can be printed. Good planning therefore requires that the peak of intensity reached by the discussion be foreseen.

It is also important that there be a way to wind up the discussion when it has served its purpose. One way to conclude it is for party or government officials to hold a meeting to decide what action is to be taken. The resolution adopted at the meeting then becomes the culmination of the campaign; it points to the changes to be made, problems to be set right. So, as much as possible, the discussion is incorporated into the regular work of publicity and decision making by the authorities and does not create a groundswell of opposition sentiment. Major discussions and campaigns, of course, employ several channels, including letters and commentary in the media, political meetings, and agitation, to draw out and steer public opinion toward predetermined conclusions.[78] During more ceremonial campaigns, such as the 1977 discussion of the constitution and the 1985–86 discussion of the draft party program, party statute, and economic plan, it is likely that party activists are encouraged to contribute letters with constructive suggestions. In other cases, media discussions are used to build the impression of popular support for a policy that the leadership is already inclined to adopt. A case in point was the decade-long airing of views about the proposal to divert northern rivers into the Volga and to Central Asia. Though opponents were successful in the end in blocking the project, they expressed considerable bitterness subsequently that the press discussion was tilted in favor of proponents. As the chairman of the Ukrainian Academy of Sciences observed, "at one time, all this could not be called a discussion—so much did the 'exchange' of opinions move in a single direction."[79]

Still another source of outside contributions is the network of freelance correspondents, many of whom maintain loose relations as stringers for particular newspapers, broadcast stations, or TASS. Their published contributions, unlike the "signals" from ordinary citizens, are paid, but they work on a nonstaff *(vneshtatnyi)* basis (meaning ineligibility for membership in the Journalists' Union), even when they sign a contract with a particular editor and consider their submissions the primary means of livelihood.

Most volunteer correspondents work on a spare-time and occasional basis. The old category of "worker-peasant correspondents" is by now a Soviet tradition, having originated in the Lenin era and been revived in the Khrushchev era. Today there is less attention to institutionalizing the *rabselkor* movement but just as much dependence on their contributions. Some work in reception offices, collecting and writing up the questions, complaints, stories, petitions, and proposals received, and submitting them to the sponsoring media organization. Some correspondents hope to break into journalism by polishing their skills as reporters and writers.[80]

Altogether there are said to be 6 million volunteer correspondents. The figure is of uncertain reliability, however, because of the variability in the level of involvement and the trend toward deinstitutionalizing the practice. There is no identification card one can carry to certify that one is a free lance; there are no required courses to pass. Although there is a nominal All-union Commission for Work with the Worker-Peasant Correspondents and the Lower Press, it is no longer active. The original aktiv is aging.[81]

Still, the correspondents contribute a sizable share of the media's copy. Most writing published in institutional papers (mnogotirazhniki) is contributed by nonstaff authors, although usually editors and some writers are full-time. At the level of district papers, probably half or more of the content is based on material submitted by free-lance writers, although, as I have pointed out, staff writers spend a good deal of time revising such material and regard this as a task almost as demanding as writing their own stories. Among higher-level newspapers, the use of nonstaff contributions falls off to one-third or less of the content. In the late 1960s, Pravda studied 100 newspapers, taking one day's issue from each, from all levels—central on down to institutional. Of 2,800 items written about leading workers, 500 were by nonstaff correspondents. A study conducted by Leningrad University analyzed critical materials in Leningradskaia Pravda in the second half of 1968. It found that, of 520 critical articles, 380 had been written by worker-peasant correspondents.[82] Estimating how much of the content of newspapers overall comes from nonstaff contributions is difficult since staff reporters and editors often fail to give credit to the original authors.[83]

Editors sometimes take pains to organize their stringers in such a way as to increase the quantity and suitability of contributions, forming, for example, nonstaff departments (for example, for people's control, environmental problems, military-patriotic education, and many other topics). One newspaper periodically turned over a whole page to the contributions from a particular nonstaff department. Often media organizations set up regular posts at which stringers receive letters and suggestions from the public and report on conditions in a particular enterprise or territory.[84] Most free lances, however, work individually.

The practice of contributing material to the media is widespread but not randomly distributed among the populace. Nonstaff correspondents, and even the authors of published letters, are significantly more likely than nonwriters to be activists and party members.[85]

Nonstaff correspondents mainly represent higher strata of the population. A survey in Donetsk oblast of twenty-eight newspapers at different levels found that fewer than 22 percent of the nonstaff writers were actually workers and peasants.[86] Another study found that 21.1 percent were workers and that, of these, most were in high-skill grades; engineering and technical employees comprised the largest category, 42 percent. Local studies show that 75 percent of the worker-peasant correspondents have a secondary or higher education and a similar percentage were continuing their studies by taking courses in the adult education system.[87] The editor of a district paper observed that his most active nonstaff correspondents were actually party secretaries.[88] A survey of free-lance correspondents in the Tatar Autonomous Republic found that over 66 percent of the respondents were party members and another 7.8 percent were Komsomol members; that 84.5 percent had higher, specialized, or secondary education; and that 82.6 had volunteer social assignments. Over 50 percent had studied in the party education system.[89] Overall, it has been found that nonstaff correspondents have better than average educations, are more skilled occupationally, and are social activists, having at least one social assignment besides journalism.[90] In the case of TASS, to become a free-lance contributor requires the approval of the party bureau of one's region, and the work is taken on formally as a social assignment.[91]

The evidence strongly indicates, therefore, that the institution of nonstaff correspondents overlaps to a great extent with the corps of social and political elites who are expected to set an example of public-spirited activism in their localities. For many, spare-time journalism is undertaken to fulfill the obligation of volunteer public service. Others do it to earn extra income. Still others may seek a career in journalism and contribute stories to develop skills and contacts. Like the ideological activists discussed in chapter 2, they are intermediaries between the anonymous upper reaches of authority and the working masses, and they carry criticism and commentary from the sphere of daily life to the media and write material that all will read.

In this chapter I have shown that it is the internal economy of the media organization, itself strongly influenced by the external political environment, that leads editors to value an abundant, politically acceptable, and predictable flow of material. News agency, reporter-generated, and voluntarily submitted materials are all used and essential. The practice of planning reflects the dual pressure on the editorial staff: for administrative control over the organization, and for integration with the political, particularly party, authorities. Planning in turn provides categorical themes and guidelines that are superimposed on departments and writers. Editors also face pressure to maximize popular participation in producing information, including the airing of a certain amount of criticism of the system's performance. To fit voluntarily contributed material to their plans and needs, editors organize stringers into departments and posts; hold public discussions to generate usable mail; and rewrite nonstaff contributions to meet predetermined needs by volume and theme.

The organizational environment within and without Soviet media organs shapes the news selection and processing values in ways that distinguish the Soviet media from the U.S. and other democratic systems. On the scale of desiderata, clarity and freshness of expression, timeliness of coverage, and correspondence with audience interests rank lower than acceptability in the eyes of the most pertinent audience, the party staff of the corresponding party organization. Repetition and didacticism, a preference for production over consumption themes, the heavy stamp of campaign slogans, all reflect these values, as does the force of conventionality and inertia. On the other hand, much in their environment helps editors meet these demands. Soviet citizens flood media organs, as other bodies, with their complaints and suggestions, so that the problem is one of selecting from among many eligible contributions; and the pressure on members of the sociopolitical elite to find socially constructive forms of public activism encourages many to turn to free-lance journalism. In addition, TASS and, to a lesser extent, APN provide a daily source of precensored, authoritative, and available copy, the only problem being that its dispatches are simultaneously accessible to every media organization in the country. Given these ready pools of copy, the small size of Soviet media organization staffs is less restrictive than it would otherwise be, and tendencies toward the professionalization of journalism, as I shall show, tend to be undercut.

5 PARTY-MEDIA RELATIONS

PARTY TUTELAGE OF THE MEDIA

Chapter 4 stressed the point that media organizations develop control techniques, such as thematic planning and distinctive operating norms, that adapt the processing of information to pressures from the political environment. It was also noted that the media depend on materials contributed by activists drawn disproportionately from the same elites that comprise the main corps of agitators and propagandists. This association, together with the strength of media "populism," also helps explain the relative weakness of institutionalized power in the fourth estate. Still, while it is safe to surmise that any given media organization normally defers to the party committee charged with supervising it, the media can also deploy independent political resources, particularly when they ally with other powerful institutions and currents of opinion. The content of a particular broadcast or publication therefore reflects the shifting balance of three sets of sometimes contending political forces: party officials, editors and journalists, and outside social interests.

To be sure, generalizations about party-media relations need to be qualified with cautionary remarks about the diversity of patterns and the limits of Western knowledge. Data are scarcest where they are most needed to appraise the balance of power among party officials, media organizations, and political forces seeking to affect policy: at the center. However, a sufficient number of cases have been discussed in Soviet literature that one can say with a fair degree of certainty what is normal and what is exceptional.

Deeply rooted in Soviet political culture is a conception of the communications media as instruments to political ends. The view that the job of gathering and reporting information must be justified by service to the collective good rather than by a diffuse civic right to know is integral to Soviet doctrine; it has deeply pervaded the working norms of media organizations, and indeed it is widely accepted in popular culture. Among émigrés from the Soviet Union, for example, the belief that the government should "raise the level of the press so that the press will educate the people" is widespread.[1] In practical terms party officials instruct media personnel about their current tasks in a variety of ways: *Pravda* editorials and other central press publications, speeches by leaders, and frequent consultations between party officials and media personnel.[2] Whose instrument the media are, however, can be unclear. Like other channels of ideology, the mass media are considered both a means by which society governs itself, shaping and expressing public opinion, and a tool of government regulation of society.[3] They are to be tribunes of the people and custodians of their interests while simultaneously extending the party's organizing and propagandistic reach into society. These potentially conflicting roles are manifested in the norm that the media always carry some "good, sharp, fighting material," critical of slack bureaucrats and lagging collectives, while serving "as an extension of the party apparatus."[4] In the phases of party support for *glasnost'*, the potential conflict between these roles is only intensified.

Like Western officials, Soviet authorities occasionally express frustration at the media's ability—which the press once was said to have in common with the harlot—to exercise power without responsibility. The media's capacity to cast favorable or unfavorable light on the activity of a wide range of individuals and bodies lends them a measure of power. In their capacity as trustees for the public interest, they are expected to propagandize "leading experience," holding the exemplary up to praise, and to investigate abuses and bottlenecks in government and society. Material printed and broadcast generates pride or embarrassment and can prompt inquiries by party and government agencies. The media play schoolmarm to society, hectoring, snooping, judging, admonishing, praising, preaching. Theirs is a tutelary authority, derived from the political authority of the party (and particularly from its monopoly over ideology) but not purely ancillary to it.

Editors and reporters must constantly judge how to select and treat subjects for coverage. A misjudgment by an editor in a fight over policy or jurisdiction between competing bureaucracies can have serious consequences for a reporter or for the editor himself. Most editors minimize risk by confining criticism to safe targets, such as organizations attached to jurisdictions well inferior to their own. Although one dramatic effect of *glasnost'* has been a sharp rise in the number of exposés of central and republican party and government organs, at lower levels, the habit of playing it safe continues to prevail. In the current climate of encouragement for critical reporting, however, few local party secretaries are as foolish as the raikom secretary who explicitly prohibited local media from criticizing anyone on the raikom's nomenklatura without his express approval.[5]

Yet the incentives remain strong for local officials to discourage muckraking journalism. The editor of the Murmansk oblast paper explained at a national media conference, for example, that his paper had run a shocking story some two years before about an incident involving hooligans who deliberately shot at the local monument of military glory. The story had been picked up by the national media: the newspaper *Sovetskaia Rossiia* asked the reporter to write an article about the incident. Then another central paper carried the story, followed by Central Television, the journal *Yunost'*, and, most recently, Central Radio. Although it was the sort of random, isolated occurrence which could take place anywhere, the story evidently touched a sensitive nerve in public opinion, and the resulting wave of national publicity required that there be an official response. The Murmansk authorities were censured for having let local military-patriotic propaganda lapse and were required to report on measures taken to improve matters. Under the circumstances, the editor asked, how could the local party authorities be expected to welcome investigative reporting by the local media?[6]

As countless instances attest, public officials fear negative publicity and take pains to avoid it. A Georgian raikom secretary, perhaps exaggerating a bit for rhetorical effect, claimed that many officials would rather be repeatedly hauled before the bureau of the raikom for a dressing down than see their name in even a short critical article in the raikom newspaper.[7] Officials not only suppress unfavorable publicity, but also seek to use the media for building favorable impressions of their performance. During the 1986 campaign to clean up corruption in Central Asia, it was revealed in the central press that the ideology secretary of a Turkmen obkom had used his power over the local media to curb critical publicity and to plant stories favorable to the first secretary, whose portrait had appeared in nearly every issue of the local paper. When a resolution critical of the Turkmen republic party organization was handed down by the CPSU Central Committee, the Turkmen Central Committee Agitation-Propaganda Department telephoned the republican theoretical journal to prevent it from publishing the resolution.[8]

Likewise, officials sometimes resort to the posturing and press agentry of their Western conterparts to generate favorable publicity. The agitprop department of an obkom in the western Siberian territorial-production complex reported on the methods it used to obtain as much coverage as possible. It held press conferences for the media every quarter and ran a permanent press office issuing information on economic subjects. The obkom had seen to it that all the journalists in the oblast had new and adequate separate apartments. It had built new buildings for several district newspapers. When reporters from the central media visited, as they did rather often, the obkom saw to it that they were hospitably treated. The agitation-propaganda department maintained a file of clippings of articles written about the complex. "We are grateful" to the media, wrote the head of the department, "for the attention they have given us." But like public figures anywhere, he wanted still more publicity. Some media outlets, he commented, such as the thick journals, could do more.[9]

Of course many factors prevent the media from realizing more than a small portion of their power to publicize abuses, contribute to the exchange of ideas, promote political goals, and generally shape and reflect public opinion. Above all the docility of the media is a product of the informal authority relations in the political system, specifically the evolution of mobilizing structures into patterns of asymmetrical mutual accommodation between the party and other governing institutions. The most effective constraints keeping the media in harness are not overt and intrusive but are internalized, implicit, and self-perpetuating. The media need guidance from the party at least as much as party officials need compliant media outlets.[10]

The integration of heads of media organizations as junior partners in the political elite normally suffices to preserve satisfactory relations between party and media. Informal relations based on shared mutual interests are backed up, however, by a powerful second line of formal controls, including party discipline, the nomenklatura system, and censorship. Expulsion from the PPO in the media organization (or nonadmittance upon expiry of the candidate period) is devastating to a journalist's career.[11] Heads of media organizations enter the nomenklatura of the next-higher party organization,[12] and an editor's further career advancement therefore depends on its assessment of his job performance. As far as censorship is concerned, the relative infrequency of interference with material submitted by media organizations attests to the effectiveness of self-censorship. According to Lev Lifshitz-Losev, editors prefer not to submit risky material since a political miscalculation or error can have serious career consequences.[13] These controls create incentives for self-restraint on the part of editors and journalists.

Many heads of media organizations are part of the ruling party bodies in territorial jurisdictions; representation is higher at lower levels. In 1981, sixty-nine newspaper editors, and in 1986, sixty-eight, were members or candidate members of province-level territorial party committees.[14] Spot reports suggest that higher rates in districts and cities are normal and that at the level of republic central committees rates are somewhat lower.[15]

At the all-union level, media representation in the party's governing organs is nominal. Six media figures (the editors of *Pravda*, *Izvestiia*, and *Kommunist*, and the chairmen of Gosteleradio, Goskomizdat, and Novosti), were full members of the Central Committee named in 1981. Seven more (eight, counting the head of a film studio) were candidate members, and six were members of the Central Auditing Commission.[16] This rate was roughly comparable to that of scientists and ambassadors (and lower than that of military and mass representatives).[17] In 1986 a roughly comparable number of media executives were elected to the slightly smaller new Central Committee: four as full members (the new head of Gosteleradio, *Pravda*'s editor, the new editor of *Kommunist*, and *Literaturnaia gazeta*'s editor); and another nine as candidate members. Another six became members of the Central Auditing Commission.[18]

At this level, of course, membership confers distinction on individuals who by their position or other qualifications have already usually attained high political status. At lower levels, membership in the ruling party body, aside from its ceremonial importance, creates opportunities for editors to hear reports about local life and to take part in decision making. At the local level, then, far more than at the center, media executives form part of the ruling nucleus of each territorial jurisdiction.

In addition to these horizontal and synchronic ties is the diachronic interlocking of media and party careers over time, as is the case with political organizers whose tour as a volunteer is followed by a junior position on the party's staff. A study of individuals appointed to prominent media positions between 1974 and 1986 (the data base consists of all those whose appointments were announced in *Zhurnalist*—a total of 873) reveals that around 21 percent had some experience as a staff member of a party organization before appointment to their current position in the media. Of those 273 individuals named to chief executive positions—newspaper chief editors, directors of publishing houses, heads of central or republic broadcasting committees and the like—36 percent had had some party staff experience. In 1986, a year of high turnover in the central and republican media, 30 of 54 new chief executives had been party officials in the past, and 17 of these were appointed directly from the party committee to the media organ.[19] For many media executives, then, an expected part of a career is a tour of duty in the party, which may lead to a permanent career in political work or back to a higher position in the media.

Apart from the participation of editors in party decision making, party organizations take steps to maintain close and direct contact with the media organs in their jurisdictions. At a minimum this contact always includes party approval of the editorial plans proposed by each media institution. On a regular basis the bureau of each party committee examines the plans submitted by the editorial boards. In some cases the bureau does little more than give the plan a cursory check. In others the officials in charge of ideological work, or even the first secretary, propose revisions. Often the party advises the editors about the directions that coverage should take in the coming plan period, explaining what issues are currently pressing both locally and nationally. Sometimes secretaries and department heads suggest specific stories to be run.

The new style of party oversight of the media under Gorbachev, according with the pragmatic, antiformalistic style of ideological work generally, aims at minimizing unduly detailed supervision. A recent article on the subject by Alexander Kapto, formerly ideological secretary of the Ukrainian party Central Committee, explains the ideal as follows:

> In our view the most successful form of long-term (perspective) planning has been found: to define annually the basic directions of the work of each organ of information. Within these outlines journalists receive sufficiently broad scope for experimentation [*poisk*] and creative initiative. . . . Petty tutelage over the press has practically disappeared.
>
> It would, of course, be premature to say that such an approach is already typical of every party committee. There are still gorkoms and raikoms that demand from the media extremely detailed plans that lay out virtually every article and letter to appear. For some leading executives to renounce well-trodden ways is oh, so hard, especially when they are incapable of feeling and accepting the new.[20]

One reason for the stubborn persistence of detailed party interference in media planning is the importance to local officials of media publicity for relaying their demands to higher authority. They therefore prefer plans that make the case for specific local interests.[21]

Given the high degree of integration of media executives into the political elite, the tensions built into party-media relations usually stem not from an adversarial posture by the media, but from the difficulty of making a normally close and cooperative relationship operate smoothly. Party officials are often dissatisfied by the trite, hackneyed style of media language, and journalists complain that they need closer support from the party, more information, better coordination, and less unrealistic plans. For both sides, consequently, the key to successful relations is closer integration, particularly a higher volume of informational contacts. Though the relationship between editor and party committee is the single most important bridge, the practice of giving more media personnel access to a wider range of party and other officials has spread.[22]

Party-media contacts take a variety of forms. In Odessa the obkom sees to it that, every Monday afternoon, officials from each department of the party committee are available to the heads of oblast- and city-level media. Before the meeting, the agitprop department, which runs the weekly sessions, gathers from the rest of the departments a rundown of the coming events of the week and a listing of the officials from the party committee and from other agencies who will take part. The agriculture department may report that a collective farm is holding a seminar for agronomists; the industry department may note that a new factory is opening. The agitprop department then briefs the editors about these events to ensure coverage. Representatives from each department are present to suggest ways of publicizing the events. The editors agree on how they will divide up coverage to avoid excessive duplication. When the editors return to their own papers and stations, they present this information to their staffs and devise a plan for the week, with assignments for stories. (A planning session of this kind is referred to as a *planerka*.) Reporters discuss the angle and genre to be used for each story.

This somewhat idealized case study is atypical, in part because of the effort to coordinate coverage across media organizations. All the editors are members of the obkom's ideological commission and, together with other members, divide themes and styles of treatment among the media and mass political channels of communication, seeking to give each channel a distinctive set of issues. Such coordination is particularly useful during a political campaign or the harvest season. Usually, though, it proves difficult to sustain and tends to break down in practice.[23]

Press conferences, planning meetings, and informal consultations are widespread at all levels, contacts between media personnel and agitprop officials often occurring at more frequent intervals than sessions with the first secretary. The CPSU Central Committee, according to the Rand study's respondents, runs "a regular biweekly meeting at the Propaganda Department, held for the chief editors of all the major media. There the editors are instructed on the latest nuances of policy and are told what types of coverage to stress in their newspapers."[24] This appears from Soviet sources to be the practice at lower levels as well. In Lithuania, the Central Committee of the republican party organization holds a quarterly conference with representatives from all ideological institutions, including the media, to coordinate all forms of communication in the republic. The Central Committee meets monthly with all republic-level editors. Its agitation-propaganda department holds regular meetings with editors, in which the reference staff of the department *(retsenzenty* or *referenty)* take part; the reference staff comprise specialists in various fields who can answer the questions from the editors, comment knowledgeably on the coverage the media have given to various subjects, and offer suggestions for current coverage.[25]

Similarly, the agitprop department of the Estonian Central Committee holds regular conferences for editors, which define the directions media coverage should take. Recently the committee was dissatisfied with the work of the republic branch of TASS and devoted a meeting to criticizing it. The department also held a special conference with agency staff and local newspaper editors to indicate specific improvements. In response, the agency started up a bulletin specifically for city and district papers, created an institute of nonstaff correspondents working for it on a contract basis, improved employee incentives, and spruced up the format of its releases.[26] In smaller republics the agitation-propaganda department of the republican Central Committee can still exercise a broadly supervisory control over the entire republic's media. In larger republics the obkoms perform the great bulk of directing and coordinating oblast- and lower-level media, again using the same devices of briefings, press conferences, and informal consultations. Republic-level assemblages are likely to be organized around specialized themes, such as improving agricultural production or consumer goods production, and to be held at longer intervals.[27]

An important aspect of these meetings is the evaluation that editors receive of past performance. The monitoring of the media by staff officials in the press sector of the agitation-propaganda department provides editors with what is doubtless their most important source of feedback. Much of the comment and criticism they receive apparently is quite specific, referring to particular articles and stories. There can be little doubt that comments by the main reference group for journalists, the party staff, are far more salient than the responses generated among the media public. For example, the Moscow State University Journalism Faculty survey of local journalists found that 65 percent of journalists on district papers and 68 percent of those on provincial papers considered themselves well informed about the directives issued by party authorities. Frequent direct personal contacts with raikom officials was reported by 85 percent of the journalists. The survey found a gratifying degree of congruence between the definitions of tasks of the media by journalists and by party officials—a list of over twenty applicable tasks was given almost identical rankings of priority by the samples of party officials and of journalists.[28]

This survey was conducted in 1969–71; since then the use of meetings, press conferences, and other forms of contact with party officials has spread. After the 1979 resolution on ideological work appeared, for example, Grigorii Romanov, then first secretary of the Leningrad obkom, pledged to increase the frequency of press conferences from a quarterly to a monthly basis. It has also proved useful to create mobile press offices on an ad hoc basis, as at harvest time, when party staff can issue daily releases about major bottlenecks or successes.[29] Similarly, agitprop departments organize field trips for journalists to important enterprises, construction sites, and other institutions, which allow party officials, media personnel, and local administrators to work out a common approach to media coverage.

Local party officials have wide leeway in determining the forms and frequency of their meetings with journalists. Where it is established, the press conference is normally held every two or three months. Editors meet more frequently with the agitation-propaganda staff of party committees, both to plan lines of coverage and even specific stories for the future, and to assess previous work. In some localities the practice of requiring editors (and sometimes media department heads) to make formal reports before the party committee plenum, the bureau, or a particular party department is customary. In others a party official attends an editorial meeting of a media organ.[30] Regional seminars, field trips, and educational courses sponsored by the party committee or the Journalists' Union supplement the more frequent forms of contact. The important point is that in their variety, these institutionalized channels for consultation meet a need felt at least as strongly by media personnel as by party officials. The first secretary of the Shchekino gorkom, describing practices in his city, probably made an accurate observation when he claimed that the meetings with party officials are in fact sought by journalists.[31] They keep journalists and particularly editors informed about the policy lines and specific decisions made by party and government authorities; beyond that, they give them the opportunity to discuss the decisions, ask questions, and receive background information and feedback in a closed, face-to-face setting.

The flow of information and cues serves what I have argued is a crucial organizational requirement of the media: the need for regular, authoritative information. Party control is more effective, therefore, when it provides context-specific guidance. Where the party simply sets out general thematic directions for the editorial plan without providing instruction on how to meet the plan targets, editors are far more uncertain about how to find appropriate content. One might expect conflicts between party and media to be more frequent as well. Constant provision of advice reduces the vulnerability of media organizations to penalties for errors or poor performance. For the party, inculcating a sense of shared political responsibility among editors helps channel the potential power of the media into the desired directions. The positive incentives for playing along are also backed up by strong sanctions for misbehavior.

GLASNOST' AND THE MEDIA

Although I have painted a picture of a basically cooperative party-media relationship beset by relatively minor frictions, the Soviet media do sometimes become independent players in political disputes, and this pattern has grown much more common under Gorbachev. In what circumstances do media organs take a stance at variance with or in opposition to the preferences of their publishers? In the pattern of media docility in the late Brezhnev period, the provincial and lower press largely abandoned a critical role. If an article appeared that criticized a sitting party secretary, for example, that meant that higher authorities had already decided to remove him.[32] Still, media organs do sometimes take positions that test the ability of party officials at a given level to employ their media as a reliable extension of the party apparatus. Editors realize that no local political establishment is autonomous: higher-level authorities may intrude and take sides in a local contretemps. When unsure which side is that of the angels, an editor must decide whether to go along with the wishes of his sponsors or appeal to higher levels.[33]

A case discussed in *Pravda* in 1981 is an example of the latter choice. *Pravda* received letters regarding a newspaper in a power station, which, drawing on investigations carried out by the people's control committee, had printed articles critical of the enterprise's food service. Evidently food grown in the plant's gardens was being diverted improperly, and the head of the station's party organization was in on the scheme. The head of the food service complained about the articles, and the district party organization initiated an investigation. Unwilling to expose the officials involved in the case, it formed an investigative commission in which raikom secretaries outnumbered representatives of the newspaper. The commission submitted a report that effectively whitewashed the culprits. The raikom chastised the paper for printing unfounded reports and complained that, if it had turned up problems, it should have come to discuss them with the raikom first, rather than rushing into print with them.

The raikom then demanded that each issue of the newspaper be submitted for approval before publication, as was the practice with the raion newspaper. The paper resisted. The raikom then sought to call in a representative of the obkom press department to sort things out, but none was available. The head of the agitprop department of the raikom then ordered that excerpts of all critical articles be shown to him before publication. Commenting on the story, *Pravda* used the case as a negative example of party supervision of the media. Editors, it explained, are given the authority to approve the content of their organs; if they err, they answer to the party committee, but the party committee should not take on the job of editor. However, if in a particular case the entire party committee collectively demands to approve every issue of a particular organ before it comes out, this is permissible. In general proper oversight requires the party to have strong ties to editors, hearing their reports and monitoring their performance, but supervision should not give way to arbitrary administration. In this instance, *Pravda* advised, the obkom authorities should step in and straighten matters out.[34]

Generally the party disapproves of party officials who usurp editorial prerogatives, since, as with *podmena* in government and economic administration, it detracts from the party's ability to exercise effective political direction and to monitor performance. Usually, where journalistic investigations or editorial crusades expose party officials to possible criticism, both sides attempt to resolve the problem by calling in outside support.

In the case just cited, the paper was allied with the people's control committee in the power station, though that probably counted for little; it also brought in the oblast-level trade union council, the department of the police concerned with combating corruption in retail trade (OBKhSS), and the trade inspection organs. These agencies sided with the paper. Ultimately, when the newspaper succeeded in enlisting *Pravda*'s aid, intervention from that level was decisive. But until then, the enterprise paper was fighting the combined forces of the enterprise-level and district-level party authorities.

A similar case was recently recounted in *Zhurnalist*. In a remote district of the far eastern USSR, a combative and idealistic reporter named Petr Braun, who made enemies with his critical investigative reports, found the powers arrayed against him insuperable. His editor turned against him; the local party authorities ignored him. When he published an article criticizing the head of the enterprise handling local communal services, the party organization of the enterprise met and passed a resolution demanding that the raikom censure Braun. As *Zhurnalist*'s reporter put it, "who knows what might have happened had the district people's control committee and the territorial board for communal services not backed the reporter?"[35]

In the end, Braun was vindicated by the obkom, but by that time the local party officials had decided not to admit him to the party when his term of candidate membership expired. Braun was beaten down by the authorities; he ceased writing critical articles and wrote only success stories ("leading experience"). One wonders whether the long and rather mournful article in *Zhurnalist* that recounts his tale will have any effect on Braun's situation.[36]

These are cases where relatively trivial matters—both cases, it will be noted, involve consumer goods and services—became politicized because of reporters' investigations. Once several concerned organizations took sides, only higher-level intervention could settle the dis-

pute. In both instances the newspaper received some sort of vindication from media at the national level, but for this very reason, such
cases must be regarded as highly exceptional. Even more exceptional,
at least in the late 1970s and early 1980s, were attacks on officials in the
area of production. Publication in *Pravda* in October 1981 of a letter
from an economist at a state farm in the Ukraine about serious abuses
in her farm and district prompted an investigation by province-level
authorities. A follow-up report in *Pravda* two months later from the
first secretary of the party obkom acknowledged the violations and
stated what corrective measures had been taken. The report was unusual for the gravity of the offenses exposed, and probably for this
reason it provoked more letters from readers than nearly any other
critical report in the early 1980s.[37]

The "Berkhin affair" will serve as the final example of a media
exposé that developed into a power struggle. In its effort to vindicate
the investigative reporting of a Ukrainian journalist, Berkhin, *Pravda*
eventually succeeded in exposing to official criticism members not
only of the procuracy and the police but also of the local KGB, whose
misbehavior was acknowledged by Viktor Chebrikov, KGB chairman,
on the front page of *Pravda*. Chebrikov's statement was the third
article that *Pravda* published on the case.

Berkhin had submitted material critical of law enforcement agencies
in the city of Voroshilovgrad to *Pravda*, which had published an article
in November 1985. In July 1986 local prosecutors prepared a criminal
case against Berkhin in order to force him to recant the material he had
given *Pravda*. Presumably at *Pravda*'s behest, the USSR Procurator's
Office intervened and got the case against Berkhin dropped. The USSR
Procurator's Office found that city and district procuracy officials had
acted improperly and illegally, and that, moreover, the Ukrainian
procuracy had failed to investigate their actions. The local prosecutors
were relieved of their duties, according to *Pravda*'s initial report on the
case, and the Ukrainian procuracy was ordered to apologize to the
journalist for the harm done him.[38]

Not content with this resolution, however, *Pravda* intervened again,
clearly targeting bigger game. In a long, rather rambling, article on 4
January 1987, it indicated that the province of Voroshilovgrad bore a
good deal of looking into—that deteriorating management and high-

level corruption were prevalent in a number of sectors there, and that the first secretary of the province himself might not be without blame. The article stated that Berkhin's arrest and the search of his apartment had been coordinated by A. Dichenko, identified simply as candidate member of the obkom bureau. Only with the final article, Chebrikov's statement, was it revealed that Dichenko was head of the province KGB administration and that he had been expelled from the KGB for his actions. Probably only with Chebrikov's consent could a KGB officer's actions be criticized in print, and probably this was the final objective of *Pravda*'s long crusade. It is certain that *Pravda* enlisted the support of the top party leadership in winning its battle and that the leadership saw in the case an object lesson of Ligachev's point that no agency was immune from criticism.[39] In this case a republic-level agency—the Ukrainian procuracy—was mentioned unfavorably; province-, city-, and district-level officials in the party, police, and other organizations were cited; and an agency previously off limits to media criticism, the KGB, was singled out for particular attention.[40] Vindication of the journalist became the occasion for a political contest among powerful agencies over the meaning of *glasnost'*.

Another category of issues in which the media may become advocates touches unresolved policy questions—those not yet closed or those reopened. In such controversies the authorities are divided. A journalist or editor can call upon highly placed specialists to support either side. Competent authority is not willing or able to exercise the "negative power," as Thane Gustafson calls it, to end or prevent the open airing of the dispute; and a coalition of forces has exerted "positive" influence to place a controversial viewpoint on the agenda.[41] Classifying public debate by scope, John Löwenhardt has distinguished two axes of communications domains: all-union or localized and general or specialized. A discussion may originate in any of the four cells created by this matrix and spill over to another, and the access of a particular coalition of forces to a particular media organ may be important in putting views before the public.[42] It is clear that the overall latitude allowed to specialist-advocates and media institutions for the public airing of controversy varies by both issue and time period and depends in part upon the inclination and power of the central leadership. The Rand study's informants generally agreed that the opportunity for critical, incisive journalism and the presentation of new ideas had diminished from the end of the 1960s to the end of the Brezhnev era. Recently, it has widened again significantly. Even in the late 1970s, however, many issues were characterized by a roughly even distribution of political influence on different sides. If a controversy involving such an issue spills out into the open in a particular locality, local party authorities may be unable to resolve it and may require intervention by higher authority.[43]

An editor's propensity to take strong, controversial stands varies considerably from one organ or locality to another according to how deeply party officials intervene in media operations and the degree of initiative editors and writers take in instigating conflict. Generally, the critical bite of a particular media organ's publications over time and across problems is a fair measure of the degree of autonomy it has been granted by the party or has assumed with party consent. As the party leadership alters the climate for media criticism, either across the Soviet Union or within a particular territorial unit, the boldness of media publications tends to rise or fall correspondingly. This is the reason that, despite constant adjurations to the contrary from senior party and media executives, the only real, operational definition of Gorbachev's *glasnost'* policy as far as the media are concerned is the freedom it gives them to criticize.

The correlation between media autonomy and political controversy is not perfect, of course. Party ideology officials may involve themselves extensively in planning media campaigns even for relatively anodyne purposes, such as the observance of a major political anniversary or publicity for a decree. Or, to take a case where the stakes are higher, a bureaucratic squabble that a media organ has publicized will often draw party officials in to arbitrate. Typically, as has been seen, this occurs when a critical article in the press or a letter from an aggrieved citizen leads to an appeal to a higher party, media, or other organization, which then forms the basis for an investigation, report, and formal response. Even when encouraged to exercise their given powers more aggressively, many, perhaps most, editors and journalists prefer to err on the side of caution.

In the absence of explicit prior authorization, an editor is likelier to be willing to run a combative or sensitive article if the target of criticism is relatively vulnerable or low in status, if the political stakes are shrouded in technical complexity, or if the central leadership is divided over the issue concerned. The latter two points coincide with observations made two decades ago by Joel Schwartz and William Keech about the conditions that favor the participation of interest groups in policy formation.[44] But, because media organs depend upon their immediate supervisors in the party for direction and evaluation, and are therefore less autonomous as political actors than other potential interest groups, editors tend to be sensitive to cues from the leadership about the limits of permissible treatment of controversial issues. To be sure, media publicity helps direct high-level attention to a problem, but careful investigation usually reveals that the political authorities have first signaled that a media discussion leading toward a predetermined position is desirable in order to build public support for a policy change as yet not adopted.

A well-documented case in point is the public discussion surrounding the northern river diversion project. This in fact represents two different schemes. One would divert up to 5.8 cubic kilometers of water annually from lakes and rivers in the region north of Moscow via canals into the Volga River in order to increase the flow of water for irrigation in southern Russia, the Caucasus, and the Ukraine. The other is a still more grandiose plan for the construction of a system of canals for the diversion of as much as 27 cubic kilometers of water from the northward-flowing Ob' and Irtysh rivers in Siberia more than 2,500 kilometers southward to relieve the growing shortage of water in central Asia. Overall, the projects envision an engineering feat of unprecedented proportions aimed at rectifying nature's cruel decision to direct Russia's rivers northward and away from the centers of its agriculture, industry, and population.

Until 1986, when the Politburo issued an order to cease further construction work, the approval of the Brezhnev-Chernenko forces moved the project forward despite opposition by many powerful figures representing regional, scientific, and intellectual interests. Access by opponents of the project to such newspapers as *Pravda, Trud, Literaturnaia gazeta,* and *Sovetskaia Rossiia,* all of which opposed the project, was limited: by and large editors avoided carrying direct statements of opposition, preferring instead to use such techniques as pairing pro and con articles.[45] *Pravda*'s editor, Viktor Afanas'ev, revealed in 1987, for example, that only with an enormous effort and the direct intervention of a Central Committee secretary could he succeed in publishing material reflecting negatively on the river diversion scheme.[46] The Chairman of the Ukrainian Academy of Sciences later commented that "all this could not be called a discussion, so much did the 'exchange' of opinions move in a single direction."[47] As late as 1985, when Chernenko's death and the promotion of leaders of the "Siberian" faction to the central leadership shifted the balance of forces toward opponents of the project, its proponents were still strong enough to force significant cuts in an article published by the writer Sergei Zalygin in the September 1985 issue of *Kommunist* denouncing the project. Even after the 1986 party congress, which failed to approve the project but did not kill it, journalists were again "advised" against reporting the fact that work on the project was continuing. Only when the leadership was near a final decision against the project was public opposition widely aired. And, ironically, since the August 1986 Politburo decision stopping it, the project's proponents have bitterly complained that they are being prevented from taking their case to the public.[48] Of course both before 1986 and since, the aggrieved side has exaggerated the extent of its exclusion from the media. But it is equally clear that in both cases, the media responded to, rather than set, the prevailing direction of policy.

To take another example, phases of discussion and decision in the formulation of a demographic policy alternated in the 1960s and 1970s. After years of favoring a high birth rate, a major shift in official Soviet attitudes about national population policy occurred in the autumn of 1965, ostensibly marked by a change in the Soviet position toward population control in the developing world, but clearly bearing on the domestic problem of uneven population growth rates among peoples in the Soviet Union. The change resulted in the launching of a nine-month debate over population policy in *Literaturnaia gazeta* in 1965–66, in which representatives of the emerging demographers' camp challenged the old orthodoxy: articles calling for change outnumbered those by traditionalists by over four to one. The new Brezhnev leadership did not give a public signal authorizing a discussion, but eleven years later, at the Twenty-fifth Party Congress, Brezhnev's statement that "an effective demographic policy" was required in order to solve "population problems, which have become exacerbated recently" opened a debate that served to identify alternative means and ends of such a policy, and, more broadly, to generate support for the position the party leader had taken. The statement therefore sharply altered the contours of the debate.[49]

Other case studies of policy decisions in which the formal adoption of a policy follows a public debate also reveal that informal signals from the political leadership have in fact preceded the media discussion. The leaders employ the discussion to mobilize support for a decision which at least a part of the leadership favors, to discredit opposition to it, and to formulate specific alternatives for adoption.[50]

In some instances, however, the media operate under a broader mandate to identify issues needing policy decisions. Some of the scandal-mongering and muckraking undertaken by courageous journalists under *glasnost'* have placed serious social problems onto the public agenda. Many recent press exposés—youth gangs, drug abuse, prostitution, prison life, declining health care standards, exploding television sets, and environmental deterioration—probably represent a general grant of authority to the media to bring to public attention hitherto unpublicized social ills rather than specific responses to signals calling for illumination of particular problems. Similarly, the media have probably received only the broadest authorization to invite new appraisals of Stalinism, allowing editors sympathetic to reform to press for a full condemnation of Stalin and rehabilitation of his victims.

Another kind of broad-gauged mandate to define new issues for policy can sometimes occur when a new chief executive is appointed to a major media organ. One good example is Richard Kosolapov's replacement as editor of *Kommunist* in 1986, which was accompanied with a Central Committee resolution on the need for *Kommunist* to improve its work.[51] Ideologically orthodox, Kosolapov had blocked the publication of proreform theoretical articles. His replacement, Ivan Frolov, was a surprising choice. Frolov was a prominent, controversial reform-minded philosopher in disfavor at the close of the Brezhnev era.[52] In his first editorial, Frolov promised that the pages of *Kommunist* would be opened to debates on current social problems.[53] One of his first acts as editor was to carry a major article by reform theorist

Tatiana Zaslavskaia; since the article was virtually identical to one she had published in another journal earlier in the year, it seems clear that he specifically solicited it for *Kommunist*.[54] Despite Zaslavskaia's prominence, she had not published in *Kommunist* for twenty-five years before the appearance of her 1986 article.[55] Further evidence of an active editorial hand is the fact that *Kommunist* underlined the importance of her views by publishing readers' responses to the article in subsequent issues, most of them favorable to Zaslavskaia's ideas.[56] *Kommunist* continued to carry innovative and reformist articles (such as an article by Academician Legasov on the need for greater attention to safety considerations in planning and siting nuclear reactors and other potentially destructive high-technology facilities[57]) until spring 1987 when Frolov was transferred to the Central Committee apparatus after only nine months on the journal. His unexpectedly early transfer and the blander tone of the journal since his departure suggest that he was thought to have taken the journal too far in the direction of reformism.

Thus, even when encouraging a broadly favorable climate for media activism, as has occurred under Gorbachev, policymakers continually intervene with personnel decisions as well as instructions about the objectives, constraints, and mandates for coverage of specific issues and in specific media organs. The danger, of course, when leaders issue open-ended mandates to the media to engage in policy advocacy and therefore to critical, investigative, and controversial coverage, is that the effects are not readily controllable. Khrushchev's rule is an instructive illustration. Khrushchev's use of the media to weaken his opponents by associating them with Stalinism resulted in cycles of liberalization and retrenchment which contributed to the damaging impression of his regime's instability. The only other recent precedent for liberalization of the media is the brief thaw during Andropov's first few months as general secretary, when criticism of slack management, labor indiscipline, drinking, and similar hindrances to economic productivity was encouraged. However, the "Andropov effect" was even more short-lived than Andropov.[58]

Gorbachev and his colleagues, however, have initiated a phase of social self-scrutiny in the mass media to which is comparable, in the scope and depth of its impact, only to NEP and Khrushchev's de-

Stalinization campaign. Even before Chernenko's death, Gorbachev's rising influence in the secretariat resulted in several articles appealing for honesty and openness in media work.[59] Gorbachev made the theme an element of his December 1984 address on ideology, as I have shown, and he returned to it in his statement upon being named general secretary. Thereafter a number of articles in the Soviet press repeated the call for *glasnost'*.[60] Gorbachev gave it close attention in his report to the Twenty-seventh Party Congress in 1986, as did several other party leaders, and continued to emphasize the theme in statements and meetings through 1987.

Glasnost' has reversed the deteriorating trends in the media which began roughly in the late 1960s. The frequency of stories and broadcasts that would have been unthinkable previously—such as reports on accidents, natural disasters, and protest demonstrations—indicates that, at least for some leaders and some editors, media openness is valued for its own sake in fact and not just in rhetoric. Another indication that Gorbachev has undertaken a sweeping effort to improve media performance is the shake-up in media personnel. Although high turnover rates among editors, staff members, and correspondents began under Andropov,[61] under Gorbachev there has occurred the most dramatic changeover of editorial leadership in the Soviet media in decades. New editors have been appointed to *Trud, Krasnaia zvezda, Sovetskaia Rossiia, Meditsinskaia gazeta, Sotsialisticheskaia industriia, Sovetskaia kul'tura, Ekonomicheskaia gazeta, Moscow News,* and other central papers. Among the journals receiving new editors are *Kommunist, Krokodil, Novyi mir, Ogonek, Politicheskoe samoobrazovanie, Znamia, Tvorchestvo,* and *Novoe vremia.* The chairmen of Gosteleradio, the State Publishing Committee, Novosti, and the state copyright agency have been replaced. Extensive changes among the deputy editors, department heads, and staffs of most of these media organs have occurred as well, as has turnover of media personnel at the republic and province level. These changes, some of which involved appointing outsiders (such as Sergei Zalygin at *Novyi mir* or Ivan Frolov at *Kommunist*) to head media organs and others of which moved party officials into media posts, have probably been directed at breaking up the networks of personal relations between media executives and political cadres which undercut media independence.[62]

A Soviet leader faces a dilemma in urging the media to take an active role in stirring political controversy. On the one hand, the consequences may be difficult to contain if the initiative passes to more radical positions as debate gathers momentum; on the other, insufficient energy and persistence in overcoming inertia leaves the response confined to purely pro forma, campaign style gestures.[63] Simply the need, at different times and in different localities, to urge the media to report problems more aggressively and then to step in to settle the resulting disputes, might account for the contradictory interpretations of *glasnost'* being issued by different members of the party leadership.[64]

But the *glasnost'* campaign has also brought out political divisions within the party. At the Twenty-seventh Congress, for example, Egor Ligachev condemned *Pravda* for publishing an attack on party privilege, but Gorbachev later repeated a portion of the same critique almost word for word in his semiprivate chat with thirty Soviet writers.[65] The limits of the permissible are rarely unequivocal and policy guidelines change constantly. How freely, for example, may the press, even such powerful central organs as *Pravda*, criticize the performance of obkom officials? Gorbachev may have been expressing a reaction of backlash against media criticism of regional party officials when he cautioned the media in January 1987 against blaming all problems on local party authorities. In his address to the Congress of Journalists in March 1987, Afanas'ev complained that obkom secretaries were succeeding in shielding their organizations from criticism by the central press. Moreover, Afanas'ev revealed that some issues, such as the space program and many environmental problems, remained off limits to media criticism.[66] At his July 1987 meeting with the media, Gorbachev expressed concern that the Central Committee was being called upon to resolve too many disputes arising from lower levels and appealed to the editors to settle more themselves. He also voiced fears that serious missteps by the media in pursuing *glasnost'* could give conservative opponents an occasion to impede the democratization and restructuring campaign. Yet, at the same meeting, Gorbachev also seemed confident that by and large the media were performing well and that there was no cause for alarm.[67]

Clearly *glasnost'* is generating power struggles among officials and institutions which cloud the future of the policy. Nevertheless, the exacerbation of tensions within the political elite is the unavoidable consequence of using the *glasnost'* campaign to attack the immobility of political life inherited from the Brezhnev period.

The evidence about party-media relations suggests a picture of a partnership in which party officials usually play an active, direction-setting role and media institutions a compliant and responsive one. Under normal conditions, even under *glasnost'*, the media remain relatively averse to risk because of the incentives for docility built into their working relations with party supervisors. Three factors in particular stand out: editors' and journalists' need for guidance and information that only party officials are in a position to supply; incentives for media personnel to act as "extensions of the party apparatus" in return for career advancement, material privileges, and other perquisites of membership in the political elite; and penalties for violating rules laid down by censorship and other officials about media coverage.

Under some circumstances in the past, however, and much more frequently since 1985, media organs do invite conflict, by publishing a complaint from a whistleblowing citizen or a contentious opinion voiced by an advocate of a policy change. They are more likely to do so when they have been authorized to publicize a viewpoint which is not yet, but will become, official policy. Even when the political climate for media criticism improves, however, authorities are reluctant to set clear rules about what is permissible, preferring instead to allow editors to assume the risk and responsibility of fighting for controversial causes. Through a large-scale turnover of top media personnel, the Gorbachev leadership has swept the media clear of many individuals with ties to the former regime, and its strategy of *glasnost'* has substantially increased the frankness and freedom of public expression. It must now steer a course between encouraging popular demands for change that cannot be satisfied except at the expense of party rule, and allowing the bureaucratic routines of a conventional media campaign to suffocate the impetus for change.

6 POLITICS AND PROFESSIONALISM IN SOVIET JOURNALISM

The Western ideal of journalistic objectivity, influenced by liberal principles of the accountability of rulers to the ruled and the empirical skepticism of science, developed as an occupational response by journalists to marketplace competition among commercially or politically motivated information suppliers and came to define the journalist's professional ethic of impartiality and independence.[1] At the same time the term *professionalism* must be used with caution. Journalism is a field with some but not all of the attributes of a profession.[2] By the usual tests of the freedom of the practitioners to govern entry to and exit from the field, to possess an exclusive right to carry on their trade, and to set the standards of performance, journalists are not as autonomous as, for example, physicians and attorneys. If they sought to close the shop to outsiders or to set standards of writing and reporting, they would be infringing upon the prerogatives of management— editors and publishers. Still, the need to define an occupational role by reference to values of objectivity and impartiality, mastery of technique, and freedom from outside interference creates strong pressures for professionalization.

At the same time the literature on the sociology of news has shown that more immediate influences than these general principles affect the journalist's labor. Above all the recent literature has emphasized the importance of organizational factors in shaping the day-to-day norms of journalistic and editorial behavior. Media organizations adopt

157

standardized routines in selecting and presenting information, routines that reflect the influence of their own internal economies based on the relative scarcities of time, staff, and air time or column space. Adaptation to the organization's own needs produces characteristic structural bias in news reporting, such as the headline approach to information, concentration of attention on a small number of organizations and individuals that regularly produce reportable events or utterances, and reportage that shows to best advantage the peculiarities of a given medium.[3] These traits illustrate the point that the environmental forces of marketplace competition and the philosophical ideal of objectivity influence the journalistic product not directly but through the media organization's own internal laws.

In the Soviet Union—where manifest norms of journalistic practice are determined by the familiar demands for party-mindedness, ideological orthodoxy, and political loyalty—how thoroughly are the working rules of journalism pervaded by the general principles laid down by party doctrine? Or alternatively, do the day-to-day requirements of the job generate tendencies toward a code of professionalism that might, given time and favorable circumstances, spur journalists to form an institutional counterweight to party authority? One of the standing phrases about the media that party officials use is that they are "an integral part of the party apparatus."[4] In this chapter let us consider whether and by what means the party works to realize this aim. I will examine four pertinent aspects of journalism bearing on these questions: the nature of journalism training in school, the lessons that early exposure to journalistic practice teaches, the role of the Journalists' Union, and finally, the social standing of journalism in Soviet society.

JOURNALISM TRAINING

At the 1977 Congress of Journalists, Professor Iasen N. Zasurskii, dean of the Journalism Faculty at Moscow State University, reported as chairman of a commission that examined education at the country's university schools of journalism. The findings showed a preponderance of female and worker-peasant matriculants. Of the 1,100–1,200 applicants admitted yearly to journalism faculties at universities in the mid 1970s, slightly over 50 percent were women, and the proportion of workers and peasants (either by own or father's occupation) rose from 56 percent to 60 percent between 1974 and 1976. Evidently these changes required more attention to remedial and preparatory work, however. Nearly all faculties and departments of journalism maintained their own preparatory divisions, and enrollments at these had risen in the same period from 133 to 452; by 1977 about half of all admitted to journalism faculties spent a year in the preparatory division.[5] The rise in the number of students admitted to the *rabfak*'s attested not only to the Brezhnev-era concern with promoting the admission of nonintelligentsia children to higher education, but also, and more tellingly, to the problem of declining quality among those applying to journalism school, a problem Soviet journalism professors have lamented along with the even more serious one of declining numbers of applications.

As of 1969 there were around ten applications to faculties of journalism for every space available, whereas by the mid 1970s this figure was cut in half. By the early 1980s there was virtually no competition at all for admission, and at the relatively prestigious Urals University Journalism Faculty, there were only three applicants per place. In part this trend is related to the declining social esteem of the profession of journalism, an issue I shall take up later in this chapter. In part it is also apparently related to a shift among young people in occupational preferences toward service areas and away from technical and science fields. One consequence is declining quality among applicants, among whom worse levels of general education and command of language have been found.[6] As a result more needs to be done to provide journalism students with basic knowledge and skills before they can go through the regular five-year course of study.

Some twenty-four universities offer journalism training. Nine have full faculties of journalism; twelve have divisions *(otdeleniia)* or departments *(kafedry)* dedicated to training journalists. In another three, departments in other subjects offer as an option a specialization in journalism. Altogether, they graduate approximately 1,200 diplomates each year.[7] Besides the 6,000 or so students of journalism in day divisions of universities are another 9,000 in evening or correspondence divisions. (Part-time or correspondence study takes six years.)[8]

However, study at a journalism school or division is not the only route to journalism training, nor does education for journalists end with graduation from university. A widespread system of courses, seminars, institutes, and schools sponsored by the Journalists' Union through the party education system offers training for a diverse range of part-time and full-time media workers. For editors and party officials responsible for administration and oversight in the media, the party maintains departments of journalism in party schools (the Academy of Social Sciences and eight Higher Party Schools) as well as courses in its lower-level universities of Marxism-Leninism and in other party schools.[9] For its part, the Journalists' Union organizes courses, through the Central House of Journalists in Moscow and through local branches of the Journalists' Union or the party education system, that serve both working journalists, offering them refresher courses, and free-lance writers seeking to improve their skills and acquire credentials. Often, for example, people who have contributed articles to newspapers as worker-peasant correspondents and who would like a permanent post in a media organization take journalism courses sponsored by the union. Some 27,000 persons take courses designed for such people. The various province- and republic-level schools, courses, institutes, and the like, organized by the Journalists' Union under the party education system and designed to improve the professional skill of working journalists and editors, serve another 10,000.[10]

Whether at university schools or divisions of journalism, or in the party schools, journalism training combines comprehensive study of party doctrine with substantive and technical training. The curriculum offers a smattering of knowledge in a wide range of subjects but leaves the students, at the end, without a firm claim to any single body of knowledge that would define them as professionals. Even the practical and technical skill that they develop often turns out to have little application to the demands on them in their initial jobs. The curriculum of the regular journalism student at Moscow State University combines general knowledge, doctrinal theory, and, in each of the five years of the curriculum as well as during the summers, practical experience in media organizations. Basic methods of work in several journalistic occupations are presented. The faculty is divided into nine *kafedry*, which together offer four basic specializations: newspapers, broadcasting, mass literature, and foreign affairs.[11]

For a student seeking to enter newspaper work, the courses include the history of the party-Soviet press, theory and practice of the press, newspaper and magazine editing, literary editing, layout and production of newspapers, and basic photojournalism. Aspiring radio and television journalists take courses in broadcast techniques, theory and practice of Soviet radio and television broadcasting, the history of cinema and film journalism, fundamentals of drama, fundamentals of directing, and operation of the equipment.[12]

An interesting recent discussion in the pages of *Zhurnalist,* the monthly magazine published by the Journalists' Union, indicates several aspects of dissatisfaction with the current state of journalism training. It opened with a critique by a recent graduate of Moscow State University Journalism Faculty, Nadezhda Azhgikhina, of the training she and her classmates received there. It evidently touched a sensitive spot among the magazine's readers, for it opened a discussion that shed a good deal of light on the current malaise among media workers. Azhgikhina observed that her class had lost its enthusiasm for writing as it progressed from year to year, in part because of the inadequate opportunity for practical work. Worse, even if students did well in their more applied subjects, bad grades in courses they considered irrelevant to their careers (such as English or agricultural economics) injured their records. Finally, when they got positions as summer employees of newspapers as another part of their practical training, by and large their editors treated them "formalistically" and gave them little useful attention, and, although good grades were easy to receive for their summer practicum, they received little benefit.[13]

Subsequent articles in the discussion acknowledged that Azhgikhina was justified in complaining that journalism school graduates were ill prepared for their jobs, but they did not accept the view that theoretical material should be reduced in favor of practice. (One noted that Azhgikhina's well-written article hardly bore out her argument about poor training.) The principal argument against cutting back the number of required substantive courses ("theory") was that, as they began their careers, journalists needed some formal knowledge about the subjects they would be covering and that they were too weakly informed as it was about the economic and technical matters they were called upon to treat. Some also called for better textbooks and technical facilities to train journalists. A deputy dean from the University of Rostov-na-Donu, reaffirming the view that theory was necessary and should even be expanded, complained that his and other universities lacked space, textbooks, and other aids; existing textbooks were obsolete but replacements were hard to find. Inadequate reference materials on journalism and the lack of any single all-union scholarly journal reporting research on journalism (he dismissed the journalism series of the *Bulletin of Moscow University* as not filling the need) were substantial hindrances, and the broadcast journalism students had to make do with a total lack of equipment—they did not even have a tape recorder. His point was that the effectiveness of existing training, particularly practical training, had to be increased.[14]

The question of the appropriate balance of substantive and practical instruction for journalists (one writer commented that the commonest —and, indeed, virtually sole—topic of conversation among journalists was how unprepared for their jobs they were when they left journalism schools and how they had to begin their real education all over[15]) is hardly confined to Soviet discussions. After all, journalism school graduates in the United States similarly unlearn all the theory taught in school and come to accept the judgments of their peers in the newsroom as the real basis for making the substantive and technical decisions of their work.[16] But the question is interesting in view of the preference that Soviet journalism schools give to applicants who have worked in the media already. Admission to the day division of Moscow State University's Journalism Faculty is supposed to be limited to individuals who have had at least two years of work experience either as free-lance or as full-time correspondents. Qualified applicants are required to obtain a recommendation from their editor or the local branch of the Journalists' Union and must submit examples (both published and, to show unedited work, unpublished) of their writing. Only upon passing this initial screening may they move to the next part of the process, a writing competition *(tvorcheskii konkurs)* and an interview; those passing this step may then take the entrance examinations.[17] Given these apparently rigorous review measures, it is striking to learn how little journalists can draw on their professional training when they move from university to their subsequent postings. Perhaps it is intrinsic to media work that no single body of theory or of practical skills "makes" a journalist in the way that several years of studying basic science and clinical practice "makes" a physician; perhaps the journalist in any system is more dependent on learning and interaction with the social environment in order to master and practice the trade.

What has the aspiring journalist learned in the faculty of journalism? So far as one can tell, the lessons are somewhat contradictory, both in their direct substance and in their implications. The mobilizing, populist role of the journalist contradicts the intense emphasis on party-mindedness and ideological orthodoxy. The journalists who apply party condemnations of foot-dragging bureaucratism too literally are apt to place themselves in the middle of fights among powerful organizations. Judging the latitude available for critical reporting becomes one of the practical lessons learned on the job. Similarly, is the journalist's occupational specialty primarily in technique or in mastery of substantive knowledge? Some attention in journalism school is given to command of craft *(professional'noe masterstvo)*. Journalism students are taught to study the examples of successful writing by such famed journalists as the late Anatolii Agranovskii and Iurii Zhukov.[18] However, in most other professional fields the formal knowledge acquired through study sets the practitioner apart from the laity. In the case of the journalist, no single corpus of knowledge or system of study distinguishes the practitioner from party or government officials, and technical skill is closely identified with individual style worked out over many years of experience. As a result, socialization received in the early phases of a journalist's career from authoritative superiors in media and party organizations probably outweighs schooling as a force shaping occupational self-conception.

SOCIALIZATION ON THE JOB

For the most part, initial postings through the *raspredelenie* system leave journalism graduates in highly unenviable circumstances, as a number of woeful letters to *Zhurnalist* attest. The *raspredelenie* or job assignment system for university and institute graduates in principle provides each graduate who has not found a post independently with a mandatory position that must be held for three years. In practice, a variety of legal and illicit dodges reduce the effectiveness of the system in filling positions. In many fields, journalism included, initial assignments are generally in remote rural districts where material and cultural amenities are few. As a consequence many students find ways to evade their assignments; women marry to stay in a more livable city; some students simply do not show up at their assigned job, apparently with reasonable assurance that the enforcement mechanisms are too weak to catch up with them.[19] Many times rural newspapers release employees to go to journalism school only to lose them to more attractive jobs.

The main complaint with respect to living conditions is that apartments are rarely provided as a perquisite of the job. This problem affects both journalists and media organizations, the latter finding that they cannot recruit and retain employees. Even senior staff members on lower-level press organs may not acquire separate apartments in some especially hard-pressed districts; party officials, one editor wrote to *Zhurnalist*, forget the importance of housing when they observe that "journalists are a part of their apparatus" *(vkhodiat v ikh apparaty).*[20] Young journalists without pull of their own or through their employers frequently have to rent a corner or a room from another family. Indeed, at the 1987 Congress of Journalists, chairman Afanas'ev reported that about one-third of all journalists are still renting living space from other families *(snimaiut chastnye ugly).* The consequence of the housing problem and the other disagreeable features of rural life is that many district papers are understaffed. Those that cannot recruit or retain the graduates of journalism faculties hire from among their local free lances.

Partly because of understaffing and partly because of their limited budgets, district papers *(raionki)* are notorious for the pressure they impose on young journalists to turn out copy. The demand for quantity, more probably than any other single factor, drives the journalist to seek short cuts and compromises. Much was learned about the lot of the district journalist in the course of a large-scale survey conducted in 1969–71 under the auspices of the Moscow State University Journalism Faculty across fourteen districts of two provinces in the Russian Republic. The authors of the study found that journalists on lower-level press organs routinely complained that they were overworked and obliged to cover too many subjects. Most newspapers set line quotas for their writers, on a per issue or per month basis or both. Many must write 100–200 lines per issue or 2,500–3,500 lines per month. Because lower-level newspapers are heavily dependent on contributions from readers and free lances, a substantial part of the local journalist's job (and this falls above all on the junior members of the staff) consists of rewriting these contributions, which are called "author's materials." Over half the local journalists surveyed spent as much time reworking copy from outside contributors as they did preparing their own copy. One writer to the *Zhurnalist* discussion cited in the preceding section called the district newspaper a "meatgrinder" (literally "juice-squeezer"—*sokovyzhimalka*) for young journalists. Not only are the line quotas excessive—the writer faced a daily target of 180 lines in his first job—but journalists cover stories for which they are totally unprepared, stories that demand a depth of knowledge and grasp of issues that journalism school has not begun to provide. The response of local editors is to assign beginners to the rewriting of author's materials, tedious work that leaves them without much experience in investigating and writing stories.[21] One of the main motivations for journalists to seek to rise to higher-level media organs is to escape the high line quotas that the understaffed district papers impose. Once at the level of city or province paper, the journalist need not turn out such high volumes of material and can begin to specialize in particular subjects.

Behind the pressure for high quantitative output is the tie of the journalist's income to his quantitative productivity. The beginning journalist earns about 120–140 rubles per month, a low wage. Although in principle journalists can submit articles to other publications and thus earn income as free-lance writers, the young writer on a district paper has little time or opportunity to do so. Only when the line quota is exceeded does the journalist qualify for a share of the bonus fund. Some editors divide the bonus fund equally among all members of the staff, a system that offers no reward to originality or skill in writing. From letters to *Zhurnalist* and other material, it appears that the pressure to meet quantitative targets in order to receive a bonus is the principal day-to-day concern of district-level journalists. At the higher levels, salaries are considerably better, and there is more time to supplement income with free-lance writing (a major source of income for writers). A senior correspondent earns 200 rubles per month. The senior staff of newspapers also normally set themselves lower line quotas and often employ relatively easy material (such as minutes of local party and government meetings, or the texts of decrees and other official matter) as the basis for fulfilling the target. An editor of a major central or republican newspaper probably earns well over 500 rubles. Each of these figures can probably be doubled once free-lance writing and shares of the bonus fund are included.[22] The prospect of raising one's standard of living quite considerably through advancement to positions that are more highly rewarded and, in addition, give greater opportunity for legal outside income must serve as a strong inducement for politically compliant behavior as well.

Overworked, writing on every conceivable topic, under pressure to turn out a sufficient quantity of copy, the journalist turns to official sources for ideas and information and to standardized, clichéd techniques for writing. Journalists at the district level are aware of and dissatisfied with the shortcomings of their work. Asked what disturbed them most about their reporting, the largest proportion of respondents cited the problem of inadequate depth and argument of articles; 61 percent chose this response.[23]

The combined shortages of time, pay, and experience, then, contribute to a tendency for journalists to seek political cues from local officials. They lack the expertise that would give them a measure of independence and the opportunity to acquire such knowledge. Dependent on official sources of news and guidance, they see yet greater ties to officials as the answer. Critical reporting or independent investigation, then, carries multiple risks. It diverts time from the need to produce copy, and it may alienate the officials whose goodwill is necessary as a condition for promotion. Journalists seek to know what it is that party officials expect of them, and they attempt to fulfill these expectations, far more than they seek to know what the audience's interests are or to satisfy them. Indeed, despite the heavy volume of letters and other contributions received from readers and the extensive sociological surveys that are used, the audience is remote and little understood.

This question was studied directly by the Moscow State University team. It found that:

In a majority of cases the judgments of the officials in governing organs and of the journalists about the most important tasks of the district newspaper coincide almost perfectly (in eight cases they are ranked identically) or are very close. This permits us to make a general conclusion that is extremely important for effective management of the newspaper. Those who head the district press and those who are called upon to carry out these tasks are unanimous [edinodushnyi] in their understanding of the functions of the district newspaper. . . . It is characteristic that the publisher and the journalists themselves give highest marks to the district press for fulfilling the tasks that they consider most important.[24]

At the same time, the journalists believed (for the most part correctly) that party officials did not place emphasis on satisfying readers' interests. At editorial meetings the tastes and demands of readers are almost never discussed. Only 15 percent of the journalists indicated that party officials had discussed readers' interests with them. Moreover, the journalists were aware that they knew rather little about their readership. They pointed out that they had few contacts with readers other than those they encountered in covering stories or receiving contributions. This led to misconceptions: for example, journalists attributed to their readers far higher levels of education than they had. In reality, over two times more readers had below-average educations and many fewer had higher education than the journalists estimated. Asked about the breakdown of their readership by gender, the journalists underestimated the proportion of women by a factor of 4. Most interesting is that journalists tended to assume that their readers used the paper as their primary source of news. Of those surveyed, 77 percent expressed certainty that the public's principal source of information about the district was the district paper; only 7 percent named radio, and 6 percent named interpersonal contacts as the primary conduit. The rest were not sure. Interpersonal conversation turned out to be the primary source of information for most people, and the newspaper was in second place.[25]

Yet, despite the journalists' lack of knowledge about their readers, few thought it essential to find out more about them. The general public is simply not the primary reference group for journalists. It is far more important for them to stay attuned to the demands of the party officials standing over them, to pay attention to their evaluations, and to maintain contact with them, than it is to respond to public demands. They know how the party defines their role, and they accept that role, even though it produces a gap between how the elite intend the media to be used by the general public and how the public actually uses them.

Moreover, the kinds of contact journalists have with the public are limited and skewed. Even at the level of the central press, few journalists pay much attention to readers' polls and surveys, many believing that their own first-hand "feel" for the readership is more reliable. A survey from the late 1960s showed that writers for *Izvestiia* and *Trud* greatly overestimated the actual degree of reader dissatisfaction with their newspapers. Interestingly, *Trud* employees felt that readers had responded to recent improvements in the quality of the paper. The readership, though, when polled, was not generally aware of the improvements.[26]

However, the acquaintance that journalists have with ordinary citizens is limited in the first place by the fact that those who write letters to the editor are often unrepresentative of the general population[27] and, in the second, by the fact that letters concentrate overwhelmingly on individuals' interests as consumers rather than as producers or participants in the political system. And even this form of contact is further restricted, since most media organs have special letters departments set aside for dealing with the general public. The newspaper attempts to balance the space it gives the two categories, but the vast majority of letters concern such issues as consumer goods and services, communal facilities, the availability and maintenance of housing, and dissatisfaction of employees with their superiors.[28] The party, by contrast, seeks to ensure that the media publicize the production interests of the authorities—the effort to realize plan targets, to improve product quality and labor productivity, to conserve resources, to evince loyalty to the system.

What are the tasks that district-level newspapers are called upon to fulfill, in the eyes of officials and of journalists? The survey of district newspapers found that both groups assigned first priority to the function of providing "operative"—that is, current and significant—information about events in the district. Propagandizing the decisions of ruling bodies on political matters was rated second by the officials and third by the journalists. Seeking the adoption of particular measures and fighting defects was rated third by the officials and fourth by the journalists. Economic propaganda was ranked fourth by the officials and fifth by the journalists. What journalists evidently thought to be their second most important task, helping in the political upbringing of the "New Soviet Person," was put in sixth place by the officials.[29]

Even greater coincidence of views appeared at the bottom end of the scale, where officials and journalists placed the least pressing tasks. Both officials and journalists assigned twenty-second place to "providing materials for relaxation and recreation, for spending leisure time." Both groups gave twenty-first place to "researching important, socially significant problems." Both placed the task of providing news about national, province-level, and world events near the bottom of the scale. What the journalists thought least pressing, giving readers advice, consultations, reference information, and advertising, the officials ranked seventeenth. The job of expressing the opinion of the populace on current problems was ranked in the middle of the scale by both groups: in eleventh place by officials and tenth by journalists. When the surveyers asked both officials and journalists what tasks each group thought the party set the newspapers, the responses differed only moderately.[30]

These results indicate both that the party succeeds in communicating to journalists the expectations it holds of them and that journalists identify these, rather than the public's interests, as their own priorities. Socialization into the craft of journalism in the Soviet Union impresses on journalists a very different set of occupational values than would be the case in the U.S. media. The norm of professional independence is very weakly rooted. It is undercut by the remoteness of the public, the low status of the profession, and by the powerful incentives for journalists to identify their professional interests with those of the party authorities. The party's conception of newsworthiness becomes the journalists'; the audience is known, for the most part, only via individual contacts in the form of letters, complaints, visits, and interviews. These contacts supply journalists with the raw material needed to satisfy the constant pressure for stories, but the position taken in each story is normally consistent with the political priorities as laid out by the local authorities. Contact with the party's staff officials is frequent and provides journalists with the direction and often the specific leads that they need to fulfill their part in the plan. Not surprisingly, therefore, journalists do not regard their institutional status as being poised between the political elite, on the one hand, and the public interest, on the other, the social position that fosters the emergence of an ethic of professional objectivity. Success for journalists derives from becoming part of the ruling elite, from acting as an extension of the party apparatus. The early exposure of journalists to the unwritten rules of the game after leaving school, when they most need to find means of coping with the material, occupational, and political pressures that they confront, is the most important phase of their occupational socialization.

THE JOURNALISTS' UNION

The Union of Soviet Journalists performs various functions for the political leadership and for journalists, but from all accounts its association with the media gives it little influence over journalistic practice vis-à-vis the party. A young and not yet fully established creative union, it has expanded in size and complexity and possibly has become more effective in lobbying for its membership's material interests. At the same time it has taken its place alongside the party as a second line of political control over the socialization and surveillance of journalists.

A brief note on the history of the union will illustrate the insecure position it has occupied in relation to the political leadership.[31] Most striking is the late date of the formation of the union itself. Organized journalists formed a section of the Educators' Union until 1927 and then, briefly, a section of the Press Workers' Union. In December 1930 the organization was disbanded, and not until Stalin's death was it revived. The magazine reaching journalists, *Bol'shevistskaia pechat'* *(Bolshevik Press)* was suspended in 1941 and resumed (under the name *Sovetskaia pechat'*) only in 1955. In 1966 this was renamed *Zhurnalist*, and it continues to be published under that name. Whatever the reasons for Stalin's suspicion of journalists, only with Khrushchev's ascendancy could they create a union parallel to those of other occupations of the creative intelligentsia. In July 1957, after a period of preparatory work, an organizational bureau met and accepted the first contingent of members. Then a succession of regional and local organizations formed and took in members. The first all-union congress of journalists met in November 1959 and declared the union founded. At that point there were about 23,000 journalists altogether in the union, although probably at least that many had not joined. It is worth noting that, of the union's membership at that time, men (88 percent of the membership) and older journalists predominated. Only 15 percent were in their thirties. Only 13 percent had begun working as journalists within the previous five years. Even four years later it was reported by one source that fully 33 percent of all journalists had been active as journalists in 1939 (40 percent in Moscow).[32] The Stalin generation continued to form the basic core of the profession, not to mention its leadership. Among those who were union members at the time of its first congress, 77 percent were party members or candidates. This rate of membership would possibly be lower were all working journalists accounted for, but it probably reflected party penetration among older journalists and those in senior or editorial positions. More surprisingly, union members were also very well educated: 70 percent had at least some higher education.[33] The composition of the membership reflected elite characteristics, then, in respect to gender, party membership, and education. Doubtless, if ethnicity were also reported, a predominance of European—especially Slavic and above all Russian—members, would have been evident. In view of this, only political suspicions can explain the absence of a union for journalists until 1957.

Khrushchev made clear his support for the journalists as a group by speaking at the congress. He called journalists "helpers of the party" and "the most reliable transmission belt of the party," thus reinforcing the message that they could be counted upon politically as well as restating the more traditional Stalinist view of the press as an extension of the party.[34] The theme of respect for the work of the journalists was also stated in the message presented to the congress from the party Central Committee. "The Communist party," the statement read, "values very highly the noble work of the Soviet journalists in newspapers and magazines, in radio and television, in publishing houses and information organs; they play an important role in the historical labor of constructing a communist society, in the upbringing of the new person, and in the struggle for world peace.[35]

Yet despite these tributes, and notwithstanding continued rapid growth, the union was undercut in its potential significance by other initiatives of Khrushchev that reinforced the older barriers to professionalization. One was the strengthening of party ideological authority; the other the stimulus to nonjournalistic channels of public life and opinion. Several weeks after the founding congress of the Journalists' Union, the party issued its major resolution on the need for more effective and particularly more widespread political-ideological education through the party school system.[36] Along with the demand for a massive effort to propagate Marxism-Leninism in as pragmatic and constructive a manner as possible, the resolution called upon the press to end the "shameful practice" of restricting journalistic propaganda to "only a small group of authors" and instead to recruit officials, scientists, specialists, innovators, and many others to write for the press.[37] To improve the coordination of ideological oversight in the media, schools, arts organizations, and the agitation-propaganda system, the Central Committee apparatus formed an ideological commission in 1962.[38]

Improved coordination of ideological work was needed in view of the encouragement Khrushchev gave to a variety of "civic" or nonstate (obshchestvennye) initiatives concerned with discovering, articulating, and aggregating popular opinion. For example, in May 1960 the newspaper Komsomol'skaia pravda founded its own amateur Institute for Public Opinion, which began sampling readers' opinion. In June of the same year the Central Committee issued a resolution on revitalizing the worker-peasant correspondent movement and increasing its size. In February 1961 the "public" Novosti Press Agency was founded, aimed at supplementing TASS materials with "articles, commentaries, interviews, conversations, surveys, reportages, sketches, photo-illustrations, and other informational material" concerning a variety of subjects. Insistent that it was not a state but a public organ, its founding members were the Journalists' Union, the Writers' Union, the Society of Soviet Leagues of Friendship with Foreign Countries, and the Znanie Society. Despite the pains taken to demonstrate the nonofficial character of the new body, it was for the most part the successor organization to the Sovinformburo, which was the principal arm of Soviet foreign propaganda.[39] Probably the most important development in the revival of public life was the tremendous spur the liberal wing of the artistic intelligentsia received in its attempt to become the forum of truthful commentary on social issues, above all the issue of Stalinism.[40] Writers rather than journalists in the Khrushchev period led the way to articulating and dramatizing the great historical dilemmas faced by the Soviet regime. No journalistic product matched the political impact or stylistic power of Solzhenitsyn's *Ivan Denisovich,* published in *Novyi mir* in November 1962. Although de-Stalinization and limited liberalization did spill over into the press (notably in *Izvestiia* under Khrushchev's son-in-law Adzhubei), the tensions among writers were far sharper than those among journalists.

These innovations of the Khrushchev period left journalists in much the same position they had been in with respect to public opinion and state power. Although the union's founding facilitated greater self-awareness and cohesiveness about journalists, this growth in structural articulation was not accompanied by any greater functional monopoly over communication. Information and propaganda remained diffused among a now wider range of state and public bodies. The journalists' former inability to lay claim through professional expertise or functional specialization to a distinctive role had simply been reproduced on a more complex, elaborate basis. Essentially the same condition continued into the mid 1980s, with the material position of journalists improving along with the rest of the Soviet elite at the same time as their social standing steadily dropped.

The Journalists' Union grew in the post-Khrushchev period, although the rate of growth declined. Its second congress was held seven years later, in September 1966, rather than four years later, as the statutes then required (five is now the norm); probably the timing of the meeting was affected by the political repercussions of Khrushchev's fall. By the time of the second congress, the union represented 43,000 members. Membership grew to 48,000 in 1971, the time of the third congress, and to 63,000 in 1977, the time of the fourth congress. The fifth congress was held in March 1982, and at that time membership had risen to 75,000. At the sixth congress in March 1987 total membership stood at 85,182, and there were estimated to be 100,000 working journalists altogether.

The union maintains branches in each of the non-Russian republics and in over fifty provinces. In major media organs the union is organized into Primary Journalists' Organizations (PJOs), which, like the party's PPOs, handle admissions, collection of dues, training, and similar administrative chores.[41] At higher levels, the union also runs sections for journalists specializing in particular fields such as science, agriculture, atheism, and the like. The sections run conferences and courses in their fields.

Generally the union's activity can be classified into three areas: education, liaison with foreign journalists' organizations, and provision of material benefits to members. The first activity consumes a great deal of the union's efforts. At the all-union level at least twenty educational events are held each year.[42] Lower-level branches organize a number of short-term courses and continuing seminars for journalists. The union also sponsors special conferences for particular categories of media workers, or holds regular meetings for editors, publishing officials, and party ideology staff.[43] In Moscow, with its concentration of major media organs, the union has a full-time staff of twelve, who oversee the full program of events run by the Moscow branch. Every journalist in Moscow is obliged to take a two-year course given by the university of Marxism-Leninism of the Moscow city party committee. In addition, ongoing seminars are run by the union for journalists in particular specialties, allowing journalists to hear from scholars and officials and to take field trips.[44]

Elsewhere the training journalists receive through union-sponsored activity and the party education system is less elaborate. In Leningrad all editors and newspaper department heads take a month-long course every three years at the obkom's Higher Party School, and all journalists in lower media organs (such as factory and district papers and radio stations) attend a continuous seminar called "Current Problems of the Day" organized through the obkom's house of political enlightenment. The union also organizes two-week internships enabling journalists on lower-level newspapers to work on the province newspaper.[45]

These examples attest to the collaboration between the Journalists' Union and the party in combining political with occupational instruction. Journalists working at the lowest level of the media system take internships and specialized courses; those working at higher levels are kept abreast of policies in the areas about which they write. Editors and other media executives receive briefings from high-ranking party and government officials. In most cases, these measures are semiobligatory or required, and they offer ways of discharging the obligation to participate in public work. Despite the ceremonial character that they share with other links of the party propaganda system, they reinforce the journalists' ties to the political elite for information and guidance.

A measure of the importance of the union's foreign responsibilities is the fact that it consumes the largest share of the union's annual budget. According to its 1987 financial report on the preceding five years, the union spent 4.25 million rubles between 1982 and 1986 on its educational and organizational activity, and 5.2 million on its international activity.[46] The union has expanded its international ties through the 1970s and 1980s, sending numerous delegations abroad and hosting foreign groups, underwriting the expenses of Soviet-bloc journalists' organizations, and subsidizing the bloc's front group, the International Organization of Journalists. In addition, the union maintains a network of contacts with third world journalists through exchanges, meetings, and material aid, as well as with sympathetic journalists in capitalist countries. For example, the union held a ski holiday in Soviet Georgia in 1977 for journalists from twenty-five countries. The increased emphasis on foreign policy is also reflected in the prominence of certain regional branch organizations in sponsoring international events. The head of the Uzbek republic journalists' branch reported in 1977 that his republic had hosted forty-seven delegations from thirty-one countries between 1972 and 1976.[47] The union thus plays its part in Soviet foreign policy.

Probably of most immediate concern to the membership, however, is the union's role in providing material benefits and lobbying for improved benefits. The union provides vouchers to resorts on Lake Balaton and 'at Varna on the Black Sea as well as to Soviet vacation spots; it distributes funds as incentives and aid to members; and its local branches operate recreational homes and clubs. But only about 10 percent of the members benefit from the vacation tickets, and the shortage of local recreational facilities is suggested by the 1982 report that only four Houses of Journalists existed throughout the country, and fewer than ten Journalists' Clubs. In many localities, therefore, the journalists rent space from other creative unions, such as the Writers' or Architects' Union.[48] A chronic complaint by the journalists is that they are not afforded the same privileges that members of other creative unions receive, despite their supposed importance to the party. In his 1987 address to the Congress of Journalists, Chairman Afanas'ev commented on the ambiguous status of journalists, observing that some consider the Journalists' Union an occupational or trade union rather than a creative union. Afanas'ev pointed out that the union still did not have its own discretionary fund, that journalists' salaries were wretched, especially in the lower-level press, and that journalists continued to lack sufficient housing.[49] The union's long struggle to improve the status of journalists finally bore fruit with a Central Committee resolution in August 1987 authorizing a substantial improvement of the material conditions of journalists and the union.[50] Notwithstanding the nominal importance of the ideological role assigned journalism and the high rate of party saturation of the profession (80 percent), the union has little influence over the party and government in either professional or personal welfare areas, another indication of the relative weakness of the journalists as an organized professional group and their dependence on party favor for their social status.

THE SOCIAL STANDING OF JOURNALISM

Evidence from a variety of sources converges on the observation that over the 1970s and early 1980s, journalism fell into disrepute. In April 1985, as the new leadership sought to put force into its drive for *glasnost'*, a *Pravda* article reported the opinion of several readers that the formerly prestigious occupation of journalist had lost its attractiveness.[51] Professors of journalism, such as V. A. Shanda of the Urals University and Vladimir Zdorovega of Lvov University, have explained the decline in the number of applications to journalism school by the fact of the profession's falling prestige.[52] Poor living and working conditions are also often cited as reasons for the low attractiveness of the field, but these cannot have deteriorated in absolute terms over the past twenty years, although they may have declined relative to other professions.

Rather, the decline seems to have begun after the force of

Khrushchev's reforms was spent and the consolidation of ideological orthodoxy under the Brezhnev leadership began, signaled perhaps by the dismissal of A. M. Rumiantsev from the editorship of *Pravda* in September 1965.[53] The Rand Corporation survey of former Soviet media employees concluded that "in the 1960s, there was evidently a policy of appointing chief editors who would make the news interesting; but in the last ten years [i.e., since the beginning of the 1970s], the stress has been on political reliability instead, even at the expense of sacrificing circulation." Professor Shanda chose 1969 as the year from which to date the beginning of the trend of dwindling applications.[54]

The emphasis through the 1970s on political conservatism narrowed the scope for journalistic independence and initiative. More and more individual ministries claimed the power to prohibit unfavorable coverage. The Ministry of Health, for example, issued instructions forbidding any mention of the problem of drug abuse in Soviet society. The State Committee for Oil Products required that any article on the supply of the country with petroleum products had to be cleared with it.[55] The number of clearances and permissions that had to be received and the lengthy revisions that investigative reports were subject to inhibited journalistic initiative and reinforced self-censorship.[56] As the mass media became less and less a tool for social self-criticism and more a means for reaffirming the policies of the regime, editors grew cautious, preferring pat, stereotyped stories to reportage with an edge.

To be sure, the field has its stars. Earlier I noted that the late Anatolii Agranovskii and Iurii Zhukov are regarded as masters of their craft, both for the salience of the topics they write on and for the skill of their writing. They represent two very different types of journalist.

Agranovskii, who died in 1984, often dealt with controversial issues, such as the private sector or the service sector of the economy. To characterize his position as liberal would be an oversimplification, but his appeals to simple common sense and old-fashioned virtues such as pride and care and quality of work implicitly criticized complacency about the status quo. His writing was deceptively simple, and its success owed much to the ability to analyze social dilemmas through the lives of ordinary citizens, as when a casual acquaintance with a waiter in a Murmansk hotel restaurant prompted an extended essay on the relationship of personal interest to the quality of the service sector.

It is regrettable he is not better known in the West, for his style exemplifies Soviet journalism at its best—essayistic, literate, and socially conscious.[57]

Iurii Zhukov represents an altogether different species of writer. Like many of the most prominent postwar journalists, Zhukov is a former war correspondent. His values are rooted in the black-and-white imagery of the Stalin era. The simplistic way in which he explains world politics and the directness of his expression appeal widely to lay audiences as well as to the political authorities, who, especially before the Gorbachev era and its "new thinking" in international relations, gave him wide scope to comment on world affairs in print and on television. He was one of the political commentators whom Stalin, following Churchill's 1946 "Iron Curtain" speech, entrusted with the right to speak without prior editorial approval. According to Zhukov, Stalin observed, "We need our own Lippmanns."[58] Such privileged journalists were provided with better than usual sources of information for preparing their commentaries. Now, under Gorbachev, the freedom of uncensored comment has been extended far more widely in the interests of increasing the timeliness and responsiveness of the media's coverage of international affairs, and Zhukov has been overshadowed by commentators such as Fedor Burlatskii and Alexander Bovin, who are more closely identified with the current line in foreign policy.

Through the Brezhnev era, foreign affairs correspondents were the most prestigious segment of the profession, with opportunities for foreign travel and contact with diplomats and statesmen. Although the postwar generation of journalists lacked their fathers' opportunities to win distinguished individual reputations, the goal of becoming a foreign correspondent attracted many young journalists. Now, however, under *glasnost'*, the tables have begun to turn. It is the younger, more aggressive journalists writing on domestic problems who have captured the attention of the public with sensational, taboo-breaking exposés. According to a political observer for *Izvestiia*, the domestic correspondents privately scorn their famous internationalist elders, recognizing that harsh attacks on President Reagan and similar articles incur no risk and have no impact whereas a critical article about a powerful official at home quickly draws fire.[59]

Several fictional works of the late 1970s and early 1980s convey something of the malaise from which journalism was suffering. A 1981 novel by an émigré journalist named Sergei Dovlatov, entitled *The Compromise*, bitingly projects demoralization and cynicism.[60] Any thought that the novel reflected an émigré's disenchantment is dispelled by a 1983 review article in *Zhurnalist* of six recent novels and stories published in the Soviet Union about journalists, only one of which depicted them in a favorable light. The author of the article observes that the main characters either become so disillusioned with their work that they flee from it or lose any spark of interest, become drudges, and turn out their stories joylessly and mechanically. They learn to accommodate any demands placed on them. One story is based on a nameless journalist's letters to his wife, in one of which he says, "Spit and don't bother opening my letters any more. But they have given me the chance to write in a way different from what the newspaper demands. . . . The material of mine that's printed, clearly, has been castrated." Eventually this character leaves the profession, realizing that although journalists are supposed to be moral guides for society, this is impossible for someone who has grown base and petty. The author of the article comments that although the total picture of journalism created by these stories is a distortion, many of the moods and situations are familiar.[61]

These literary sources, together with the figures on declining applications to faculties of journalism from the late 1960s to the early 1980s, make it clear that the drift of the Brezhnev era toward hackneyed, conformist journalism directly affected the quality, prestige and attractiveness of the profession. As one might expect, therefore, *glasnost'* has had the effect of beginning to restore the prestige of a profession which had sunk far in both social standing and self-esteem. According to a recent report, applications to journalism faculties have tripled.[62]

The evidence indicates that journalism is shaped by a variety of influences. Some of them reflect national policy, and others are inherent in the environment, such as the close ties media organs maintain to their party supervisors, the cross-pressures of journalistic and political professionalism, and the diffusion of communications functions among other institutions—the fine arts, party and other meetings, mass agitation and propaganda, and word-of-mouth networks. Even when the leadership calls for a renewal of social self-criticism, writers, scientists, philosophers, and officials upstage journalists with provocative materials in the press and broadcast media. The theater, cinema, literature, and other arts compete for public attention, benefiting from the freer cultural policy. Even the party education system and mass agitation revive thanks to the greater official tolerance for candid public expression.

In fact, so threatened is the political position of the journalistic establishment, at least of its academic elite, that it seems to resist liberalization. The bulletin of the Moscow State University Journalism Faculty, which is the sole scholarly journal on journalism published in the Soviet Union, has taken a noticeably cool line toward *glasnost'*, interpreting it largely as a campaign for economic productivity and industrial modernization. The journal managed to ignore the entire subject of *glasnost'* until the summer of 1986. An article appearing in the journal's spring 1987 issue by one of the faculty members rather sourly reminded readers that in Soviet society it falls to the party to plan and organize the propagation of political ideas, and that these political ideas "program the activity" of journalists. Not only was he underlining the orthodox tenet that journalists are ideological partners of the party, but he also appeared to be admonishing the party not to neglect its responsibilities with respect to journalists.[63]

More important than academic training or the professional union in shaping journalistic practice, however, is on-the-job assimilation of the working norms of the trade. These are influenced above all by the expectations of the primary reference group for editors and journalists—their superiors in the party. Under *glasnost'*, as before, success for journalists lies in following the axiom that they act as an extension of the party apparatus. Viktor Afanas'ev commented at the Sixth Congress of Journalists (1987) that it was galling under present conditions to hear party officials complain that journalists have no right to criticize party committees: after all, Afanas'ev pointedly asked, "since when has the journalist ceased being considered a party employee?"[64]

7 BUILDING THE SOCIALIST COMMUNITY

The division of labor, which we have already seen above as one of the chief forces of history up till now, manifests itself also in the ruling class as the division of mental and material labor, so that inside this class one part appears as the thinkers of the class (its active, conceptive ideologists, who make the perfecting of the illusion of the class about itself their chief source of livelihood), while the others' attitude to these ideas and illusions is more passive and receptive, because they are in reality the active members of this class and have less time to make up illusions and ideas about themselves. Within this class this cleavage can even develop into a certain opposition and hostility between the two parts.

—Marx and Engels, *The German Ideology*

The preceding chapters have surveyed the ways in which the party exercises ideological influence over the main channels of political communication in Soviet society, arguing that effective control requires a balance between diffusion of responsibility for upholding party doctrine among members of socially privileged groups and their incorporation into a broad political elite. To put it in the most abstract terms, this balance involves an exchange of a measure of ideological responsibility for a measure of political status. The exchange assumes a variety of forms. Technical, administrative, managerial, and scientific personnel are recruited into ideological work both as activists in oral agitation and propaganda and through exposure to continuous political instruction in party schools. The growth of the ideological *aktiv* in the postwar era parallels the growth of the managerial and engineering-technical stratum and corresponds to the party's policy of incorporating these rapidly expanding groups into political activism and particularly into ideological work. The higher the individual's rank, the more responsible the assignments that are assumed.

The grooming of prospective cadres for higher-level jobs offers another means of integrating members of the social and political elite. The party depends extensively on the efforts of unpaid, nonstaff organizers to back up staff instructors, to serve as deputy PPO secretaries in large enterprises overseeing ideological work, to run reference offices, political schools, lecture bureaus, and public committees of various kinds. By assigning administrative chores to young and ambitious would-be officials, seeing to their advancement, selection, and training, the party maintains a reserve nomenklatura from which it replenishes the pool of political professionals in the party apparatus, enterprises, government, Komsomol, media, and other organizations. At the same time, it is clear that much of this organizational work is an elaborate charade, that a great many organizers do little or no actual work, and that a good deal of the work that is done is purely ceremonial. Little wonder that under Gorbachev, ideology officials have been under new pressure to justify themselves economically and to concern themselves with practical problems of production and social services.

The specialized nature of the mass media generates distinctive pressures on the exchange relationship between party and society. Although ideology officials continue to refer to the media as an extension of the party apparatus, glasnost' has encouraged editors and journalists to adopt a more critical and independent stance. The media grew incomparably bolder through 1986 and 1987, and the new freedom for social comment has been reinforced by a massive turnover of personnel at all levels and in all branches of the media. The greater autonomy for media organs has invigorated a profession which had grown cynical and demoralized, and the new leadership has addressed some of the long-standing grievances on the part of journalists about their corporate status and identity.

Yet in many ways, the glasnost' campaign has simply underscored standing barriers to media professionalism and autonomy. Periods such as the present, when the national climate encourages open and honest communications, allow a variety of communications channels outside the media to spring up, including numerous informal organizations and semitolerated unofficial periodicals; they reinforce the importance of nonjournalists such as public officials, intellectuals, and scholars as sources of information and opinion within and outside the media; and they require the media in their capacity as popular tribunes to respond to the vastly greater volume of mail from the general public. Although the content of letters chosen for publication must meet some criterion of significance or typicality, the preoccupation with the particular—with the small-scale dramas of daily life in a bureaucratized society—hinders the media as such from aggregating larger social interests. Within the media, moreover, the dominance of the voices of the center, the news services, Central Radio and Television, the major all-union newspapers and journals, inhibits the exchange of news and ideas horizontally across the communications system.

To be sure, the greater openness of political communications has begun to replace the spurious solidarity of the political elite which was the public face of the Brezhnev period with revelations of serious divisions over the proper orientation of ideological theory and activity. Whenever doctrine turns in the direction of pragmatism, seeking answers to the problem of declining productivity, it poses a threat to the normative basis of solidarity within the political community and invites the revival of alternative ideologies. The rapidity with which an extreme form of Russian nationalism sprang up in Moscow and other cities in 1986 supports this generalization (and recalls the similar rise of "Fatherland" clubs in the mid 1960s). The challenge for the party's ideological managers, therefore, is to combine the lifting of restrictions on permissible public expression with the assault on the conservative orthodoxy of the Brezhnev era without also contributing to a breakdown in the field of ideological authority itself.

So far in this book I have mainly concentrated on the output side of the communications system, emphasizing the degree to which members of the social elite and media professionals share portions of the ideological responsibility ultimately borne by the party staff. Now it is pertinent to ask what if any effect the "ideological complex" has in influencing the outlooks and behavior of Soviet citizens. The difficulty of answering this question is compounded by the scarcity of reliable survey data on Soviet society. This chapter seeks to address the question of attitudes, as well as that of the reliability and validity of the data, by analyzing data from multiple sources. Among these are surveys taken within the Soviet Union under both official and unofficial auspices and surveys conducted outside the country among both citizens and émigrés. As much as possible, findings from comparable studies are used to determine the strength and trustworthiness of the patterns uncovered.

MEDIA CONSUMPTION

Before inquiring into the effects of ideological work in molding the attitudes and beliefs of the Soviet population, one needs first to examine the actual exposure of citizens to the products of the oral agitation and propaganda system and the mass media. On this relatively less sensitive point, Soviet data provide detailed answers. Putting aside for the moment the question of depth of attention or impact on opinion or behavior, there can be no question about the near total reach of the mass media. Survey after survey demonstrates that Soviet citizens consume the material communicated by print and broadcast channels. Three will be cited.[1]

By far the most comprehensive body of survey data pertaining to media habits in the Soviet Union derives from the project carried out in the Russian city of Taganrog in the late 1960s and early 1970s. This survey found that 99.3 percent of the population were consumers of some combination of print and broadcast media. Virtually all adults read at least one central newspaper as well as at least one other newspaper—on average two to three people read every copy of *Pravda*, *Izvestiia*, and *Taganrogskaia pravda* received in the city. Of magazines received, over 50 percent of the titles were published in Moscow, and these accounted for 92 percent of all copies read; 96.4 percent of the population listened to radio; 90.7 percent watched television. Overall only 3.4 percent of the population called themselves irregular consumers of the media.[2]

Another study, conducted in 1977 in the Russian city of Kaluga, found television well established among cultural and media institutions: 83.3 percent of respondents said they watched television regularly, another 11.8 percent "from time to time"; 81.2 percent regularly listened to the radio; 65.7 percent said they read (apparently books, newspapers, or any printed matter); 60.7 percent reported attending the movies no less than once a month; and 42.1 percent said they listened to records and tapes. After that the audiences for other cultural forms declined sharply: fewer than 20 percent each claimed to attend concert halls, museums, theater, and clubs.[3]

A third survey was conducted in Leningrad between 1978 and 1980. Self-reported usage of various media for local news was as follows: 82 percent for newspapers, 77 percent for television, and 75 percent for radio. Magazines were the least-cited source, at 12 percent.[4] The same survey also asked respondents about their preferred sources for various categories of information: international affairs, domestic affairs, the economy, art and culture, education and health, and law and morals. Respondents were asked to choose among radio, television, and newspapers and could give an unlimited number of preference ratings across thematic categories. In all categories, television was the big winner, as table 6 indicates. Variables such as age, gender, occupation, and education of the respondent bore scarcely any relationship to preference for television. However, newspaper consumption was strongly correlated with education, as table 7 shows. When the respondents were subdivided into four groups by educational attainment, the percentage of those with the least education (seven to nine years) who named newspapers as their preferred source of news was on the order of 20 percentage points or more below the percentage of those with the most

TABLE 6   Preference for Information Sources
(in percentages; N = 1355)

	Newspapers	Radio	TV
International affairs	79	64	86
Domestic affairs	72	64	77
The economy	53	44	56
Art and culture	48	45	74
Education and health	34	31	55
Law and morals	50	38	72

Source: V. A. Losenkov, *Sotsial'naia informatsiia v zhizni gorodskogo naseleniia* (Leningrad: Nauka, 1983), p. 64.

education (full or incomplete higher education) who named newspapers for four of the six thematic categories. Interest in newspapers rises monotonically with education. In short, as the "hard" medium of information, newspapers appeal to the better educated.

Not only, then, do the mass media saturate the population, but also, by all indications, Soviet people avidly consume the media, with television staking out a position of increasing dominance for all but the most highly educated, among whom it is also popular. How, then, does this huge stream of print and broadcast messages compare in volume and acceptance to other forms of organized and unorganized communication? In particular, can the volume of information produced and distributed through the print and broadcast media be compared with that channeled through the oral communication system? Second, with respect to time and attention devoted to them, does the latter equal or overshadow the former? Only after examining the scale of party-regulated communications can one begin to assess the broader issue of the impact of these forms of communication on public consciousness.

THE ORAL PROPAGANDA NETWORK

A distinctive feature of the Soviet communications system is the enormous number of spare-time communicators producing a large volume of differentiated, personally mediated messages. It will be recalled from chapter 2 that, after a certain retrenchment and consolidation, the numbers of propagandists, agitators, and other party-sponsored oral communicators settled by 1985 to roughly the following numbers (in millions):[5]

Propagandists	2.2
Agitators	3.7
Political information speakers	1.8
Reporters	0.3
Znanie Society lecturers	3.0
Total	11.0

As impressive as this figure is, of course, it is necessary to remember that some empirical Soviet studies have found that for a large number of activists—without for the moment being more precise about how many—fulfillment of assignments in the oral propaganda system is sporadic at best. The Taganrog study, for example, found that most members of the city's ideological aktiv addressed the public only from time to time, most devoting no more than several hours a month to this activity. It will also be recalled that, in one survey of Znanie Society lecturers, it was found that only one-third actually gave lectures. The Taganrog study found a small minority of Znanie Society lecturers, 14–15 percent, giving half of all the lectures.[6] The Znanie Society probably tolerates a higher degree of nominal participation than do the speakers' groups organized directly by primary and local party committees, and surely the political education (propaganda) system, concerned as it is with regular doctrinal instruction, manifests the least amount of minimal or nominal performance. Still, most talks are short—fifteen to twenty minutes for agitation and political information sessions, one hour for lectures and political education classes. These two features of the oral communication system—sporadic effort and short duration of sessions—account for the apparent anomaly that, despite the vastly larger number of spare-time communicators than professionals, the actual volume of communicated messages, as measured by the time devoted by the public, is higher in the mass media

TABLE 7   Relation of Interest in Newspaper to Level of Education (in percentages)

	7–9 years	Secondary general	Specialized secondary	Higher (full or incomplete)
International affairs	68	79	85	88
Domestic affairs	65	71	77	84
The economy	45	48	61	70
Art and·culture	41	47	57	60
Education and health	31	38	42	46
Law and morals	47	45	58	60
Total respondents	195	330	287	384

Source: V. A. Losenkov, Sotsial'naia informatsiia v zhizni gorodskogo naseleniia (Leningrad: Nauka, 1983), p. 65.

system than in the oral propaganda system by several orders of magnitude.[7]

This discrepancy does not mean, though, that oral propaganda is failing to penetrate the populace. Examining the audience for the most formalized of oral communications—political education, political information, and lectures—the Taganrog researchers found that about 66 percent of the city's population were being reached by some combination of these. (Lectures reached 57 percent of the sample, political information 45 percent, and political education 23 percent, combining regular and irregular participation.)[8] Counting workplace meetings and agitation sessions (the latter were excluded from this inquiry as being too irregular to measure properly) would certainly increase the net audience for oral communications. Other studies have found equal or higher levels of penetration. A survey of a Kramatorsk plant in 1977 found that some 96 percent of the work force regularly attended political information sessions, 87 percent attended agitation talks, and 94 percent attended lectures. The likelihood that these figures are inflated is suggested by the report that 84 percent of the respondents considered themselves satisfied with these efforts. In Odessa province, surveys show that almost 33 percent of workers do not attend agitation talks.[9] It is probably most accurate to say, as surveys conducted by the Academy of Social Sciences reportedly show, that the penetration of mass-political work is highly variable, differing by region and by labor collective within regions. At the high end, nearly all members of the labor force of some enterprises are being reached by one or more forms of oral propaganda; at the low end, in labor collectives where it is weakly organized, it reaches only 60 percent of the potential audience.[10] One reason for this high variability of penetration is the intermittent nature of agitation. More than activists working in more formalized channels, such as lectures and political information sessions, agitators take a rather casual approach to their assignments. In most cases they do not plan their work in advance or coordinate it with the primary party committee.[11]

So, though an enormous number of activists address a vast audience through a large and differentiated network of organized channels, factors such as haphazard or occasional participation in the system, imperfect penetration, and the limited nature of contact at any one session lead the general public to devote much more time to consuming the products of the mass media. The work of the activists is guided and frequently organized by party committees. In the case of the vast bulk of mass-political work and political education, however, the organizing is performed by primary and even subprimary party committees based in the workplace, rather than, as is the case with supervision of the mass media, by full-time officials employed by territorial party committees.

PRIMARY CHANNELS AND INTERPERSONAL COMMUNICATION

The victims of a bureaucratized, dogmatized communications system are credibility and validity of information. The quality of information reaching the center declines. Audiences tune out, discrediting or discounting information received through official channels. Instead they seek out information and opinion from informal or unauthorized sources. This explains why, despite the system's success in penetrating society with media output, information remains a deficit good, compensated for by a persistent and universal habit of gathering news and opinion through face-to-face conversation.[12] As a Soviet social scientist commented, people are not saturated with information: in fact they want more. The information stream they turn to is both official and unofficial. When official sources do not satisfy the need, the public uses channels such as conversation and foreign radio.[13]

Soviet social scientists have gathered a great deal of data bearing on patterns of information use. One of the hardy findings threaded throughout the data is the prevalence of conversation with family members, friends, and co-workers as a valued source of information. These findings persist regardless of social milieu: indeed, as will be shown (and as the Harvard refugee project found forty years ago), people in higher-status strata tend both to seek and to trust interpersonal conversation at least as much as those of lower status. Several illustrative surveys will be cited.

A 1979 survey of machinists and metallurgical workers in two factories, one in Riazan and one in Dnepropetrovsk, inquired about the sources used by workers to obtain information on economic questions.

It is unusually complete in that it lists a large number of possible sources and allows comparison between two different enterprises. It yields quite typical ranges. Table 8 shows the sources used by workers in each factory to gather information on economic matters. (Note that, as with virtually all such surveys, respondents could choose as many sources as they wished.)

A survey in several workplaces in a district of Kishinev, Moldavia, sought to find out the sources used to obtain "social information" (not otherwise defined). Responses (in percentages) were as follows:[14]

Newspapers	84
Television	78
Radio	65
Conversations with comrades	45
Political education system	28
Lectures	26
Journals	19
Political information talks	14

An interesting survey of workers on the Baikal-Amur Main Line (BAM) project asked respondents for their main source of information about living and working conditions on BAM before coming. Some 2,000 workers and 359 supervisors responded as follows (in percentages):[15]

Komsomol officials	19.6
Recruiters	15.2
Mass media	8.6
Relatives, friends, acquaintances	51.1

In this case, the information received beforehand, not only from second-hand sources but also from recruiters eager to promise the moon, was quite often unreliable. Once they got to the project site, 40–50 percent of the respondents changed their opinions for the worse. The authors of the report concluded that official information sources needed to paint a more realistic picture of life on BAM to avoid disenchantment.

Returning to the 1978–80 survey of Leningrad residents concerning their information habits, one can now fit all the categories of sources

TABLE 8   Sources of Information on Economic Questions
(in percentages)

	Machinists	Metallurgists
Television	83.8	87.9
Radio	71.9	71.1
Central newspapers	60.9	66.9
Pravda	54.7	59.4
Other central press	27.2	39.7
Oblast and city press	23.7	36.5
Enterprise newspapers	24.3	36.3
Party and work meetings	23.5	30.8
Talks by agitators, political information speakers, and propagandists	19.5	29.1
Economic study classes	16.6	20.6
Other political study classes	12.9	20.2
Theoretical journals	8.1	10.2
Interpersonal contact	34.1	45.0

Source: V. A. Beliaev, "K voprosu ob effektivnosti ekonomicheskoi propagandy v pechati (opyt sotsiologicheskogo issledovaniia," in Zh. T. Toshchenko, ed., *Voprosy teorii i metodov ideologicheskoi raboty,* vyp. 12 (Moscow: Mysl', 1980), pp. 167–70.

discussed so far into a common framework, further breaking the results down by occupation, age, and gender. The question posed was, From what source(s) do you obtain information about local affairs? Respondents could choose multiple sources. Tables 9 and 10 show the results.

This survey is unusually interesting for several reasons. First, Leningrad usually ranks high on social indicators in which urbanization and modernization are independent variables; it was shown earlier, for example, that Leningrad residents tend to own more television sets than the national average. It is a highly industrialized city with, as hardly needs to be pointed out, a tradition of high cultural development and Western influence. It would be in Leningrad, if anywhere, that the withering away of traditional patterns of face-to-face news gathering could be expected to have occurred. Second, the survey is relatively recent, and its findings cannot therefore be ascribed to weak penetration by either the mass media or the oral propaganda system. (One might, for example, wish to attribute to such factors the finding cited in chapter 6 that, in a number of rural districts, newspapers took second place to personal contacts as a source of news.[16]) Third, the survey gives unusually detailed distributions by social category. Note, for example, that men and women are about equally likely to cite interpersonal conversation as a news source even while differing significantly in newspaper use. Note also that age plays a significant role in affecting interpersonal communication: retirement, by isolating individuals from the work environment, appears to be strongly related to the drop-off in interpersonal communication.

Of greatest interest for my purposes, however, is the social status variable, measured here by a combination of occupational and educational characteristics. Far from declining among higher-skill or higher-status groups, interpersonal news gathering rises: 45 percent of skilled workers cite it; 55 percent of specialists (employees with higher education) cite it. This is by no means an anomalous finding. A survey of scientific workers in two scientific institutions in Moscow found that almost all read the central press for information, and that 46.1

TABLE 9   Sources of Information on Local Affairs, Leningrad, by Occupational Category (in percentages)

	A	B	C	D	E	All
Newspapers	83	81	83	85	76	82
Television	84	77	72	82	79	77
Radio	75	81	74	76	69	75
Friends, workmates, neighbors, acquaintances	45	52	55	25	59	50
Lectures and political information	21	21	28	21	8	22
Magazines	16	17	11	13	12	13
Total respondents	179	147	253	89	74	742

Source: V. A. Losenkov, Sotsial'naia informatsiia v zhizni gorodskogo naseleniia (Leningrad: Nauka, 1983), p. 45.
Note: A = skilled workers; B = white-collar employees without higher education; C = white-collar employees with higher education; D = pensioners; E = students.

percent cited conversations with co-workers and others as sources of news about social and political matters in the USSR and the world. A slightly lower proportion (44.2 percent) said that they derived such information from the questions they put to political information speakers. These scientists were a critical lot: 45 percent complained that they learned little that was new from political information, and only 33 percent said that the current state of ideological work was adequate for current needs. It is reasonable to infer, therefore, that interpersonal news gathering reflects a search for information to meet an appetite unsatisfied elsewhere, a hypothesis proposed by Inkeles and Bauer on the basis of the Harvard project.[17]

The concept of an information deficit is familiar in Soviet studies; it is not a hostile bourgeois invention. Grushin and Onikov indicate that nearly all the Taganrog respondents said they wanted more information. In any society rumor serves to compensate for an information deficit.[18] Among published Soviet studies, the Leningrad survey is nearly unique in addressing the role of rumor. It found that 24 percent of the respondents heard rumors often and 65 percent sometimes. (These categories were not further defined.) Not surprisingly, students

TABLE 10   Sources of Information on Local Affairs, Leningrad, by Age and Gender (in percentages)

	A	B	C	D	E	All
Newspapers	78	83	82	85	78	82
Television	71	75	81	78	77	77
Radio	71	75	79	72	78	75
Friends, workmates, neighbors, acquaintances	62	52	33	51	49	50
Lectures and political information	14	23	28	20	23	22
Magazines	13	14	14	14	13	13
Total respondents	261	323	213	423	374	793

Source: V. A. Losenkov, Sotsial'naia informatsiia v zhizni gorodskogo naseleniia (Leningrad: Nauka, 1983), p. 45.
Note: A = up to 29 years old; B = 30–49 years old; C = 50 year and older; D = men; E = women.

encounter rumor most often (31 percent said often, 67 percent said sometimes); but more surprisingly, employees with higher education reported hearing rumor in larger numbers than others: 71 percent reported hearing rumor sometimes as against the average for the sample of 65 percent. Evidently not only is the quality of rumor higher in better-educated circles, but so is the appetite for it. Although the reporting of this portion of the survey is extremely sketchy, it is evident that those who take a more active part in rumor networks are also more likely to believe that rumors turn out to be true: 28 percent of those "often" encountering rumors say that they are usually found to be true; only 15 percent of those "sometimes" hearing rumors are so convinced. It follows, then, that in high-status groups, where information searching and interpersonal news gathering is most intensive, the credibility of such news is greatest.[19]

It might be supposed from these findings that the more critical elements of the intelligentsia, who are more apt to take a skeptical view of the credibility of the official media, supplement them with conversations with colleagues, friends, acquaintances, and family. As I shall point out in a moment, there is indeed evidence for this common-sense conclusion. First, however, let us ask whether in official circles the taste for unofficial information is equally strong.

The evidence indicates that, the greater one's involvement in public affairs, the greater one's use of informal interaction with others as a source of information. The Leningrad study confirmed that the more people are engaged in public work, the more they turn to informal information channels.[20] In this regard it is also interesting to consider the results of a survey of party officials at different levels (krai, city, and districts) in Stavropol that inquired how they obtained information. Responses (in percentages) were as follows:[21]

Personal meetings with citizens	89.6
Questions asked at lectures, political days, and the like	88.3
Press, radio, and television	76.8
Comments at party, trade union, Komsomol, and production meetings	74.6
Local party organizations and enterprises	51.1
Conversations with local soviet deputies	49.7

There appears to be an underlying scale of credibility at work here. At the high end is information received in the relatively more intimate setting of face-to-face meetings on an individual basis. At the low end are highly formalized, organized channels of information. "Officialness" *(kazennost')* stands in inverse proportion to credibility. In this connection it is worth recalling the 1985 article in *Nedelia*, the weekly supplement to *Izvestiia*, on the discrepancy between the truthful communication characteristic of intimate, face-to-face interpersonal contacts and the false, ritualistic contacts when people speak in their official capacity at meetings, in official interviews, and the like. Citing several examples, the author mentions an occasion when he went to interview a high-ranking official in charge of the bread-making industry. With him he carried a bundle of letters of complaint about the declining quality of bread in several cities. His interlocutor provided pat, insincere answers to every question, claiming that production of high-quality bread was constantly rising. "But, all the same, why doesn't bread taste as good as it used to?" the reporter interrupted. At that point the official suddenly began speaking candidly and heatedly about the real problems of the industry.[22] Why, the reporter lamented, cannot all official speech manifest the same qualities of candor and sincerity that intimate face-to-face conversation, frequently over a glass or two, possesses?

THREE TYPES OF INFORMATION USERS

One of the most interesting observations arising from the Taganrog study was published in 1973. Instead of correlating measures of volume or type of information use with ordinal variables such as education or occupational status, I. E. Kokorev reported that patterns of information use fell into three modal orientations based on clusters of traits. These he labeled the consumer, the intellectual, and the professional-functional user.[23]

Consumers passively and superficially receive information from the mass media and lack the informational or educational background to evaluate or fully understand it. Their use of the media is mainly for current affairs and entertainment. They therefore tend to rely on cues, as well as day-to-day information, from friends and workmates, to acquire and interpret contextual information. Consumers are uncomfortable with being thought different from others and generally do not take on much independent social activity or serve as opinion leaders among their colleagues. In grasping media messages, consumers rely on stereotypes and conventional images: much current information goes over their heads because of their low background information.

Intellectual users need little help in grasping information from the media and tend to use leisure time for cultural or intellectual pursuits. Unlike consumers, they tend to think in abstract terms and to take an active interest in national and world issues. They are very critical of the media for oversimplifying complex matters and evaluate media content independently on the basis of extensive background knowledge. Like consumers, however, they also shy away from taking on much sociopolitical responsibility or serving as opinion leaders. They prefer to analyze information for themselves.

Professional-functional users have little problem in orienting themselves to the channels of the mass media, but they select and absorb information with a view to using it to instruct and inform others. They are uncritical toward the media, accepting its content as their guide to knowledge and behavior. As Kokorev put it, they have no trouble grasping the ideas presented in the media because they speak and think in the same language themselves. Usually professional-functional users hold positions of authority in administrative or instructional work and maintain wide rather than deep social relationships. They take interest in social and political news and use the newspaper as the most serious source of information and interpretation. The media keep them abreast of current events and enable them to explain matters to others. They read rapidly, selecting the cues and examples they will use in their lessons.

Another study based on the Taganrog survey concludes that the category of heaviest media users consists entirely of those with political functions: soviet deputies, organizational executives, members of elected boards and committees, and ideological activists. In addition to being heavy media users, they also tend to be the largest producers of information, generating the largest share, for example, of letters to the newspaper, contacts with local officials, and talks at meetings.[24]

A good deal of subsequent evidence supports this typology. One portion of Taganrog study, under the direction of an innovative

sociolinguist named Tamara Dridze, examined the problem of cognitive barriers to understanding the content of the mass media. She
concluded that educational differences only partly explained differences in comprehension. On the basis of a carefully structured sample
of three hundred, she broke the population into seven categories by
level of comprehension of ordinary newspaper articles. Only 12 percent
of the sample could fully and properly understand each article. Another
17 percent grasped the general points of the articles, understanding key
terms if used in familiar contexts. Fully 33 percent, of whom most had a
secondary or higher education, could define key words but not understand their sense in the articles because their juxtaposition with other
terms confused them. Altogether nearly 40 percent lacked some degree
of knowledge crucial to comprehending media content, either because
they were not familiar with particular terms or because they could not
properly read the texts.[25] Not surprisingly, Dridze found these differences related to sociooccupational status. Over 50 percent of her top
group, those possessing a good knowledge of both specialized terms
and general vocabulary and readily able to interpret the test articles,
consisted of members of the nonproduction intelligentsia. Among
workers, 90 percent lacked the cognitive equipment to interpret the
texts properly.[26] Reliance on interpersonal contacts to supplement and
replace media information is a logical outgrowth of the low capacity
for understanding media texts that is particularly prevalent among
workers.

Support for the association of high background information and
education with a discriminating and critical attitude toward the media
has also been reported in a number of other studies.[27] One of the most
interesting confirmations of the problems posed by the "intellectual
user" comes in the report of a 1980 survey of 3,600 residents of Belorussia that was structured to represent the whole employed population of
the republic. The survey was concerned with the relationship between
volume of media consumption and sociopolitical involvement. It
found that, as media consumption rose from low to moderately high
levels, level of activism rose with it. Among those with the highest
levels of informedness and information needs, sociopolitical activism
declined and even became, in the author's term, *dysfunctional.* The
author proposes a "boomerang effect," by which the most active media
users "to a certain extent begin to escape its effect and begin to satisfy

their information needs in other forms and with the help of other means" including "ideologically hostile sources."[28] (This implies foreign radio broadcasting and samizdat, for example.[29])

The Kokorev typology and related studies indicate that the effects of education and informedness, which are generally treated as independent variables in explaining patterns of media use, are influenced by intervening factors such as political attitude, political responsibility, and social milieu. A survey among recent emigrants from the Soviet Union showed, for example, that discussion of news heard on foreign radio broadcasts was confined almost entirely to their immediate family and friends.[30] Ties of interpersonal intimacy and trust were indispensable to the spread of the human rights movement. First, according to Ludmilla Alexeyeva's careful and comprehensive account, in the aftermath of Stalin's death, numerous overlapping circles of friends were formed, which shared an interest, for example, in songs by Okudzhava, Vysotskii, and others and later addressed directly political issues in conversation. Gradually these circles broadened into large groups consolidated by trust, enabling samizdat to circulate and an unofficial "public opinion" to form. From this base, an organized movement pressing the regime to honor civic and political rights developed. Even in its further development, as new recruits replaced members who were arrested or had emigrated, the movement's cohesion continued to depend on ties of friendship among the members. Alexeyeva also points out that the free intellectual atmosphere in research towns creates a receptive milieu for the circulation of samizdat and support for aid to families of political prisoners, although support for open dissent has declined among scientists.[31] Likewise the émigré sociologist Vladimir Shlapentokh notes that friendship in the Soviet Union in some ways substitutes for the mass media and that groups of like-minded friends can become social "cells" of opposition thought.[32]

A different milieu appears to exist among those holding positions of political responsibility. I noted in chapter 2 and again in this chapter the high correlation between sociopolitical responsibility and work as an ideological activist, in large degree thanks to the Brezhnev-era policy of recruiting ideological workers as widely as possible from the managerial, engineering, and specialist elites. I estimated that 50 percent or more of the individuals in managerial and specialist categories carry out some assignment in the ideological area; they probably comprise 75 percent of the propagandist corps alone.[33] The party now appears to set a 10 percent benchmark as the desired party membership rate among the employed population.[34] Therefore, even allowing for high rates of purely nominal participation and inflation in reporting, it is reasonable to accept the figure presented in a recent report that in some workplaces, as many as 10 percent of the labor force are listed as propagandists, lecturers, reporters, political information speakers, and agitators.[35] Not all party members take on ideological assignments; those who do not are partially offset by the substantial number of non–party members among agitators and, though to a lesser degree, among political information speakers. (Probably around 33 percent of the 5.5 million listed as having these assignments are not party members.) Of this 10 percent, however, a substantial proportion perform their assignments perfunctorily, sporadically, or not at all, so that whatever behavioral implications we infer from patterns of ideological activism should be confined to a smaller pool—consisting of those who, as Kokorev put it, "speak and think in the same language [as the media] themselves." They use interpersonally gathered information less as a substitute for the media than as a complement to it.

Hence one can distinguish two quite different social types among heavy media users: those whose vocational or avocational responsibilities make them into conduits for official information into their social surroundings; and those who, on the contrary, treat official information independently and skeptically. There appears to be a fork in the path from levels of information, education, and media use to patterns of attitude and behavior. One path links higher social status with high social involvement and responsibility and a functional use of the mass media. The other leads to lower levels of social activism and use of alternative sources of information. The final question takes one still farther into the realm of supposition. If the structure of information use differs systematically in different social milieux, do political attitudes differ among them as well?

THE ELITE SUBCULTURE

Let us hypothesize that mechanisms such as self-selection to the aktiv and interaction with the elite milieu affect not only the patterns of searching and selecting information, but, through them, the formation of beliefs and values. Can this proposition be tested? Unfortunately there are no more than a few surveys bearing on this problem, and almost never is there data on the effect of the variable of political activism. In each case, though, the surveys indicate that the single strongest factor bearing on opinion is party affiliation; it outweighs social status, education, age, and gender as a predictor. Even as measured by so crude an indicator as membership in the party, where one stands seems to depend on where one sits; and it appears possible to identify among the activist elite a political subculture that possesses an outlook on politics congruent with officially promoted viewpoints.

A pair of polls of attitudes among Soviet citizens toward Sakharov demonstrates how misleading it is to infer a direct correlation between education and attitudes without controlling for the intervening factor of political responsibility. Both surveys were conducted under relatively free conditions. One was carried out within the Soviet Union among a quasi-random sample of 853 people on the basis of informal responses later coded on a nine-point scale of favorable/unfavorable opinion by the survey takers. Of the respondents, about 20 percent overall expressed a positive view of Sakharov; but 65 percent of the group termed intelligentsia did so. This group consisted largely of university faculty, teachers, physicians, journalists, painters, musicians, and other members of professional groups. The respondents also included a certain number of middle-level executives (scientists, laboratory heads, institute directors, and other administrative personnel). Among them attitudes were distributed quite differently, 66 percent being negatively disposed toward Sakharov, only 33 percent positively. Among party members an even wider discrepancy was observed: about 5 percent expressed favorable views, 75 percent negative. According to the report, "almost all of the latter group were party activists, members of the party administration, secretaries, and so on."[36]

The second survey was conducted under the auspices of the Soviet Area Audience and Opinion Research (SAAOR) unit of Radio Liberty among Soviet citizens traveling in the West (not émigrés). The circumstances in which these polls are conducted are far from ideal, as is of course the case with surveys taken within the Soviet Union, since the questions are asked in the course of casual conversation and answers are recorded afterward.[37] Nonetheless, the results of these surveys show a remarkable degree of congruence with those of other Soviet and émigré polls when differences among questions, time periods, and sample composition are held to a minimum. One SAAOR poll asked 265 Soviet citizens a series of questions in 1975–76 about Sakharov and elicited an almost identical overall distribution of opinion to that of the internal but unofficial Soviet survey: about 20 percent favorable, 33 percent unfavorable, and about 50 percent having no opinion. When the data were disaggregated by educational and occupational category, however, there were substantial discrepancies: SAAOR found a considerably higher proportion of unfavorable opinion among the intelligentsia and technical intelligentsia and a lower proportion of favorable responses among the technical intelligentsia. (Favorable responses among the intelligentsia, however, were roughly the same in the two surveys, 28 percent for the internal poll and 31 percent for SAAOR's sample.) Given the strength of the political variable in the internal poll, these discrepancies would very likely diminish if the variable of political affiliation—even if measured only by the variable of party membership—were controlled for in the SAAOR group.[38]

In view of the consumer pattern described earlier, reinforced by low levels of background information and cognitive skill, it is notable that in both the internal Soviet poll and SAAOR's own, about two-thirds of the manual workers surveyed expressed no opinion.

The salience of party membership for attitudes was also shown in another SAAOR poll. In a survey of 505 Soviet citizens conducted shortly after martial law was declared in Poland in December 1981, it was found that 90 percent of party members declared themselves hostile toward the Solidarity movement and the trends of the Solidarity period. Neither education nor social status proved to be a useful predictor of opinion, but party membership was strongly related to attitude.[39]

Similarly, a very wide difference in the attitudes of party members and nonmembers was evident in SAAOR's poll concerning the shooting down of KAL 007 (see table 11). Among 158 respondents for whom party affiliation was ascertained, 84 percent of the party members (including candidate members) expressed approval of the Soviet government's action in downing the plane. Among nonmembers, opinion was rather evenly divided between approval, disapproval, and no opinion. The SAAOR surveys consistently find that those who listen regularly to Western radio are more likely to express views at variance with the regime's positions than those who do not. In the KAL case this finding was marked: about one-half of the Western radio listeners in the survey disapproved of the Soviet action and accepted the Western version of the events. If one could conduct a factor analysis of Soviet opinion, taking into account education, social and occupational status, attention to Western radio, and party membership, the evidence presented here suggests that party membership would be the strongest factor predicting opinion and that much of the strength of the education and social status variables would wash out. This premise is based on the body of evidence already presented that the social milieu in which individuals take part shapes the attitudes toward information as well as the sources used to gather it. Party membership is a surrogate measure of membership in a social milieu in which discordant information is screened out or discounted. *For any given level of educational and social status,* the party membership variable does a good job of predicting the type of attitudinal matrix in which an individual receives and processes information. Even in the surveys cited here, where informality and privacy protected respondents from the fear that the ideologically incorrect answer would provoke unwelcome inquiry, party members and, still more, members of the administrative elite, expressed views congruent with the regime's line. Nonparty intellectuals, on the other hand, were substantially more likely to take dissent-

TABLE 11   Attitudes Toward Downing of KAL 077
by Party Membership (in percentages)

	CPSU Members	Nonmembers
Approve	84	40
Disapprove	6	29
No opinion	10	30
Total respondents	49	109

Source: Radio Free Europe–Radio Liberty Soviet Area Audience and Opinion Research, "The Korean Airline Incident: Western Radio and Soviet Perceptions," AR 4-84, (April 1984), p. 16.

ing views; and non–party members of the working class frequently had
no opinion.

THE AKTIV AND SOCIALIST COMMUNITY

The evidence presented here shows that patterns of information seeking and opinion differ in a systematic way between those who identify
themselves with the regime by taking on full-time or spare-time assignments on its behalf or joining the party and those who, with similar
levels of information, education, and social status, do not. To be sure,
educational levels affect how people take in and interpret information.
More education increases the likelihood that an individual will consume more information from the media, will be critical of the media,
and will seek compensatory information from informal social contacts. Of still greater importance is the quality of participation—for
many, ideological activism is a purely formal commitment. Even despite the large error factor introduced by the prevalence of nominal or
cynical performance, and using a crude indicator of political stance
such as party membership, one finds large and stable differences in
outlook between those who hold positions of political responsibility
and those who do not. In the absence of ties of responsibility that bind
an individual to the political system, greater education and information are associated with tendencies to escape the ideological influence
of the media by seeking information from channels that are unap-
proved, and even disapproved of. In turn, these patterns of information
use result in distinctive distributions of opinion, with party members,
administrators, and activists likely to identify themselves with the
regime, its interests, and the positions the leadership takes on current
issues. Differences in opinion are shaped and reinforced by contacts
with friends; family, and colleagues and the sources of information
relied upon for news and interpretive cues.

Can one identify the size and composition of the political elite more
specifically? Is it at all integrated by a common political self-
awareness, or is it merely an artifact of differences on the scales of
information use and opinion that I have reviewed? Certainly it would
be foolish to overstate the cohesiveness of an aggregate as artificial,
stratified, and diverse as that of the 8–10 percent of the employed

population who take on organizing and opinion leading positions. At the same time it is too easy to fall back to the opposite view and argue that the commonalities among the activists are outweighed by differences in their occupational, political, institutional, ethnic, or other interests. The significance of the ideological aktiv as a stabilizing element for the state lies not only in the organizing and instructing duties its members share that create a certain bond among them but also in the weakness of political associations *outside* the regime.

In particular, the aktiv gives political focus to the existing stratification of social status in the workplace. Party policy has increasingly emphasized the role of the labor collective as a social cell, a microcommunity in which a well-managed moral climate and system of material rewards not only shape the character and behavior of each individual member, but also become the basic unit of social organization.[40] Social scientists approvingly cite surveys showing, for example, that the attitudes of young workers are shaped to a significant degree by the norms prevalent in their workplace. Another survey found that, among the various material and moral sanctions that can be applied to those violating moral rules, the one named by far the most frequently as being effective was public discussion of offenders before their comrades.[41] The workplace has long been the primary channel for distribution of such goods as housing, vacations, child care, and medical care.[42] More recently it appears that it is playing a growing role in the distribution of certain scarce food and other commodities as well.[43] The most important indication of the policy of the regime reinforcing the power of the work collective as a mechanism of social control came in the new law on labor collectives enacted in June 1983 and the press commentary then and since linking the law to the need to strengthen social discipline. An article in the trade union newspaper, *Trud*, in November 1983, pointed out that the new law "has significantly raised the workers' activity in the management of production and in the resolution of social problems, but the role of the collective has particularly grown in the strengthening of labor discipline."[44]

Accordingly, it is the duty of the aktiv to exercise leadership in shaping the climate of opinion in the collective.[45] Alexander Zinoviev asserts that in fact a handful of activists in the collective, watching over their fellow workers, speaking up at meetings, writing letters, joining investigative committees, can sometimes "determine the whole social and psychological atmosphere of the institution." Successful political work, according to a recent Soviet study, requires capturing the majority: "inasmuch as in moral upbringing in the collective, and especially in the struggle against specific negative manifestations, it is essential to rely on the moral support of the majority. . . . A majority starts at 51 percent, and that is the first boundary of the effectiveness of ethical upbringing."[46] Therefore, the goal of the party in incorporating those holding positions of responsibility in the workplace into the ideological aktiv is to capitalize upon their greater capacity for political influence over the work force at large.[47] Within the workplace, then, the creation of an organized ideological aktiv not only draws the elite into political work but also has tended to undercut the formation of oppositional bases of social authority over a period when the technical-managerial stratum in the economy grew much faster than any other segment of the work force.

In addition the aktiv incorporates individuals at different levels of responsibility, from junior party and Komsomol organizers to the general director of the enterprise, and ties them with the staff of the territorial party committee, helping reduce a certain amount of the social distance across the ranks. In the Soviet Union the ideological aktiv represents a stratum of society cutting across ethnic, generational, regional, and institutional cleavages. Moreover, the requirement that the public be addressed in a standardized language with a common line, regardless of any private cynicism expressed offstage, probably helps create a shared interest in keeping up appearances for appearances' sake. Ideological work is a way in which members of the elite justify a system that gives them privileges and opportunity. These unifying aspects of political participation surely do not create a strong consciousness of shared interest. They temper but certainly do not eliminate status differentials, institutional interests, differences in political orientation, ethnic consciousness, and other divisive forces. In a society in which other forms of association are weak, however, they foster unity. Other social divisions in the Soviet Union are not mutually reinforcing: in contrast with the polarized situation of Russia on the eve of the 1917 revolutions, when coinciding revolutions in the countryside, the cities, and the national borderlands combined to topple the autocracy, in Soviet society nationality grievances are competitive rather than cumulative, and class tensions cut across nationality lines. The regime appeals to blue-collar resentments of Jews and intellectuals and to the intelligentsia's fears of popular unrest. In this politically fragmented situation, even a weakly integrated political elite helps maintain stability.[48]

Moreover, the former strategy of consolidating the political elite around a common interest in preserving the status quo has paradoxically become a positive liability to reform. Having previously nurtured a fear of social conflict, whether released by inflation or political liberalization, the regime must now carefully mobilize popular opposition to bureaucratic power and the Stalinist dogmas that supported it. To do so it has revised ideological theory to emphasize such concepts as marketplace competition, individual legal rights, and the legitimacy of political opposition, which not only contradict many previously standard tenets of Marxism, but subvert the binding power of ideology itself. Yet without preserving the premise of an unchallengeable theoretical reference point, an ideological first principle, the entire structure of political control over communications would break down. Better the embourgeoisement of Marxism than a vacuum of ideological authority altogether.

Over the course of Soviet history the ideal of a socialist self-governing society, a socialist *obshchestvennost'*, has remained elusive because the regime has sought either to destroy the most important forms of social association or to convert them into extensions of the state. Party ideological work has been analyzed here as a process of exchange between society and state, by which responsibility for maintaining popular loyalty to the symbols and ideals of the political system is extended outward among a large and fast-growing segment of the country's social elite in the expectation of reinforcing its commitment to the power and stability of the regime. Many of these elites serving in activist roles do in fact mediate between power and society, "speaking and thinking in the same language as the media." A socialist community formed of society's elite, however, is a contradiction in terms, and the danger of an extended period of stagnation and dogmatism is a widening gap between the elite and the general populace in attitudes and behavior.

When, therefore, a phase of liberalization and renewal occurs, the primary-level structures of social association that have resisted cooptation respond most rapidly: out of the networks of friendship and ethnicity emerge new informal organizations and publications, a quickening of culture, and demands for democratization. Under Gorbachev the regime is seeking to channel these new energies into politically useful forms, seeking leverage against entrenched bureaucratic power through an alliance with the liberally oriented elements of the creative and scientific intelligentsia. One cannot but foresee, however, that, as has happened in liberalization phases in other communist systems, the consolidation of new political interests will raise serious problems for central control. The turn to ideological pragmatism and greater openness in communications will generate strong counterpressures for a conservative restoration.

NOTES/INDEX

NOTES

CHAPTER 1 IDEOLOGY IN A NEW KEY

1 *Pravda*, 18 April 1979.
2 Ibid., 6 May 1979.
3 On the methods of media campaigns, see Thomas Remington, "Policy Innovation and Soviet Media Campaigns," *Journal of Politics* 45, no. 1 (February 1983):220–27.
4 M. E. Dobruskin, *Nesostoiatel'nost' antikommunisticheskikh kontseptsii roli sovetskoi intelligentsii* (Kiev: Vishcha shkola, 1983), p. 136; S.A Fediukin, *Partiia i intelligentsiia* (Moscow: Izdatel'stvo politicheskoi litertury, 1983), p. 226.
5 Paul Roth cites an unnamed Soviet researcher for the assertion that it was confidential party surveys which lay behind Brezhnev's sharp condemnation of the state of ideological work in the mass media and propaganda at the November 1978 plenum. See Paul Roth, "Propaganda as an Instrument of Power," in Hans-Joachim Veen, *From Brezhnev to Gorbachev: Domestic Affairs and Soviet Foreign Policy* (New York: St. Martin's Press, 1987), p. 228.
6 Zh. T. Toshchenko, *Ideologiia i zhizn': Sotsiologicheskii ocherk* (Moscow: Sovetskaia Rossiia, 1983), p. 14. As the handbook *Party Construction* points out, the development of theory is but one of the party's duties in the ideological sector: the others are the inculcation of convictions, the conversion of convictions to action, and the protection of doctrine against alien ideas. *Partiinoe stroitel'stvo: Nauchnye osnovy partiinoi raboty. Kurs lektsii*, pt. 1 (Moscow: Mysl', 1985), p. 311.
7 Jerry F. Hough, *The Struggle for the Third World: Soviet Debates and American Options* (Washington, D.C.: Brookings Institution, 1986), pp. 7, 20. One problem with this formulation is its neglect of the intellectual compromises made to acquire and preserve the establishment status necessary to take part in such debate. In short, in the terms of Barach and Baratz, ideology may be most efficacious in *excluding* topics or ideas from the public agenda. See T. H. Rigby, "A

211

Conceptual Approach to Authority, Power and Policy in the Soviet Union," in T. H. Rigby, Archie Brown, and Peter Reddaway, eds., *Authority, Power, and Policy in the USSR* (New York: St. Martin's Press, 1975), p. 23.

Jerry Hough's position is similar to that of John A. Armstrong, who in his succinct textbook lays out the basic tenets of Marxist-Leninist doctrine—including materialism, dialectics, the theory of imperialism, party leadership, democratic centralism, socialism in one country, statism, the progressive construction of communism, and, most recently, the concept of developed socialism—but concludes that, despite the durability of most of these ideas, the outstanding characteristic of Soviet doctrine is its flexibility and indeterminacy. As a belief system, therefore, Armstrong argues, it fails to meet the legitimating purposes for which it is maintained. John A. Armstrong, *Ideology, Politics, and Government in the Soviet Union,* 4th ed. (New York: Praeger, 1978), ch. 2, "The Ideology."

8   For example, Adam Ulam regards Soviet communism as an amalgam of Marxism and Russian nationalism, which employes the internationalist frame of reference of Marxism to continue the expansionist and state-centered ideology of Russian czarism. In Seweryn Bialer's analysis of the problem of post-Stalin change, the legitimating norms of the system are said to have been fundamentally shifted under Stalin from party-centered communist doctrine to state-centered nationalism, with which today a set of other norms broadly consistent with Marxism-Leninism are joined in integrating the political elite: among these are imperialism, hostility to market capitalism, belief in a one-party state, fear of spontaneity, and the cult of unity. Adam Ulam, "Russian Nationalism," in Seweryn Bialer, ed., *The Domestic Context of Soviet Foreign Policy* (Boulder, Colo.: Westview Press, 1981), pp. 3–18; Seweryn Bialer, *Stalin's Successors: Leadership, Stability, and Change in the Soviet Union* (Cambridge: Cambridge University Press, 1980), p. 196.

9   Robert C. Tucker, "Swollen State, Spent Society: Stalin's Legacy to Brezhnev's Russia," *Foreign Affairs* 60, no. 2 (Winter 1981/82):431–32.

10 See Stephen White, "Political Socialization in the U.S.S.R.: A Study in Failure?" *Studies in Comparative Communism* 10, no. 3 (Autumn 1977):328–42, esp. p. 341; idem, "Continuity and Change in Soviet Political Culture: An Emigré Study," *Comparative Political Studies* 11, no. 3 (October 1978):381–95; idem, "The Effectiveness of Political Propaganda in the USSR," *Soviet Studies* 32, no. 3 (July 1980):323–48; and his major treatment of the subject, *Political Culture and Soviet Politics* (London: Macmillan, 1979).

11 Gayle Durham Hollander, *Soviet Political Indoctrination: Developments in Mass Media and Propaganda since Stalin* (New York: Praeger, 1972), p. 3.

12 Georg Lukács, *History and Class Consciousness,* trans. Rodney Livingstone (Cambridge, Mass.: MIT Press, 1971), p. 197.

13 N.B. Bikkenin, *Sotsialisticheskaia ideologiia,* 2d ed., rev. (Moscow: Politizdat, 1983), pp. 5–6, 13, 18, 35–41, 56, 76–77, 80–83.

14 A prize-winning textbook on social science for senior secondary students elides

the distinctions between these three social collectivities. "Having given a scientific picture of the world, uncovering the laws of social development, Marxist philosophy turned into the spiritual weapon of the proletariat. As a philosophy of the broad popular masses, Marxism acquired the actuality that philosophical systems of the past lacked. Dialectical and historical materialism became a theoretical foundation for the construction of socialism and communism. Communist and workers' parties rely on it in working out their policies in the complicated conditions of the contemporary epoch." G. Kh. Shakhnazarov et al., *Obshchestvovedenie: uchebnik dlia vypusknogo klassa srednei shkoly i srednikh spetsial'nykh uchebnykh zavedenii,* 22d ed. (Moscow: Izdatel'stvo politicheskoi literatury, 1985), p. 69. This textbook received the State Prize of the USSR in 1980.

15 Bikkenin, *Ideologiia,* pp. 402–3; Shakhnazarov et al., *Obshchestvovedenie,* pp. 280–83.

16 Shakhnazarov et al., *Obshchestvovedenie,* 283, 284.

17 In this connection, Leszek Kolakowski comments that, despite the triumph of power over ideology under Stalin, ideology can still threaten the rulers. "The logic of Stalinism is that truth is what the party, i.e., Stalin, says at any given moment, and the effect of this is to empty ideology of its substance altogether. On the other hand, ideology must be presented as a general theory with a consistency of its own, and as long as this is done there is no guarantee that it may not acquire a momentum of its own and be used—as actually happened in the post-Stalinist period—against its chief spokesmen and sole authorized interpreters." Leszek Kolakowski, *Main Currents of Marxism,* vol. 3, *The Breakdown,* trans. P. S. Falla (Oxford: Clarendon Press, 1978), p. 91.

18 Morton Schwartz, cataloguing influences on Soviet foreign policy, generally describes Soviet behavior as a reflection of great power and Russian nationalist impulses, but he leaves room for the effect of Marxist-Leninist convictions, first in reinforcing the conflictual, "kto-kogo" style of appraising world politics, and second in providing analytical tools—notably class struggle—for analyzing political trends. Morton Schwartz, *The Foreign Policy of the USSR: Domestic Factors* (Encino, Calif.: Dickenson, 1975), ch. 4, "Soviet Political Beliefs: Ideological Influences."

19 Carl A. Linden, *The Soviet Party-State: The Politics of Ideocratic Despotism* (New York: Praeger, 1983), p. 159.

20 Robert Daniels, *Russia: The Roots of Confrontation* (Cambridge, Mass.: Harvard University Press, 1985), pp. 281–84; quotation on p. 283.

21 Kolakowski, *Main Currents,* 3:85, 90.

22 See Kolakowski's comments in Michael Charlton, *The Eagle and the Small Birds* (London: BBC, 1984), pp. 132–33.

23 Aleksandr I. Solzhenitsyn, *Letter to the Soviet Leaders,* trans. Hilary Sternberg (New York: Harper & Row, 1974), esp. pp. 41–49, 53.

24 Alexander Zinoviev, *The Reality of Communism* (London: Victor Gollancz, 1984), pp. 216–22.

25 Ibid., p. 225.

26   Ibid., p. 229. Note the similarity of this point of view to Marcuse's notion of "repressive tolerance" in advanced capitalist society. The greater the freedom, the more the theory of class oppression is thereby confirmed. Moreover, Zinoviev's position here is at variance with the argument cited earlier that a cultural "thaw" is eroding ideological dogmatism.

27   Alain Besançon, *The Rise of the Gulag: Intellectual Origins of Leninism*, trans. Sarah Matthews (Oxford: Basic Blackwell, 1981).

28   Zbigniew Brzezinski and Samuel P. Huntington, *Political Power: USA/USSR* (New York: Viking, 1964), pp. 21, 37–42, 409–410.

29   Ibid., p. 41. See also the recent article by Thomas A. Baylis, "Agitprop as a Vocation: The East German Ideological Elite," *Polity* 18, no. 1 (Fall 1985):25–46, which finds a high degree of career specialization among ideological cadres, as in the USSR, but also higher career mobility than in the USSR: a relatively larger proportion of agitprop specialists in the German Democratic Republic can be found among regional first secretaries and as Politburo members.

30   Talcott Parsons, "Evolutionary Universals in Society," in idem, *On Institutions and Social Evolution*, ed. Leon H. Mayhew (Chicago: University of Chicago Press, 1982), pp. 323–24.

31   Samuel P. Huntington, "Social and Institutional Dynamics of One-Party Systems," in Samuel P. Huntington and Clement H. Moore, eds., *Authoritarian Politics in Modern Society: The Dynamics of Established One-Party Systems* (New York: Basic Books, 1970), pp. 26–27, 40–41, 44.

32   Richard Löwenthal, "On 'Established' Communist Party Regimes," *Studies in Comparative Communism* 7, no. 4 (Winter 1974):357.

33   William B. Simons and Stephen White, eds., *The Party Statutes of the Communist World* (The Hague: Martinus Nijhoff, 1984).

34   Erik P. Hoffmann and Robbin F. Laird, *The Politics of Economic Modernization in the Soviet Union* (Ithaca, N.Y.: Cornell University Press, 1982), pp. 4–5.

35   Donald R. Kelley, *The Politics of Developed Socialism: The Soviet Union as a Post-Industrial State* (Westport, Conn.: Greenwood Press, 1986), pp. 6–12.

36   Ibid., p. 11.

37   Ibid., p. 201; Hoffmann and Laird, *Economic Modernization*, p. 72.

38   Erik P. Hoffmann and Robbin F. Laird, *Technocratic Socialism: The Soviet Union in the Advanced Industrial Era* (Durham, N.C.: Duke University Press, 1985), pp. 7–10.

39   Hoffmann and Laird, *Economic Modernization*, p. 73.

40   Hoffmann and Laird, *Technocratic Socialism*, p. 197.

41   Kelley, *Developed Socialism*, p. 203.

42   *Pravda*, 15 June 1983.

43   Cf. Zhores A. Medvedev, *Gorbachev* (New York: Norton, 1986), p. 140. Discussion of the role of ideological secretary and related formal and informal offices in the party machinery will be deferred to chapter 2.

44   Konstantin Chernenko, "Na uroven' trebovanii razvitogo sotsializma," *Kommunist*, 1984, No. 18:3–21, trans. in *Current Digest of the Soviet Press* 37, no. 4 (20 February 1985): 1.

45   *Pravda,* 17 January 1985.

46   Ibid., 23 February 1985.

47   Ibid., 11 December 1984.

48   Mikhail Gorbachev, *Zhivoe tvorchestvo naroda* (Moscow: Izdatel'stvo politi- cheskoi literatury, 1984), pp. 12–13; M. I. Piskotin, *Sotsializm i gosudarstvennoe upravlenie* (Moscow: Nauka, 1984). Tatiana Zaslavskaia came to the attention of the general public in the West with her reform-minded 1983 "Novosibirsk memorandum," a copy of which was published in the West. A full version is "Doklad o neobkhodimosti bolee uglublennogo izucheniia v SSSR sotsial'nogo mekhanizma razvitiia ekonomiki," in Radio Free Europe/Radio Liberty (RFE/RL), *Materialy samizdata,* AS no. 5042, vyp. 35/83 (26 August 1983). She attributes the problems of declining growth and structural disproportions in the economy to the lag of productive relations (and the state's "mechanism of administering the economy") behind the development of productive forces (pp. 3–4). If the recent debate over whether socialism could generate antagonistic contradictions in the relations of production had resulted in an affirmative answer, liberal reformers would have had still stronger ideological authority for a case that remains ideolog- ically fragile if practically compelling. Instead, the Andropov-Gorbachev line was that the relations of production were not fundamentally in contradiction with the forces of production but only lagged behind them. A useful theoretical explication of this recondite issue is provided by Helmut Dahm, "Ideology as a Code of Politics—Socio-Economic and Intellectual-Cultural Crisis Awareness in the Soviet Union and Its Political Adulteration," *Berichte des Bundesinstituts für ostwissenschaftliche und internationale Studien: Summaries, 21-49/1985,* report no. 25 (Cologne): 1986), pp. 14–23.

49   Gorbachev, *Zhivoe,* pp. 14, 30–1, 35.

50   The Propaganda Department at the time of Gorbachev's speech was headed by Boris Stukalin. In July 1985, Stukalin was removed, made ambassador to Hungary, and replaced by Alexander Yakovlev. Although appointed propaganda secretary under Andropov in December 1982, Stukalin was said to have been a protégé of Mikhail Zimianin, a traditionalist in ideological matters. His instructions to *Pravda*'s editorial staff about how to summarize Gorbachev's revisionist text must clearly have reflected the position of the Brezhnev-Chernenko group. On the Stukalin-Yakovlev turnover, see Elizabeth Teague, "Soviet Propaganda Chief Appointed Ambassador to Hungary," *Radio Liberty Research Bulletin,* RL 237/85 (22 July 1985).

51   *Pravda,* 26 October 1985.

52   "Programma Kommunisticheskoi partii Sovetskogo soiuza, Novaia redaktsiia," in *Materialy XXVII s"ezda Kommunisticheskoi partii Sovetskogo soiuza* (Mos- cow: Izdatel'stvo politicheskoi literatury, 1986), pp. 122, 128.

53   "*S ponimaniem my otnosimsia*"—hardly a resounding endorsement.

54   *Pravda,* 26 February 1986.

55   Hoffmann and Laird, *Economic Modernization,* p. 66.

56   See Thomas F. Remington, "Varga and the Foundation of Soviet Planning," *Soviet Studies* 34, no. 4 (October 1982):585–600; cf. Silvana Malle, *The Economic Or-*

ganization of War Communism, 1918–1921 (Cambridge: Cambridge University Press, 1985), ch. 6, "Planning."

57 Alfred Evans, Jr., "The Decline of Developed Socialism? Some Trends in Recent Soviet Ideology," *Soviet Studies* 38, no. 1 (January 1986): 20.

58 A. Yakovlev, "Dostizhenie kachestvenno novogo sostoianiia sovetskogo obshchestva i obshchestvennye nauki," *Kommunist*, 1987, no. 8: 3–22. Quotation on p. 13. The article was based on a report he made to the section of social sciences of the Presidium of the Academy of Sciences.

59 "Obshchestvennye nauki na novom etape," *Pravda*, 28 November 1987.

60 "Rabotat', myslit', otvechat'," *Pravda*, 3 December 1987.

61 In a meeting with a French delegation immediately upon his return to Moscow from an extended summer vacation, Gorbachev was asked whether pluralism was the goal of his reforms. His response, that not pluralism, but socialist pluralism, was the goal, may have been more an off-handed comment for foreign benefit than an expression of the new philosophy of change. See *Pravda*, 30 September 1987.

62 A. Yakovlev, "Glavnoe v perestroike segodnia-prakticheskie dela i konkretnye rezul'taty," *Partiinaia zhizn'*, 1987, no. 10: 15. Anatolii Butenko, a philosopher whose views on the possibility of "antagonist contradictions" persisting under developed socialism were decisively rejected by the conservative forces under Brezhnev and Chernenko, has recently written about the conflict of social interests in the face of the current drive for social restructuring. See, for example, A. Butenko, "Beseda o perestroike," *Moskovskaia pravda*, 7 May 1987.

63 Bohdan Nahaylo, "Interview with Tat'yana Zaslavskaya," *Radio Liberty Research Bulletin*, RL 365/87 (15 September 1987), p. 8.

64 "Dostizhenie," *Kommunist*, p. 21.

65 A cartoon appearing in *Pravda* on the day the draft guidelines for economic development through the year 2000 were published—with their highly ambitious goals—carries a tellingly Khrushchevian defense of utopianism. A train flying a banner marked "Program of the CPSU" crosses a bridge labeled "27th Party Congress." As it rushes forward, an Uncle Sam figure, brandishing a bomb, founders in the water beneath, crying "Utopia!" The word *utopia* is written "utop . . . i . . . ia," making a pun and meaning, "And I have drowned." The caption reads, "The prophet of doom: since 1917 I have been saying that this is utopia." Gorbachev appears willing to accept the risk of tying propaganda to the promise of rapid progress in order to shake up the sterile ideological routines inherited from the Brezhnev period. *Pravda*, 9 November 1985.

66 As the immense publicity surrounding the world-wide publication of Gorbachev's book *Perestroika* has shown. This volume contains no textual information, although much of it is excerpted from earlier speeches. Neither source references nor even the name of the translator is provided in the English-language edition, let alone the means by which Soviet media sources assisted the American publishers in bringing out the book. Mikhail Gorbachev, *Perestroika: New Thinking for Our Country and the World* (New York: Harper & Row, 1987).

67 *Pravda*, 15 June 1983. Chernenko was no doubt unaware that the orchestra simile for propaganda was first used by Goebbels.

CHAPTER 2   AKTIV AND APPARAT

1   V. D. Voinova, "Iz opyta kompleksnogo izucheniia deiatel'nosti sobranii trudovykh kollektivov po formirovaniiu obshchestvennogo mneniia," in V. S. Korobeinikov, ed., *Sotsiologicheskie problemy obshchestvennogo mneniia i deiatel'nosti sredstv massovoi informatsii* (Moscow: Institut sotsiologicheskikh issledovanii, 1979), p. 92.

2   Interview by Mervyn Matthews with "A. Pravdin," a former employee in the Central Committee apparatus, "Inside the CPSU Central Committee," *Survey* 20, no. 4 (Autumn 1974):94–105.

3   Lilita Dzirkals, Thane Gustafson, and A. Ross Johnson, *The Media and Intra-Elite Communication in the USSR*, Rand report no. R-2869 (Santa Monica, Calif.: Rand Corporation, September 1982), p. 13.

4   Philip Taubman, "A New Pravda Mirrors Openness, up to a Point," *New York Times*, 13 February 1987; Ned Temko, "Soviet Insiders: How Power Flows in Moscow," in Erik P. Hoffmann and Robbin F. Laird, eds., *The Soviet Polity in the Modern Era* (New York: Aldine, 1984), p. 179.

5   A. N. Yakovlev, "Protiv antiistorizma," *Literaturnaia gazeta*, 15 November 1972. He had been punished for this, evidently, by diplomatic exile to the ambassadorship to Canada before being brought back to Moscow to the Institute of World Economics and International Relations (IMEMO) by Andropov. Thus, like many of Gorbachev's team, he was linked to Andropov. See Elizabeth Teague, "Soviet Propaganda Chief Appointed Ambassador to Hungary," *Radio Liberty Research Bulletin* RL 237/85, 22 July 1985.

6   On the careers of Tiazhel'nikov and Stukalin, see Alexander G. Rahr, comp., *A Biographic Directory of 100 Leading Soviet Officials*, trans. Stelianos Scarlis (Munich: Radio Liberty Research Bulletin, 1981), pp. 221–23; and ibid., 1984, pp. 207–09.

7   According to Roy Medvedev, in addition to overseeing certain Central Committee departments (Propaganda, Science and Educational Institutions, Culture, International, Cadres Abroad, and Liaison with Ruling Communist Parties) Suslov oversaw the government agencies that adminster publishing, broadcasting, censorship, newsgathering, cinematography, and the fine arts. He supervised the unions of writers, journalists, architects, artists, cinematographers, and other branches of the cultural intelligentsia. The ideological content of education, particularly the social sciences, and the supervision of religion and lectures, came under his jurisdiction. In addition, he oversaw the observance of public holidays, anniversaries, and even birthdays of the leaders. See Roy Medvedev, *All Stalin's Men*, trans. Harold Shukman (Oxford: Basil Blackwell, 1983), pp. 62–63.

8   See Rahr, *Directory*, pp. 207–10.

9   Timothy Colton speculates, probably correctly, that Gorbachev made Yakovlev a counterweight in the ideological sector to Ligachev. Timothy J. Colton, *The Dilemma of Reform in the Soviet Union*, rev. ed. (New York; Council on Foreign Relations, 1986), p. 105. Some evidence is accumulating that Ligachev is the force behind the favor for Russian cultural nationalism and that Yakovlev, known for

his 1972 article against Russian nationalism, opposes him. For example, Yakovlev did not appear at the founding conference of the new Soviet Cultural Foundation.

10 *Pravda*, 29 June 1985.

11 E. Ligachev, "Gotovias' k partiinomu s"ezdu," *Kommunist*, 1985, no. 12: 8–22, esp. 20–21.

12 Meetings of heads of media, cultural, scientific, and other organizations in the ideology sphere with top party officials at the Central Committee have become a regular practice, not only after each plenary meeting of the Central committee, but often between them as well. The frequency of such meetings and the high level of participation attest to the important role assigned to the media in pushing for implementation of the leadership's policy goals.

13 Dzirkals, Gustafson, and Johnson, *The Media*, pp. 26–27.

14 *Pravda*, 6 September 1984.

15 Medvedev, *All Stalin's Men*, p. 79.

16 See *Partiinoe stroitel'stvo*, 4th ed. (Moscow: Politizdat: 1976), pp. 166–69.

17 A. Shyrybyrov, "Opiraias' na aktiv," *Partiinaia zhizn'*, 1982, no. 5: 53.

18 A. V. Cherniak, *Tovarishch Instruktor* (Moscow: Politizdat, 1984).

19 See "Protiv formalizma, bumazhnogo stilia," *Partiinaia zhizn'*, 1982, no. 2:70–71; "Povyshat' avangardnuiu rol' kommunistov, ikh aktivnost' v proizvodstven-noi i obshchestvennoi zhizni," ibid., pp. 14–21; M. Nenashev, *Ratsional'naia organizatsia ideologicheskoi raboty* (Moscow: Sovetskaia Rossiia, 1976), p. 60.

20 *Kompleksnyi podkhod v ideologicheskoi rabote: stil' i metody* (Moscow: Iz-datel'stvo politicheskoi literatury, 1976), pp. 100–101.

21 Ibid., pp. 20, 330–31.

22 Nenashev, *Ratsional'naia organizatsiia*, p. 156.

23 *Kompleksnyi podkhod*, p. 318.

24 Z. Bogdanova, "Na osnove kompleksnogo podkhoda," *Partiinaia zhizn'*, 1982, no. 1: 46.

25 *Kompleksnyi podkhod*, p. 296; Matthews, "Inside," p. 95.

26 Cherniak, *Tovarishch Instruktor*, pp. 6, 7, 39, 40; A. Kandrenkov, "Sover-shenstvuem rabotu apparata partiinykh komitetov," *Partiinaia zhizn'*, 1981, no. 3: 24.

27 Philip Stewart, *Political Power in the Soviet Union* (Indianapolis: Bobbs-Merrill, 1968), p. 191.

28 Cited in Alex Simirenko, *Professionalization of Soviet Society*, ed. C. A. Kern-Simirenko (New Brunswick, N.J.: Transaction Books, 1982), p. 45.

29 See discussion in Bohdan Harasymiw, *Political Elite Recruitment in the Soviet Union* (New York: St. Martin's Press, 1984), pp. 154–49; *Kompleksnyi podkhod*, p. 331; Cherniak, *Tovarishch Instruktor*, pp. 110–11.

30 Harasymiw, *Recruitment*, pp. 154–55.

31 Cherniak, *Tovarishch Instruktor*, p. 25.

32 *Pravda*, 22 February 1985; Harasymiw, *Recruitment*, p. 155.

33 Cherniak, *Tovarishch Instruktor*, p. 224, 44.

34 Cherniak, *Tovarishch Instruktor*, pp. 7–8, 6, 234.

35 See Jerry F. Hough, "The Party Apparatchiki," in H. Gordon Skilling and Franklyn Griffiths, eds., *Interest Groups in Soviet Politics* (Princeton: Princeton University Press, 1971), pp. 53–55, 74–75. Thomas Baylis has recently found a similar pattern among ideological specialists in the German Democratic Republic, and has discovered, moreover, that there were semispecialized career tracks *within* the ideology sector. Thomas A. Baylis, "Agitprop as a Vocation: The East German Ideological Elite," *Polity* 18, no. 1 (Fall 1985):25–46.

36 Joel C. Moses, "Functional Career Specialization in Soviet Regional Elite Recruitment," in T. H. Rigby and Bohdan Harasymiw, eds., *Leadership Selection and Patron-Client Relations in the USSR and Yugoslavia* (London: George Allen & Unwin, 1983), p. 19.

37 John Armstrong, *The Soviet Bureaucratic Elite* (New York: Praeger, 1959), pp. 95, 101.

38 A recent and authoritative expression of this policy is given by Egor Ligachev in his address to the party's personnel managers on 26 July 1985. See E. Ligachev, "Gotovias' k partiinomu s"ezdu," *Kommunist*, 1985, no. 12: 21.

39 The workers brought into the work regions spend long hours traveling and waiting between segments of their trips. Soviet authorities use this time for political work. For example, workers living in dormitories in Surgut (a city on the Ob River about 750 km north of Omsk) ride forty-five minutes to get to the helicopter pad, and those in outlying areas have rides of up to two hours. On the bus, accordingly, the Surgut authorities play them tape recordings and provide for information briefings, lectures, and question and answer sessions. M. P. Gabdulin et al., comps., *Agitator, politinformator, dokladchik,* 3 (Moscow: Politizdat, 1983), pp. 52–53.

40 V. P. Vasil'ev, "Ustnaia politicheskaia agitatsiia v sisteme ideologicheskoi raboty trudovogo kollektiva," in *Voprosy teorii i metodov ideologicheskoi raboty*, vyp. 9 (Moscow: Mysl', 1978), p. 69.

41 Gabdulin et al., *Agitator*, pp. 23–4. This pattern is repeated in most other areas. See *Kompleksnyi podkhod*, p. 252; E. N. Marikhin, "Nekotorye voprosy sovershenstvovaniia partiinogo rukovodstva ustnoi politicheskoi agitatsiei," in *Voprosy teorii i metodov ideologicheskoi raboty*, vyp. 12 (Moscow: Mysl', 1980), p. 194.

42 Gabdulin et al., *Agitator*, p. 134.

43 See Gayle Durham Hollander, *Soviet Political Indoctrination* (New York: Praeger, 1972), pp. 157–60.

44 *Kompleksnyi podkhod*, p. 155.

45 Ibid.; B. A. Grushin and L. A. Onikov, *Massovaia informatsiia v sovetskom promyshlennom gorode* (Moscow: Izdatel'stvo politicheskoi literatury, 1980), p. 145; B. Podkopaev, "Klub politicheskoi informatsii," *Partiinaia zhizn'*, 1979, no. 12: 67–67.

46 *Kompleksnyi podkhod*, p. 155; Gabdulin, et al., *Agitator*, p. 30.

47 Grushin and Onikov, *Massovaia informatsiia*, p. 136.

48 V. Rodionov, "Edinyi politden'," *Partiinaia zhizn'*, 1979, no. 12: 62.

49 Rodionov, "Edinyi politden'," p. 63; A. Rybakov, "Povyshat' soznatel'nost' i

aktivnost' mass," ibid., 1980, no. 12: 35; *Pravda*, 23 July 1979, p. 2; Gabdulin, et al., *Agitator*, pp. 82–84.

50   K. Vaino, "Delovoi nastroi," *Zhurnalist*, 1982, no. 2: 10–12; "Reshaetsia na meste," ibid., p. 16.

51   V. Kolesnikov and B. Batkibekov, "Den' otkrytogo pis'ma—vazhnaia forma partiino-politicheskoi raboty," *Partiinaia zhizn'*, 1980, No. 15: 21–22.

52   B. M. Morozov, V. E. Fadeev, and V. V. Shinkarenko, "Voprosy kompleksnogo planirovaniia ideologicheskoi, politiko-vospitatel'noi raboty v sovremennykh us-loviiakh," *Voprosy istorii KPSS*, 1982, no. 6: 57.

53   *Kompleksnyi podkhod*, p. 188.

54   Rodionov, "Edinyi politden'," pp. 63–64.

55   *Pravda*, 17 January 1985: Louise Shelley, *Lawyers in Soviet Work Life* (New Brunswick, N.J.: Rutgers University Press, 1984), p. 97.

56   Rybakov, "Povyshat'," p. 35; L. Kravchuk, "Lektory nesut v massy slovo partii," *Partiinaia zhizn'*, 1980 no. 16: 34.

57   V. F. Sbytov, *Upravlenie sotsial'nymi i ideologicheskimi protsessami v period razvitogo sotsializma: nekotorye voprosy teorii i opyt sotsiologicheskogo issle-dovaniia* (Moscow: Nauka, 1983), p. 181. *Kommunist* reported 26 million in 1982. I. Kapitonov, "Osnova partii, politicheskoe iadro trudovogo kollektiva," *Kommunist*, 1982, no. 7: 10. But Kapitonov may have inaccurately stated that this many lectures were offered in labor collectives; the Taganrog survey found that lectures in enterprises account for only one-third of all lectures given. Grushin and Onikov, *Massovaia informatsiia*, p. 138.

58   Grushin and Onikov, *Massovaia informatsiia*, pp. 202–4.

59   *Kompleksnyi podkhod*, p. 96.

60   Sbytov, *Upravlenie*, p. 181; M. F. Nenashev, *Effektivnost' ideino-vospitatel'noi raboty* (Moscow: Izdatel'stvo politicheskoi literatury, 1974), p. 65; Grushin and Onikov, *Massovaia informatsiia*, p. 138.

61   *Kompleksnyi podkhod*, p.96.

62   Alex Inkeles reported that there were around 2 million more or less regular agitators active as of 1950. Alex Inkeles, *Public Opinion in Soviet Russia: A Study in Mass Persuasion*, 3d ed. (Cambridge, Mass.: Harvard University Press, 1958), pp. 62–63. Together with the very small number of Znanie Society members at that time (36,700) and party propagandists (fewer than 1 million), there were perhaps 2.5–3.5 million ideological activists in 1953.In the 1950s and 1960s this ideological *aktiv*, according to reported figures, grew at an average annual rate of 3.5–4.5 percent By around 1970 there were said to be 2.5 million political informa-tion speakers in addition to another 2 million or so agitators. Hollander, *Indoctri-nation*, pp. 148–159. Znanie enrolled another 2 million lecturers; 1 million party propagandists taught in political schools. There were therefore 7–8 million ac-tivists in ideological work at the close of the 1960s. A 1980 report indicated that there were 4 million agitators and 2.1 million political information speakers in the USSR. Marikhin, "Nekotorye voprosy," p. 193. The party handbook, *Partiinoe stroitel'stvo 1985*, claims 4.1 million agitators for 1981, along with 2.1 million

political information speakers, 300,000 reporters, and 2.4 million propagandists. A fairly careful 1983 book presents a rather smaller count, 3.7 million agitators and political information speakers. Sbytov, *Upravlenie*, p. 152. Another 1983 book claims that over 6 million persons fulfill party assignments as agitators, political information speakers, and reporters. Gabdulin, et al., *Agitator*, p. 11. Membership in the Znanie Society appears to have stabilized at about 3.2 million (V. M. Ivanov, *Sovetskaia demokratiia: ocherk stanovleniia i razvitiia* (Moscow: Politizdat, 1983), p. 210), and the number of propagandists is more or less fixed at 2–2.5 million (the official figure for the 1980–81 school year was 2.4 million; for 1983 it was 2.3 million; and for the 1984–85 year it was reported by M. V. Zimianin to be 2.5 million). See "KPSS v tsifrakh," *Partiinaia zhizn'*, 1981, no. 14: 26; Sbytov, *Upravlenie*, p. 152; and M. V. Zimianin, "Voprosy organizatsii ideologicheskoi, agitatsionno-massovoi raboty," ibid., 1985, no. 2: 14. The 1985 figures cited by Nenashev therefore show another small decline in the totals. M. F. Nenashev, "Nasushchnye voprosy sovershenstvovaniia organizatsii i stilia ideologicheskoi raboty," in Zh. T.Toshchenko, et al., comps., *Voprosy teorii i praktiki ideologicheskoi raboty*, vyp. 17 (Moscow: Mysl', 1985), p. 6.

63   A. K. Orlov, *Sovetskii rabochii i upravlenie proizvodstvom* (Moscow: Profizdat, 1978), p. 140.

64   Zh. T. Toshchenko, et al., comps., *Nravstvennoe vospitanie v trudovom kollektive: opyt sotsiologicheskogo issledovaniia* (Moscow: Profizdat, 1981), p. 90.

65   V. N. Zaitsev, "Ideologicheskim kadram—postoiannuiu zabotu i vnimanie," in V. I. Korzhov, eds., *Voprosy ideologicheskoi raboty: o kompleksnom podkhode k problemam kommunisticheskogo vospitaniia trudiashchikhsia Leningrada i oblasti* (Leningrad: Lenizdat, 1982), pp. 25–26.

66   *Pravda*, 16 September 1985.

67   On this point see Orlov, *Sovetskii rabochii*, pp. 140–44; Thomas Remington, "Sources of Support of the Soviet Regime," paper presented to the American Political Science Association meeting, Chicago, September 1983, pp. 10–11.

68   G. A. Ziuganov, "Gorodskoi obraz zhizni i ego planomernoe sovershenstvovanie," in *Voprosy teorii i metodov ideologicheskoi raboty*, vyp. 13 (Moscow: Mysl', 1981), p. 106.

69   Sbytov, *Upravlenie*, pp. 198–99.

70   V. A. Chulanov, *Sovremennoe sovetskie rabochie: peredovye cherty i sotsial'naia aktivnost'* (Moscow: Mysl', 1980), pp. 148–49, 180–81.

71   T. P. Arkhipova and V. F. Sbytov, *Voprosy teorii i praktiki politicheskogo rukovodstva: opyt deiatel'nosti raikoma partii* (Moscow: Izdatel'stvo politicheskoi literatury, 1981), p. 230; *Pravda*, 14 October 1979; *Kompleksnyi podkhod*, p. 86.

72   Sbytov, *Upravlenie*, p. 72.

73   Zimianin, "Voprosy," p. 14; Masherov, *Ideino-politicheskoi rabote—vysokuiu deistvennost'* (Moscow: Izdatel'stvo politicheskoi literatury, 1975), pp. 67–68; *Kompleksnyi podkhod*, p. 188.

74   Cf. M. E. Dobruskin, *Nesostoiatel'nost' antikommunisticheskikh kontseptsii*

roli sovetskoi intelligentsii (Kiev: Vishcha shkola, 1983), who states (p. 136) that over 2 million scholars, teachers, economic managers, and other specialists work as propagandists in the political education system, and that substantially more perform other kinds of ideological work, in which they are joined by several hundred thousand workers and peasants.

75 *Partiinoe stroitel'stvo 1985*, p. 337; also see Nenashev, *Effektivnost'*, p. 46; and Marikhin, "Nekotorye," p. 194.

76 *Kompleksnyi/Rostov*, p. 252; Marikhin, "Nekotorye," p. 194.

77 Harasymiw, *Recruitment*; John H. Miller, "The Communist Party: Trends and Problems," in Archie Brown and Michael Kaser, eds., *Soviet Policy for the 1980's* (Bloomington: Indiana University Press, 1982), pp. 1–20; T. H. Rigby, *Communist Party Membership in the U.S.S.R., 1917–1967* Princeton: Princeton University Press, 1968).

78 Harasymiw, *Recruitment*, pp. 187–92.

79 E. V. Foteeva, *Kachestvennye kharakteristiki naseleniia SSSR* (Moscow: Finansy i statistika, 1984), p. 77; on the growth of employment by branch, see *Narodnoe khoziaistvo SSSR 1922–1982* (Moscow: Finansy i statistika, 1982), p. 399.

80 G. Bartoshevich, "Ideologicheskaia komissiia partkoma pervichnoi partor-ganizatsii," *Partiinaia zhizn'*, 1979, no. 18: 55–56.

81 V. Iakubov, "Kompleksnyi podkhod v ideino-vospitatel'noi rabote," ibid., 1980, no. 9: 57–61.

82 A. Shyrybyrov, "Opiraias' na aktiv," ibid., 1982, no. 5: 53.

83 Sbytov, *Upravlenie*, pp. 154–55.

84 Matthews, "Inside," pp. 97–98.

85 K. Chekh, "Uluchshaem vnutripartiinuiu informatsiiu," *Partiinaia zhizn'*, 1979, no. 12: 42–44; V. Grishin, "Organizatsionno-partiinuiu rabotu—na uroven' tre-bovanii XXVI s"ezda KPSS," *Kommunist*, 1981, no. 8: 19; V. P. Polianichko, "Partiinyi komitet—organizator kompleksnogo podkhoda k vospitaniiu," in *Voprosy teorii i metodov ideologicheskoi raboty*, vyp. 11 (1979): 80.

86 Stephen White, *Political Culture and Soviet Politics* (London: Macmillan Press, 1979), p. 78; A. Kapto, "Povyshat' deistvennost' ideologicheskoi raboty, *Kommunist*, 1981, no. 18: 52; M. V. Gramov and N. C. Chernykh, eds., *Ideino-vospitatel'naia rabota v proizvodstvennom kollektive: opyt, problemy* (Moscow: Sovetskaia Rossiia, 1976), p. 72.

87 Sbytov, *Upravlenie*, p. 217; Darrell Slider, "Party-Sponsored Public Opinion Research in the Soviet Union," *Journal of Politics* 47, no. 1 (February 1985); 215.

88 *Kompleksnyi podkhod*, p. 27.

89 "Otvety na voprosy," *Partiinaia zhizn'*, 1979 no. 10: 69–70.

90 Marikhin, "Nekotorye," pp. 188–95; *Knizhka partiinogo aktivista 1981* (Moscow: Izdatel'stvo politicheskoi literatury, 1980), p. 170; Morozov, Fadeev, and Shinkarenko, "Voprosy," pp. 37, 40, 114–16.

91 Christopher Binns, tracing the historical development of what he terms "ceremonial" in Soviet life, notes that with the routinization of ritual came an increased role for status and hierarchy, embodied in the greater use of "structure." For

example, the raised platform separated the audience from the "unanimously elected presidium" and the official representatives of the masses. Christopher A. P. Binns, "The Changing Face of Power: Revolution and Accommodation in the Development of the Soviet Ceremonial System: Parts I and II," *Man* 14, no. 4 (December 1979): 585–606 and ibid. 15, no. 1 (March 1980): 170–87. Cited material in ibid. 14: 598.

92   V. D. Voinova, "Iz opyta kompleksnogo izucheniia deiatel'nosti sobranii trudo-vykh kollektivov po formirovaniiu obshchestvennogo mneniia," in V. S. Koro-beinikov, ed., *Sotsiologicheskie problemy obshchestvennogo mneniia i deia-tel'nosti stredstv massovoi informatsii* (Moscow: Institut sotsiologicheskikh issledovanii, 1979), pp. 93–94. The meeting format described here was abstracted from a survey undertaken by Soviet scholars; they found that in one-half of the cases studied, the time for debate lasted no more than five minutes.

93   The article cited in n. 92 discusses the unwillingness to take meaningful part in workers' meetings that the author found to be common. An American working at the Novosti Press Agency managed to attend an open party meeting of his office. Despite his presence, many in the audience felt uninhibited about displaying attitudes of boredom and indifference to the proceedings. His presence, nonethe-less, was an embarrassment to the management, which asked him to refrain from attending future meetings. Marc Greenfield, "Life among the Russians," *New York Times Magazine*, 24 October 1982, p. 99.

94   Colton has called attention to the prevalence of anniversary celebrations in the Brezhnev period, in keeping with the conservative and backward-looking charac-ter of the leadership. Colton, *Dilemma of Reform*, p. 16.

95   A. Kurshakova, "Gotovim partiinoe sobranie 'zhit', rabotat', i borot'sia po-leninski, po-kommunisticheski'," *Partiinaia zhizn'*, 1980, no. 4: 35–38.

96   *Izvestiia*, 23 March 1985; *Pravda*, 7 July 1985.

97   *Pravda*, 22 September 1985.

98   *Knizhka partiinogo aktivista, 1980* p. 152; see related accounts in *Pravda*, 22 November 1979; V. Arkhipenko, "Slovo i delo truzhenikov 'Integrala,'" *Kom-munist*, 1979, no. 10: 28; Gramov and Chernykh, *Ideino-vospitatel'naia rabota*, pp. 116–22; Polianichko, "Partiinyi komitet," p. 72.

99   A. Ivanov, "Massovo-politicheskaia rabota v period izbiratel'noi kampanii," *Partiinaia zhizn'*, 1980, no. 1: 61.

100 R. Dement'eva, "Povyshaia otvetstvennost' otraslevykh otdelov partiinykh komitetov za sostoianie vospitatel'noi raboty," ibid., no. 11: 30.

101 *Pravda*, 17 and 18 October 1979.

CHAPTER 3   POLITICAL EDUCATION

1   N. B. Bikkenin, *Sotsialisticheskaia ideologiia*, 2d ed., rev. (Moscow: Politizdat, 1983), Quotation on p. 18.

2   M. V. Zimianin, "Voprosy organizatsii ideologicheskoi, agitatsionno-massovoi raboty," *Partiinaia zhizn'*, 1985, no. 2: 14.

3   On the 1956 decree, and on the politics of "ideological education" in the Khrushchev period, see the highly informative study by Jonathan Harris, "After the *Kratskii kurs:* Soviet Leadership Conflict over Theoretical Education, 1956–1961," *Carl Beck Papers in Russian and East European Studies,* Russian and East European Studies Program, University of Pittsburgh, no. 401 (Pittsburgh: 1984), esp. pp. 9–10.

4   R. V. Degtiareva, *Deiatel'nost' KPSS po formirovaniiu politicheskoi kul'tury nauchno-tekhnicheskoi intelligentsii v usloviiakh razvitogo sotsializma* (Leningrad: Izdatel'stvo leningradskogo universiteta, 1985), p. 61.

5   "Itogi konkursov na sozdanie uchebnikov dlia sistemy partiinoi ucheby," *Partiinaia zhizn',* 1984, no. 15: 65–66. This is not to say, of course, that students of the subject of scientific communism are deprived of an authoritative textbook. A prominent team of ideological authorities under the direction of an academician, P. N. Fedoseev, and including Viktor Afanas'ev, editor of *Pravda,* N. B. Bikkenin (whom I quoted above), Karen Brutents, Fedor Burlatskii, Aleksandr Iakovlev, G. L. Smirnov, Vadim Zagladin, and eight other distinguished figures, has collectively written the principal textbook for use in institutions of higher learning and in party education courses. See P. N. Fedoseev et al., *Nauchnyi kommunizm: uchebnik dlia vuzov,* 7th ed. (Moscow: Politizdat, 1985).

6   Harris, "After the *Kratkii kurs,*" p. 4.

7   "Marksistsko-Leninskoe obrazovanie trudiashchikhsia—na uroven' sovremennykh zadach," unsighed *podval, Pravda,* 7 August 1985.

8   *Pravda,* 29 June 1985.

9   E. Ligachev, "Gotovias' k partiinomu s"ezdu," *Kommunist,* 1985 no. 12: 20–21.

10   *Pravda,* 10 June 1985.

11   Ibid., 16 September 1985. Again, notice the emphasis on the subjective factor of mood as a major object of propaganda.

12   Degtiareva, *Deiatel'nost',* p. 50.

13   Zimianin, "Voprosy," p. 13.

14   Ibid., p. 16.

15   Degtiareva, *Deiatel'nost',* p. 47.

16   Quoted in Frederick C. Barghoorn, *Politics in the USSR,* 2d ed. (Boston: Little, Brown, 1972), p. 121.

17   Ibid., p. 122; Leonard Schapiro, *The Communist Party of the Soviet Union* (New York: Vintage Books, 1960), p. 471; on the demise of the cult of Lenin by 1933, see Nina Tumarkin, *Lenin Lives! The Lenin Cult in Soviet Russia* (Cambridge, Mass.: Harvard University Press, 1983), esp. p. 250.

18   Schapiro, *Communist Party,* pp. 471–72.

19   Harris, "After the *Kratkii Kurs,*" p. 15. The pragmatic orientation of ideological work reached its height just after the Twenty-first Party Congress, when official pronouncements about political education were at their most antitheoretical.

20   Ibid., pp. 17–18.

21   Figures drawn from Ellen Propper Mickiewicz, *Soviet Political Schools: The Communist Party Adult Instruction System* (New Haven, Conn.: Yale University

Press, 1967), pp. 10–13; Barghoorn, *Politics*, pp. 125–26; and "KPSS v tsifrakh," *Partiinaia zhizn'*, 1977, no. 21: 42; and "KPSS v tsifrakh," ibid., 1981, no. 14: 26.

22   "KPSS v tsifrakh," *Partiinaia zhizn'*, 1977, no. 21: 42.

23   "KPSS v tsifrakh," ibid., 1981, no 14: 26; "KPSS v tsifrakh," ibid., 1986, no. 14: 32.

24   Zimianin, "Voprosy," p. 12; *Pravda*, 7 August 1985.

25   V. N. Zaitsev, "Ideologicheskim kadram—postoiannuiu zabotu i vnimanie," in V. I. Korzhov, ed., *Voprosy ideologicheskoi raboty: o kompleksnom podkhode k problemam kommunisticheskogo vospitaniia trudiashchikhsia Leningrada i oblasti* (Leningrad: Lenizdat, 1982), pp. 25–26.

26   "Programme of the Communist Party of the Soviet Union," in *The Road to Communism: Documents of the 22nd Congress of the Communist Party of the Soviet Union* (Moscow: Foreign Languages Publishing House, 1961?), pp. 537–45.

27   These are well discussed by Jerome M. Gilison, *The Soviet Image of Utopia* (Baltimore: Johns Hopkins University Press, 1975).

28   Donald R. Kelley, "Developments in Ideology," in idem, ed., *Soviet Politics in the Brezhnev Era* (New York: Praeger, 1980), pp. 182–99.

29   Quoted in ibid., pp. 186–87. Italics in original.

30   *Pravda*, 26 February 1986.

31   Peter Kenez, *The Birth of the Propaganda State: Soviet Methods of Mass Mobilization, 1917–1929* (Cambridge: Cambridge University Press, 1985), pp. 129–32.

32   Yuri Glazov, *The Russian Mind since Stalin's Death* (Dordrecht: D. Reidel, 1985), p. 11.

33   Vladimir E. Shlapentokh, "Two Levels of Public Opinion: The Soviet Case," *Public Opinion Quarterly* 49, no. 4 (Winter 1985): 443–59.

34   Michael Voslensky, *Nomenklatura: The Soviet Ruling Class*, trans. Eric Mosbacher (Garden City, N.Y.: Doubleday, 1984), p. 296.

35   Alexander Zinoviev, *The Reality of Communism* (London: Victor Gollancz, 1984), p. 218.

36   Kenez, *Propaganda State*, p. 133; Schapiro, *Communist Party*, p. 472.

37   Stephen White, *Political Culture and Soviet Politics* (London: Macmillan, 1979), p. 111; and idem, "The Effectiveness of Political Propaganda in the USSR," *Soviet Studies* 32, no. 3 (1980): 323–48, reprinted in Erik P. Hoffmann and Robbin F. Laird, eds., *The Soviet Polity in the Modern Era* (New York: Aldine, 1984), p. 683.

38   Degtiareva, *Deiatel'nost'*, p. 62; for 1965–66 the figure was 5 million, and for 1976–77, 2.4 million. *Knizhka partiinogo aktivista 1980* (Moscow: Politizdat, 1979), p. 56.

39   Stephen White, *Political Culture and Soviet Politics*, p. 76; "KPSS v tsifrakh," 1981, p. 26; "KPSS v tsifrakh," 1986, p. 32.

40   Gayle Durham Hollander, *Soviet Political Indoctrination* (New York: Praeger, 1972), pp. 152–53; *Zhurnalist*, 1979, no. 7: 12.

41   Hollander, *Indoctrination*, pp. 151–52; M. N. Zinov'ev, ed., *Vospitatel'naia rabota partiinykh organizatsii promyshlennykh kollektivov* (Leningrad: Izdatel'stvo leningradskogo universiteta, 1983), p. 51.

226 NOTES TO PAGES 88–92

42 R. P. Skudra, "Narodnye universitety v sisteme ideino-vospitatel'noi raboty," in *Voprosy teorii i metodov ideologicheskoi raboty*, vyp. 11 (Moscow: Mysl', 1979), pp. 121–130.

43 "O dal'neishem uluchshenii ekonomicheskogo obrazovaniia i vospitaniia trudiashchikhsia," *Kommunist*, 1982, no. 10: 3–5. This is the text of a joint resolution of the party Central Committee, the Council of Ministers, the All-Union Central Council of Trade Unions (VTsSPS), and Komsomol on the structure and thematic orientation of economic education in the light of the spring 1982 Central Committee plenum. It reaffirmed the existing structure of the system and called for greater focus on such policy problems as "intensifying" production and conservation of materials.

44 *Pravda*, 11 August 1981.

45 I. Kapitonov, "Osnova partii, politicheskoe iadro trudovogo kollektiva," *Kommunist*, 1982, no. 7: 11.

46 This figure tallies with other regional reports as well as the national proportion of ideological activists to employed population, which suggests a benchmark of about one activist to twelve or thirteen employed persons. Total population of the province is 5.25 million.

47 G. Erkhov, "Shkoly ideologicheskogo aktiva," *Partiinaia zhizn'*, 1982, no. 8: 52–56.

48 *Pravda*, 11 August 1981.

49 V. Zakharov, "Metodologicheskie seminary v sisteme partiinoi ucheby," *Kommunist*, 1985, no. 5: 53–62.

50 F. F. Svetik, "Napravleniia raboty partiinykh organizatsii raiona po sovershenstvovaniiu kommunisticheskogo vospitaniia nauchno-tekhnicheskoi intelligentsii" in R. G. Ianovskii et al., eds., *Ideino-politicheskoe vospitanie nauchno-tekhnicheskoi intelligentsii: opyt i problemy* (Moscow: n.p., 1982), pp. 57–69; T. P. Arkhipova and V. F. Sbytov, *Voprosy teorii i praktiki politicheskogo rukovodstva: opyt deiatel'nosti raikoma partii* (Moscow: Izdatel'stvo politicheskoi literatury, 1981), pp. 240, 231–32.

51 Iu. A. Osip'ian and V. F. Sbytov, "Sotsial'noe razvitie nauchnykh kollektivov i effektivnost' ideologicheskoi i ideino-vospitatel'noi raboty sredi nauchno-tekhnicheskoi intelligentsii," in Ianovskii et al., *Vospitanie*, pp. 40–56.

52 Degtiareva, *Deiatel'nost'*, p. 53; V. I. Markin, "Edinstvo nravstvennogo, ideino-politicheskogo i trudovogo vospitaniia v protsesse vyrabotki aktivnoi zhiznennoi pozitsii lichnosti," in V. G. Baikova, ed., *Voprosy teorii i metodov ideologicheskoi raboty*, vyp. 11 (Moscow: Mysl', 1979), p. 59.

53 *Pravda*, 26 September 1981.

54 A. I. Iakovlev, *Effektivnost' ideologicheskoi raboty* (Moscow: Izdatel'stvo politicheskoi literatury, 1984), p. 289; *Partiinoe stroitel'stvo: nauchnye osnovy partiinoi raboty, Kurs lektsii*, pt. 1 (Moscow: Mysl', 1985), pp. 265–66.

55 For Razumovskii's statement on the new goals of party education, see his article "Sovershenstvovat' podgotovku i perepodgotovku rukovodiashchikh kadrov partii," *Kommunist*, 1987, no. 9: 3–13.

56 The 1987 Central Committee resolution restructuring political education is presented in "O perestroike sistemy politicheskoi i ekonomicheskoi ucheby trudiashchikhsia," *Pravda,* 26 September 1987.
57 The claim that the new resolution is aiming at a "radical restructuring" of political education is noted in a *Pravda* editorial, "Znaniia—delu perestroiki," about the start of the new political education year, 6 October 1987.
58 A. Kapto, "Povyshat' deistvennost' ideologicheskoi raboty," *Kommunist,* 1981, no. 18: 53. Kapto, until 1986 ideology secretary of the Ukrainian party, and subsequently named ambassador to Cuba, was a frequent writer on ideological subjects, emphasizing the importance of a principled "class" approach to propaganda.
59 V. Makeev, "Kommunisticheskaia ideinost'," *Partiinaia zhizn',* 1979, no. 14: 26.
60 T. F. Iakovleva, "Obespechenie vzaimosviazi khoziaistvennykh, organizatsionnykh i vospitatel'nykh zadach v perspektivnykh planakh ideologicheskoi raboty," in Zh. T. Toshchenko, ed., *Voprosy teorii i metodov ideologicheskoi raboty,* vyp. 13: *Ideologiia i ekonomika* (Moscow: Mysl', 1981), p. 60; V. A. Chulanov, *Sovremennye sovetskie rabochie: peredovye cherty i sotsial'naia aktivnost'* (Moscow: Mysl', 1980), p. 128; Markin, "Edinstvo," p. 59.
61 Kapto, "Povyshat'," p. 53; Makeev, "Kommunisticheskaia ideinost'," p. 26.
62 "KPSS v tsifrakh," *Partiinaia zhizn',* 1977, no. 21: 42.
63 Razumovskii indicates that this goal was largely met over the preceding twenty years. "Sovershenstvovat'," pp. 7–8.
64 *Kompleksnyi podkhod v ideologicheskoi rabote: stil' i metody* (Moscow: Izdatel'stvo politicheskoi literatury, 1976), p. 109.
65 Ibid., pp. 218–19.
66 Ibid., p. 196.
67 Ibid., p. 356. There are minor discrepancies in the figures reported in this case, but not of sufficient magnitude to cast doubt on the general proposition about the coincidence of nomenklatura status with higher party education.
68 *Pravda,* 23 August 1981.
69 Iakovlev, *Effektivnost'',* p. 246.
70 Degtiareva, *Deiatel'nost',* p. 83.
71 *Pravda,* 16 February 1983.
72 For example, Ellen Mickiewicz writes that "the search for Party efficacy goes on within the Party itself, as well, and as the level of education within that elite rises, so, too, emerge more refined and critical attitudes—attitudes that may support a redefinition of role, more pragmatic, more concretely defined, and more widely based on empirical research." See Ellen Mickiewicz, "Introduction," in idem, ed., *Handbook of Soviet Social Science Data* (New York: Free Press, 1973), p. 34.
73 Zimianin, "Voprosy," p. 16. Describing the procedures for obtaining a doctorate through the Academy of Social Sciences, for example, Michael Voslensky, who was a member of its learned council for some years, writes that "everyone knows that theses written at the Academy of Social Sciences are invariably accepted, and that their standard is invariably low." *Nomenklatura,* p. 220.
74 Stephen White, *Political Culture,* pp. 123–36; idem, "Effectiveness," pp. 342–43.

CHAPTER 4   PLANNING THE NEWS

1 V. V. Egorov, *Televidenie i zritel'* (Moscow: Mysl', 1977), p. 66, 47.

2 Ibid., pp. 45–46.

3 *Pravda*, 21 November 1985.

4 *New York Times*, 21 November 1985. Lapin's successor, Aleksandr N. Aksenov, probably understands the priority of party political interests. Aksenov worked for the Komsomol for fifteen years, from 1944 to 1959. From the Komsomol, like many of Aleksandr Shelepin's clientele at that time, he entered police work, spending six years (1959–65) in leading positions in the KGB and internal affairs ministry. Then for thirteen years he was a professional party official, rising from first secretary of the Vitebsk obkom in Belorussia to second secretary of the Belorussian Central Committee. Thereafter for five years he chaired the Belorussian Council of Ministers before becoming ambassador to Poland in 1983. Already a member of the Central Committee of the CPSU as Belorussia's head of government, he was reelected in 1986 in his new capacity as chairman of Gosteleradio, as his predecessor Lapin had been. His background shows broad experience in politics and security and none at all in the media. He is probably closely linked to Ligachev. See *Zhurnalist*, 1986, no. 2:61.

5 M. V. Shkondin, *Pechat'*: *Osnovy organizatsii i upravelniia* (Moscow: Izdatel'stvo moskovskogo universiteta, 1982), p. 154.

6 Figures taken from *Ezhegodnik* (1984) of the *Bol'shaia sovetskaia entsiklopediia* (Moscow: Sovetskaia entsiklopediia, 1984), p. 92.

7 Data drawn from ibid., pp. 91–93; B. A. Miasoedov, *Strana chitaet, slushaet, smotrit: statisticheskii obzor* (Moscow: Finansy i statistika, 1982), pp. 42–43, 54, 66; *Zhurnalist*, 1981, no. 5:4; Shkondin, *Pechat'*, p. 154; *Pechat' SSSR v 1981 godu* (Moscow: Finansy i statistika, 1982).

8 Maiak, instituted in 1964, is a program similar to the all-news radio stations in the United States. It carries five-to-seven-minute news bulletins and commentary, regularly updated, on the hour and half-hour, and intersperses these segments with music. It was specifically designed to appeal to non-homebound listeners, such as those listening to portable radios. It is a production of Central Radio, but similar stations exist in the union republics.

9 Miasoedov, *Strana*, pp. 54–54; P. S. Gurevich and V. N. Ruzhnikov, *Sovetskoe radioveshchanie: stranitsy istorii* (Moscow: Iskusstvo, 1976).

10 *Pravda*, 31 May 1985.

11 V. V. Egorov, *Televidenie*, pp. 53–54; A. Iurovskii, *Televidenie: Poiski i resheniia* (Moscow: Iskusstvo, 1975), pp. 99–100.

12 D. Biriukov, "Ishchem optimal'nye resheniia," *Televidenie radioveshchanie*, 1984, no. 9:7–8; interview with Vadim Volkov, "Televidenie i zritel'," *Zhurnalist*, 1985, no. 8:61.

13 Volkov, "Televidenie," p. 60.

14 E. Efimov, "Dva televideniia—dve kul'tury," in idem, comp. *Televidenie vchera, segodnia, zavtra*, vyp. 1 (Moscow: Iskusstvo, 1981), pp. 54–55.

15   *Vecherniaia Alma-Ata,* 10 May 1986.
16   *Ezhegodnik* (1984), p. 92. To say that 85 million sets are in use is misleading in view of the unusually large number of complaints about the low quality of television sets and difficulty of getting them repaired. Scams in which a repairman is induced by shady means to report that a set is unrepairable, hence entitling the owner to replace it, are often denounced in the press.
17   Miasoedev, *Strana,* pp. 55, 64, 70; B. M. Firsov, *Massovaia kommunikatsiia v usloviiakh nauchno-tekhnicheskoi revoliutsii* (Leningrad: Nauka, 1981), pp. 58–78.
18   Ned Temko, "How Power Flows in Moscow," in Erik P. Hoffmann and Robbin F. Laird, eds., *The Soviet Polity in the Modern Era* (New York: Aldine, 1984), p. 179; Robert Gillette, "Beneath Myth and Illusion, Soviet Power Resides in Hands of Elite Few," in *Remaking the Revolution: The Soviet Union Seventy Years Later* (Los Angeles: Los Angeles Times, 1987), p. 66.
19   Data drawn from listing of newspapers in John L. Scherer, *USSR Facts and Figures Annual* (Gulf Breeze, Fl.: Academic International Press, 1978), 2:359–74. The newspapers listed represent approximately 83 percent of all newspapers at these levels. Changes in names of newspapers will affect these findings, since the dates listed pertain to the year the newspaper was first published under its current name.
20   V. I. Ganichev, *Molodezhnaia pechat': istoriia, teoriia, praktika* (Moscow: Mysl', 1976), p. 99.
21   "O rabote gazety «Trud,»" in *Spravochnik partiinogo rabotnika 1983* (Moscow: Izdatel'stvo politicheskoi literatury, 1983), pp. 463–68.
22   *Pechat' SSSR v 1981 g.,* p. 118. The breakdown of newspapers by branch is as follows (data as of 1981):

Komsomol	132 (+ 28 Pioneer)
Industry and construction	7
Transportation	50
Agriculture	9
Literature, culture, arts	17
Teaching	17
Physical culture, sports	15

23   Roman Szporluk, "The Press and Soviet Nationalities: The Party Resolution of 1975 and its Implementation," *Nationalities Papers* 14, no. 1–2 (1986):47–64.
24   As Zbigniew K. Brzezinski showed, the hub-and-spoke arrangement, under which Moscow emphasized bilateral ties with each Soviet satellite rather than strong multilateral institutions, was also characteristic of Soviet relations with the bloc under Stalin. Zbigniew K. Brzezinski, *The Soviet Bloc: Unity and Conflict,* rev. ed. (New York: Praeger, 1961). On the principle of segmentation in Soviet communications more generally, see Thomas Remington, "Federalism and Segmented Communication in the USSR," *Publius* 15, no. 4 (Fall 1985): 113–32.

25 Figures for 1983, from *Ezhegodnik* (1984), p. 92, are as follows:

all-union	31
republican	160
oblast, krai, and okrug	331
autonomous oblast and autonomous republic	98
city	713
district	3,019
institutional	3,330
kolhoz	591

26 Under *glasnost'*, the incomparably greater openness of public communication has stimulated demand for publications of the central press, with the result that only 60 percent of the volume of orders for 1987 subscriptions to central newspapers could be met. This point is evidence of the fact that the quality of the supply strongly influences the level of demand. G. Frolov, "O problemakh tsentralizovannogo snabzheniia," *Rasprostranenie pechati*, 1987, no. 8:6.

27 *Sovetskaia Rossiia*, 15 March 1987.

28 This judgment is based on a 1977 survey of local newspapers that found that 20 percent of the staff of oblast-level papers and 33 percent on that of *raion*-level papers were not union members. Over the past ten years, accordingly, union penetration of the field has grown, but the size of the journalistic establishment has not. L. G. Svitich and A. A. Shiriaeva, *Zhurnalist i ego rabota* (Moscow: Izdatel'stvo moskovskogo universiteta, 1979), pp. 167–68.

29 See table 3.

30 On the other hand, if one does include it, the figure would probably have to be doubled. No firm data on the size or even organization of the censorship agency are at hand; émigré reports suggest wide variation in the methods of operation of censorship. The estimate offered by the former journalist Leonid Finkel'stein in Martin Dewhirst and Robert Farrell, eds., *The Soviet Censorship* [Metuchen, N.J.: Scarecrow Press, 1973], p. 65), of 70,000 censors is perfectly reasonable for the 1960s. Other émigré reports suggest, however, that employees of local printing establishments work as part of the censorship apparatus, receiving the circulars and instructions that designate forbidden items and appropriate revisions. In other cases a "control editor" *(kontrol'nyi redaktor)* works as a censor on the staff of a media organ, either seconded by the censorship agency or as an in-house representative of it. The conventional form of censorship described by Finkel'stein and by Lev Lifshitz-Losev separates the functions of editing, printing, and censoring. See Lev Lifshitz-Losev, "What It Means to Be Censored," *New York Review of Books*, 29 June 1978, pp. 43–50; and Leonid Vladimirov [Finkel'stein], *The Russians* (New York: Praeger, 1968), pp. 94–106.

Valery Golovskoy, in a useful paper on the structure and operations of Soviet censorship, distinguishes between "ideological control"—a concept similar to that of "ideological process" discussed here—from censorship. Whereas the latter has become "decentralized and departmental," according to Golovskoy, ideological control remains powerful and pervasive. Valery Golovskoy, *Is There Censorship in the Soviet Union? Methodological Problems of Studying Soviet Censorship,*" Kennan Institute for Advanced Russian Studies, Wilson Center, occasional paper no. 201 (Washington, D.C.).

More information pertinent to Soviet censorship may be inferred from the rather abundantly documented Polish case. In addition to the important volume translated and edited by Jane Leftwich Curry, *The Black Book of Polish Censorship* (New York: Vintage Books, 1984), see the bizarre interview with a former Polish censor, conducted in the Solidarity period, "I, The Censor," *Index on Censorship* 10, no. 6 (December 1981), 46–49. The former censor makes a self-serving distinction between those censors, the majority, engaged in purely repressive work, and those who, like himself, held "creative" positions in which they produced the information bulletin that laid down the guiding rules for other censors. This individual also indicates that some people with journalism degrees take jobs in censorship because of the higher starting pay. Overall, though, neither his comments nor those pertaining to the Soviet case by Finkel'stein or Lifshitz-Losev—both former journalists—give much reason to consider employees of the censorship agency to be akin to journalists in either function or outlook.

31 An excellent study of the importance of selection criteria and operational procedures in U.S. news organizations is Herbert J. Gans, *Deciding What's News* (New York: Vintage, 1980).

32 An exhaustive study demonstrating the importance of managerial adjustments to Stalin-era production plans is Eugene Zaleski, *Stalinist Planning for Economic Growth, 1933–1952,* trans. and ed. Marie-Christine MacAndrew and John H. Moore, (Chapel Hill: University of North Carolina Press, 1980).

33 B. M. Morozov, V. E. Fadeev, and V. V. Shinkarenko, *Planirovanie ideologicheskoi raboty: nekotorye voprosy teorii i praktiki* (Moscow: Mysl', 1980), p. 185; I. V. Kurilov and V. V. Shinkarenko, "Nekotorye metodologicheskie problemy planirovaniia politicheskoi literatury," *Vestnik moskovskogo universiteta,* Journalism Series, 1975, no. 4: 15.

34 Igor' Magai, "Kandidatskii stazh," *Zhurnalist,* 1982, no. 2:52.

35 Hedrick Smith, *The Russians* (New York: Quadrangle, 1976), p. 355. Information about TASS is from Shkondin, *Pechat',* pp. 91–95; Morozov, Fadeev, and Shinkarenko, *Planirovanie,* p. 185; Georgii Khatsenkov, "Partnery," *Zhurnalist,* 1982, no. 1: 26–27; interview with S. Losev, chairman of TASS, "Glavnoe-Povyshenie kachestva i operativnost' informatsii," *Zhurnalist,* 1981, no. 4: 16.

36 Kurilov and Shinkarenko, "Nekotorye," pp. 15–24.

37 See Paul Roth, *Sow-Inform: Nachrichtenwesen und Informationspolitik in der Sowjetunion* (Düsseldorf: Droste Verlag, 1980), pp. 179–80.

38 An example is the aptly named Sphinx Press, with a New York address, which in 1980 published a book on Soviet weightlifter Vasili Alexeev and another on the Trans-Siberian Railroad, "with the assistance of Novosti Press Agency Publishing House, Moscow."

39   On APN, see Shkonkin, *Pechat'*, p. 95; V. Popov, "Prezhde vsego operativnost'," *Zhurnalist*, no. 10 (1982):20–21.
40   Dewhirst and Farrell, *Soviet Censorship*, p. 68.
41   M. V. Shkondin, "Redaktsiia i avtorskii aktiv," *Vestnik moskovskogo universiteta*, Journalism Series 1978, no. 5:8. The main focus of this article is the use of materials from nonstaff correspondents.
42   Svitich and Shiriaeva, *Zhurnalist*, p. 173; "Ob avtorakh i strochkakh," *Zhurnalist*, 1981, no. 10:57.
43   Magai, "Kandidatskii stazh," pp. 49–50.
44   S. V. Tsukasov, *Nauchnye osnovy organizatsii raboty redaktsii gazety* (Moscow: Mysl', 1977), p. 16.
45   In addition to the sources providing information on censorship listed in n. 30, see also Robert Conquest, *The Politics of Ideas in the U.S.S.R.* (New York: Praeger, 1967), esp. ch. 3, "The System of Restriction"; Paul Lendvai, *The Bureaucracy of Truth: How Communist Governments Manage the News* (Boulder, Colo.: Westview Press, 1981), esp. ch. 3, "Censorship, Secrecy and the Special Bulletins"; and George Schöpflin, ed., *Censorship and Political Communication* (New York: St. Martin's Press, 1983). The literature fails to take account of the fact, noted in n. 30, that censorship is highly variable in its organization and merges with institutions such as printing and editorial offices. All sources agree, however, that editorial control and censorship and self-censorship by journalists are more immediate sources of censorship than interference by censors themselves, which, since it suggests a lapse in vigilance, is normally avoided as much as possible.
    The *Bulletin of the Supreme Soviet* indicated in October 1986 that one of the laws to be promulgated in the next few years concerned "the press and information." *New York Times*, 7 October 1986. A well-informed Soviet source indicated that among the provisions of the new law would be a more restrictive definition of what constitutes a state secret, together with language authorizing journalists to write about anything not otherwise declared off limits. The exposure of KGB and procuratorial complicity in suppressing the investigations of a Ukrainian journalist named Berkhin are evidently meant to dramatize the *glasnost'* policy against institutions previously off limits to media criticism. See *Pravda*, 4 and 8 January 1987.
46   A *Pravda* editor once boasted that he had forty different editorials ready to run. In other cases, editors have been known simply to reuse the same editorials year after year. See "Kopii peredovits," *Zhurnalist*, 1982, no. 3:29; Dewhirst and Farrell, *Soviet Censorship*, p. 59.
47   Alexander Dallin, *Black Box: KAL 007 and the Superpowers* (Berkeley and Los Angeles: University of California Press, 1985), pp. 1–15.
48   According to the report prepared by the Soviet Area Audience and Opinion Research (SAAOR) office of Radio Free Europe/Radio Liberty, Western radio broadcasts were cited by 45 percent of a sample of Soviet citizens as their source of information about the KAL incident; only 20 percent cited the Soviet press. Some 62 percent cited political meetings as a source, a figure that suggests the impor-

tance of the oral political work discussed in chapter 2 as a channel of deniable news. Soviet television was cited by 48 percent of respondents. Among those who listened to Western radio, the credibility of Soviet reports was low (18 percent found the Soviet version most credible); among nonlisteners, it was high (79 percent). See Radio Free Europe/Radio Liberty, SAAOR, "The Korean Airline Incident: Western Radio and Soviet Perceptions," AR 4-84 (April 1984).

49 Information on the Chernobyl story derives from the following sources: Foreign Broadcast Information Service (FBIS), 28 April–22 May; "Avariia na chernobyl'skoi AES i ee posledstviia: Informatsiia, podgotovelennaia dlia soveshchaniia ekspertov MAGATE (25–29 August 1986), Vena)," prepared under the auspices of the State Committee for the Utilization of Atomic Energy of the USSR, dated August 1986, and marked "Not for Publication"; Ellen Jones and Benjamin L. Woodbury II, "Chernobyl' and Glasnost'," *Problems of Communism* 35, no. 6 (November-December 1986): 28–38; and Erik P. Hoffmann, "Nuclear Deception: Soviet Information Policy," *Bulletin of the Atomic Scientists* 43, no. 1 (August-September 1986): 32–37.

In addition, since I was travelling in the Soviet Union during the first three weeks of the crisis, I collected a number of newspapers carrying coverage of the story.

50 Falin made his comments in an interview, " 'Wir Waren Innerlich Nicht Vorbereitet,' " *Der Spiegel*, 12 May 1986, pp. 139–43, where he observed that Monday's dispatch could have been issued on Sunday. Gorbachev had been informed of an event on Saturday, but he implied that the local authorities concealed the true extent of the disaster and that only on Monday did the Politburo appreciate its magnitude. Gubarev, who was one of the two *Pravda* writers who covered the story continuously, observed to Philip Taubman of the *New York Times* that, in retrospect, it was a mistake to have withheld the news at first, a decision he attributed to higher authorities. Philip Taubman, "A New Pravda Mirrors Openness, Up to a Point," New York Times, 13 February 1987.

51 "Avariia," p. 52.

52 Among the associated themes were these: the accident showed the awesome destructive power of nuclear energy, which must never be used in war; nuclear energy for peaceful power production was needed and would continue to grow; the situation at Chernobyl was basically safe, the population did not panic, and the environment was not significantly affected; the evacuated population was being well cared for, with minor hitches; the accident's victims were receiving top-flight medical attention; Western propaganda about the accident made deliberate and falsifying use of it to impugn the Soviet Union and deflect attention from its own nuclear recklessness; and the efforts of the scientific, technical, military, and other personnel to clean up were of epic and heroic proportions.

53 "Avariia," p. 34.

54 S. I. Galkin, "Teoreticheskie problemy planirovaniia v redaktsii gazety," *Vestnik moskovskogo universiteta*, Journalism Series, 1972, no. 2: 13.

55 Svitich and Shiriaeva, *Zhurnalist*, p. 121.

56   A Latvian district paper presented the following figures on income and expenses in rubles for 1981:

Planned revenue	38,000
Actual revenue	
Subscription and sales	40,807
Advertising and notices	38,989
Expenses	71,390

With the profit the paper declared a 10 percent pay raise for the staff and filled its incentive funds. Income from notices and advertisements was distributed in the following percentages:

Government agencies, cooperatives, enterprises	45.0
Obituary and sympathy notices	32.0
Notices of job vacancies	15.0
Offers to buy or sell goods, exchange apartments	6.5
Congratulations on holidays, achievements, weddings	1.5

It was indicated that the local soviet requested the paper to stop advertising job openings in other districts. An advertisement 1 square centimeter in size cost a citizen 60 kopeks, the government, 50. An accompanying commentary explains that there are no regulations governing advertising in newspapers. Editors should simply bear in mind that advertisements should be "appropriate" (considerations of *tselesoobraznosti*). See "Kakie ob''iavleniia pechatat'?" *Zhurnalist*, 1982, no. 11: 58.

57   Tsukasov, *Nauchnye osnovy*, pp. 39–42.

58   See S. V. Tsukasov, "Effektivnost' organizatsii—effektivnost' tvorchestva," in K. K. Barykin et al., eds., *Problemy nauchnoi organizatsii zhurnalistskogo truda: ocherki teorii i praktiki* (Moscow: Mysl', 1974), pp. 22–24; idem, "osnovnye tendentskii razvitiia organizatsii raboty tsentral'noi gazety," *Vestnik moskovskogo universiteta*, Journalism Series, 1972, no. 5: 5; idem, *Nauchnye osnovy*, p. 14.

59   Tsukasov, *Nauchnye osnovy*, pp. 10–12; O. V. Kalinin, "Postoiannye razdely—v osnovu tematicheskoi modeli gazet i zhurnalov," in *Problemy zhurnalistiki*, vyp. 9 (Leningrad: Izdatel'stvo leningradskogo universiteta, 1977), pp. 94–95.

60   Viktor Shklovsky, "Writers Must Write So That People Read Slowly," *Literaturnaia gazeta*, 24 August 1983, *Current Digest of the Soviet Press* 35, no. 50 (11 January 1984): 24.

61   Kalinin, "Postoiannye razdely," pp. 87–104; interview with V. Kozhemiako, "Postoiannye temy," *Zhurnalist*, 1982, no. 2: 42.

62   Shkondin, *Pechat'*, p. 125.

63   V. A. Parfenov, "Zhurnalistika i ideologicheskoe obespechenie ekonomicheskoi politiki KPSS," *Vestnik moskovskogo universiteta*, Journalism Series, 1978, no. 1: 15.

64 *Ezhegodnik* (1984), p. 93; A. G. Mendeleev, *Chto za gazetnym slovom?* (Moscow: Mysl', 1979), p. 115.

65 Nicholas Lampert, *Whistleblowing in the Soviet Union* (New York: Schocken Books, 1985), p. 173.

66 *Partiinoe stroitel'stvo: Nauchnye osnovy partiinoi raboty. Kurs lektsii* (Moscow: Mysl', 1985), 1: 282–83; 2: 244.

67 See *Pravda*'s editorial for 17 January 1987, entitled "Strogii ekzamen zimy," which discusses the many complaints reaching *Pravda* from people whose state apartments were inadequately heated during the fierce winter cold. Many of these were desperate pleas for central intervention after appeals to local housing and soviet offices had proven unavailing.

69 P. Broditskii, "Gazeta i sotsiologiia," *Rasprostranenie pechati*, 1980, no. 7: 4–6. The source of this figure is not indicated, and the point is expressed in very hazy language. Most likely the figure derives from the Taganrog study (discussed in chapter 7), which estimated that about one-sixth of the adult population wrote the media or the government at some point. See B. A. Grushin and L. A. Onikov, *Massovaia informatsiia v sovetskom promyshlennom gorode* (Moscow: Izdatel'stvo politicheskoi literatury, 1980), pp. 382–83.

70 Stephen Sternheimer, "Communications and Power in Soviet Urban Politics," in Everett M. Jacobs, ed., *Soviet Local Politics and Government* (London: George Allen & Unwin, 1983), p. 145.

71 S. I. Igoshin, "Pis'mo v sisteme organizatorskoi raboty sredstv massovoi propagandy," in *Problemy zhurnalistiki*, vyp. 10, *Organizatorskaia funktsiia pechati, radio, i televideniia* (Leningrad: Izdatel'stvo leningradskogo universiteta, 1979), p. 72.

72 Lampert, *Whistleblowing*, p. 136.

73 Ibid., p. 137.

74 *Pravda*, 28 February 1986.

75 Tsukasov, *Nauchnye osnovy*, p. 30; idem, "Effektivnost'," p. 31.

76 As *Trud* is said to have done, for example. See Mendeleev, *Chto za gazetnym slovom*, p. 115. But only a few. At lower levels, even punch-card filing systems are regarded as curiosities, since they are presented as cases of "advanced" or leading experience. See, for example, M. G. Rozenfel'd, "Uchet, analiz, vyvody," in Barykin et al., *Problemy*, pp. 199–205; and P. I. Ladygin, "Vozmozhnosti tvorcheskogo sorevnovaniia," in ibid., pp. 195–96. Indeed, the "post-industrial society" is a long way off for most local media organizations, where even typewriters are scarce.

77 These are the estimates supplied by Mendeleev, *Chto za gazetnym slovom*, p. 118.

78 A. Rashidov, "Partiinoe rukovodstvo politicheskoi kampaniei (teoretiko-metodologicheskoii aspekt)," in Zh. T. Toshchenko, ed., *Voprosy teorii i metodov ideologicheskoi raboty*, vyp. 12 (Moscow: Mysl', 1980), pp. 202–15; *Pravda*, 11 July 1979; Tsukasov, *Nauchnye osnovy*, p. 28. In earlier research, I compared the media campaigns for two major party decrees of 1979 and found evidence of competition between them. See Thomas Remington, "Policy Innovation and Soviet Media Campaigns," *Journal of Politics* 45, no. 1 (February 1983): 220–27.

79 B. Paton, "The Safety of Progress," *Literaturnaia gazeta*, 29 October 1986, *Current Digest of the Soviet Press* 38, no. 48 (31 December 1986): 1–4.

80 S. V. Karavashkova, "Pechat' i sotsial'naia aktivnost' lichnosti," *Vestnik moskovskogo universiteta*, Journalism Series, 1972, no. 1: 24–25; F. Tsarev, "Kto mozhet byt' chlenom soiuza zhurnalistov," *Zhurnalist*, 1979, no. 7: 35.

81 The figure of 6 million was cited by V. G. Afanas'ev in his report to the Sixth Congress of Journalists in March 1987. See *Sovetskaia Rossiia*, 15 March 1987. On the nonstaff correspondents movement, see A. Roskoshnyi, "Otvety, kotorye staviat voprosy," *Zhurnalist*, 1982, no. 2: 6.

82 Karavashkova, "Pechat'," pp. 24–25.

83 Roskoshnyi, "Otvety," p. 6.

84 Iu. Meshcherin and N. Kiselev, "Novyi pod''em rabsel'korovskogo dvizheniia (1959–1972 gody)," in A. Shaposhnik, ed., *Zhurnalistika i zhizn'* (Voronezh: Izdatel'stvo voronezhskogo universiteta, 1973), pp. 68, 71.

85 On those who write letters, see the detailed study by A. I. Verkhovskaia, *Pis'mo v redaktsiiu i chitatel'* (Moscow: Izdatel'stvo moskovskogo universiteta, 1972), esp. pp. 153–58.

86 Roskoshyni, "Otvety," p. 6.

87 Karavashkova, "Pechat'," pp. 26, 25.

88 P. Pozhidaev, "Partiinaia zhizn'—rubrika postoiannaia," in Shaposhnik, ed., *Zhurnalistika i zhizn'*, p. 174.

89 F. I. Agzamov, *Leninskie printsipy zhurnalistiki v deistvii* (Kazan: Izdatel'stvo kazanskogo universiteta, 1980), p. 106.

90 Karavashkova, "Pechat'," p. 26.

91 Kurilov and Shinkarenko, "Nekotorye," p. 24.

CHAPTER 5   PARTY-MEDIA RELATIONS

1 Stephen White, *Political Culture and Soviet Politics* (London: Macmillan, 1979), p. 101.

2 A valuable general study of party-media relations is Lilita Dzirkals, Thane Gustafson, and A. Ross Johnson, *The Media and Intra-Elite Communication in the USSR*, Rand report no. R-2869 (Santa Monica, Calif.: Rand Corporation, September 1982), esp. ch. 4, "Discussions, Debates, and Controversies in Soviet Media."

3 I. P. Magai, *Metodologicheskie problemy zhurnalistiskogo masterstva (funktsii pressy i sotsial'naia rol' zhurnalista)* (Moscow: Izdatel'stvo moskovskogo universiteta, 1979), pp. 5–16.

4 A. V. Grebnev, "Sostavnaia chast' partiinoi raboty," in K. K. Barykin et al., eds., *Problemy nauchnoi organizatsii zhurnalistskogo truda: ocherki teorii i praktiki* (Moscow: Mysl', 1974), pp. 82–83.

5 Elena Korol'kova, "Kak smenili redaktora," *Zhurnalist*, 1981, no. 3: 53.

6 *Sovetskaia kul'tura*, 8 December 1987.

7   Interview with V. P. Esvandzhia by E. Kamenetskii, "Chto znachit rukovodit' konkretno," *Zhurnalist*, 1983, no. 9: 5–6.
8   See V. Loginov, "By the Light of the Truth," *Pravda*, 24 October 1986; "Resolutely Combat Violations of Party and State Discipline," *Turkmenskaia iskra*, 21 October 1986, *Current Digest of the Soviet Press* 38, no. 43 (26 November 1986): 1–3.
9   Leonid Khmel'nitskii, "TPK nabiraet moshchnost'," *Zhurnalist*, 1981, no. 5: 21–22.
10 Perhaps this relationship is best expressed in the habitual use of the familiar second person singular *ty* form when the first secretary of a party committee addresses the editor of the local newspaper and the formal *vy* in the address of the editor to the secretary, a general pattern of speech expressing familiarity and inequality between superiors and subordinates in Soviet public life. See A. Bondarenko, "Nachal'stvennoe 'ty'—norma ili khamstvo?" *Zhurnalist*, 1983, no. 8: 59. See also an earlier article in which a newspaper editor and the head of the local party agitprop department were on a *ty* basis but the editor and the first secretary were on the *ty/vy* footing. N. Barmina, "A chto budet zavtra . . ." ibid., 1982, no. 7: 56–58.
11 For example, see Igor' Magai, "Kandidatskii stazh," ibid., no. 2 (1982), 49–52.
12 A. G. Mendeleev, *Chto za gazetnym slovom?* (Moscow: Mysl': 1979), p. 22.
13 Lev Lifshitz-Losev, "What It Means to Be Censored," *New York Review of Books*, 29 June 1978, p. 49.
14 "Izbrany na XXVI s"ezde KPSS," *Zhurnalist*, 1982, no. 4: 3.
15 In Gorkii oblast, for example, nearly all newspaper editors are members of the bureaus of party committees. In Kostroma oblast all newspaper editors are members of the bureaus of party committees. In Brest oblast in Belorussia, of the sixteen newspaper editors of district and combined city-district papers, thirteen belong to city and district party committees, and all are deputies to soviets. In Latvia, thirty-three media figures are members of the Republican Central Committee and lower territorial party committees. Since there are about eighty cities and districts, and around one hundred newspapers in Latvia, representation rates are lower than average. See interview with Iu. N. Khristoradnov, "Reshaia novye zadachi," *Zhurnalist*, 1980, no. 12; 6; B. S. Arkhipov, "Partiinyi komitet i organizatsiia raboty redaktsii," in Barykin et al., *Problemy*, p. 94; *Pravda*, 29 September 1980, p. 2; A. E. Voss, "V tsentre vnimaniia—tvorchestvo," *Zhurnalist*, 1980, no. 4: 16–17; *Zhurnalist*, 1986, no. 4: 41.
16 "Izbrany,"·p. 3.
17 See the following Radio Liberty Research Bulletins: "CPSU Central Committee Full Members Elected by the Twenty-Sixth Party Congress in March 1981," RL 123/81 (23 March 1981); "Central Committee Candidate Members Elected by the Twenty-Sixth Party Congress in March 1981," RL 127/81 (25 March 1981); "Members of the CPSU Central Auditing Commission Elected by the Twenty-Sixth Party Congress in March 1981," RL 129/81 (25 March 1981); "Additions and Amendments to the Membership of Leading Organs of the CPSU Elected by the

Twenty-Sixth Party Congress in March 1981," RL 148/91 (7 April 1981)," all compiled by Herwig Kraus.

18 *Zhurnalist*, 1986, no. 4: 11.

19 A fuller report of this study will be found in Thomas F. Remington, "Gorbachev and the Strategy of Glasnost'," in idem, ed., *Politics and the Soviet System: Essays in Honor of Frederick C. Barghoorn* (London: Macmillan, forthcoming). I am indebted to William Stowe for assistance in coding and entering the data.

20 Aleksander Kapto, "Vse reshaiut kadry," *Zhurnalist*, 1985, no. 11: 19.

21 V. Novikov, "Kompetentno i otvetstvenno," ibid., 1979, no. 7: 12–13.

22 "Keeping journalists informed, and not just editors but also other creative employees, has become one of the indispensable conditions of party direction of the press. Now the creative staff members of the media are constantly up to date about everything that the party committee, soviet, and othe rorgans, are doing or intend to do, and, accordingly, they know what concrete tasks in that connection face journalists." Kapto, "Kadry," p. 19.

23 E. Kamenetskii, "V nachale nedeli," *Zhurnalist*, 1981, no. 9: 8–10.

24 Dzirkals, Gustafson, and Johnson, *The Media*, pp. 46–47. As always, *Pravda* is handled in a special way. The editor reports that he frequently converses with Alexander Yakovlev by phone and considers him his immediate supervisor; Gorbachev himself often phones. Philip Taubman, "A New Pravda Mirrors Openness, up to a Point," *New York Times*, 13 February 1987.

25 "Anketa Zhurnalista," *Zhurnalist*, 1981, no. 3: 11.

26 K. Vaino, "Delovoi nastroi," ibid., 1982, no. 2: 11–12.

27 As in the Ukrainian case presented by Kapto, "Kadry," p. 19.

28 L. G. Svitich and A. A. Shiriaeva, *Zhurnalist i ego rabota* (Moscow: Izdatel'stvo moskovskogo universiteta, 1979), pp. 52–54.

29 "Povyshat' kachestvo raboty," *Zhurnalist*, 1979, no. 7: 3. "Reshaia novye zadachi," ibid., 1980, no. 12: 5–6.

30 S. V. Mitroshin, "Partiinyi komitet i pechat'," in *Partiinyi komitet i sredsvta informatsii* (Moscow: Izdatet'stvo politicheskoi literatury, 1980), p. 7; G. Grotseskul, "Eshche raz o khlebe," *Zhurnalist*, 1982, no. 3: 15.

31 Grotseskul, "Eshche raz," p. 15. As an article in *Zhurnalist* put it, journalists want to be told when to be bold and critical. Boris Chubar, "Khochu byt' smelym . . . esli pozvoliat," *Zhurnalist*, 1986, no. 12: 35.

32 *Pravda*, 6 August 1986, in *Current Digest of the Soviet Press* 38, no. 31 (29 August 1984): 21–22; A. Khomiakov, "Glasnost'—oruzhie perestroiki," *Zhurnalist*, 1986, no. 10: 3.

33 One important observation made in Lampert's study of media stories involving whistle-blowing suggests the opposite, however: that, though higher-level authorities can intervene against a local power structure, local authorities have surprising powers of resistance, even against direct and high-level demands. Nicholas Lampert, *Whistleblowing in the Soviet Union* (New York: Schocken, 1985), pp. 7, 145.

34   *Pravda,* 24 August 1981.
35   Magai, "Kandidatskii stazh," p. 50.
36   A few years later, Braun, still a journalist, wrote a letter to *Zhurnalist,* about another matter. Losing his party card did not deprive him of a livelihood in journalism, probably because of the severe shortage of journalists in many rural districts. But his chances for advancement are likely to be slim.
37   Lampert, *Whistleblowing,* pp. 78–86; E. Kamenetskii, "Partiinyi otdel «Pravdy»," *Zhurnalist,* 1984, no. 1: 26.
38   Such was the essence of the rather short article appearing on Pravda's back page. "V prokurature SSSR," *Pravda,* 29 November 1986.
39   See chapter 4, no. 74. Of course it is possible that *Pravda* was simply acting at the behest of political authorities seeking to embarrass Chebrikov rather than taking the active role, as is suggested here. The pattern of the case indicates, however, that it was *Pravda* that initiated higher-level intervention.
40   M. Odinets and M. Poltoranin, "Za poslednei chertoi," *Pravda,* 4 January 1987; V. Chebrikov, " 'Za poslednei chertoi'," ibid., 8 January 1987.
41   See the discussion of how "new ideas" are placed on the agenda in Thane Gustafson, *Reform in Soviet Politics* (Cambridge: Cambridge University Press, 1981), ch. 6, "Bringing New Ideas into Soviet Politics." Gustafson analyzes the problem of agenda setting as a matter of the changing relations between two categories of actors, political authorities and specialists. In Dzirkals, Gustafson, and Johnson, *The Media,* ch. 4, "Discussions," the authors present the problem as a more complex three-way interaction of media personnel, particularly editors; party and other political leaders; and specialists or other policy advocates. Since a variety of combinations are possible in this relationship, it becomes extremely difficult to determine how much independence an editor has in a given dispute vis-à-vis party officials on the one hand and contributors on the other.
42   John Löwenhardt, *Decision Making in Soviet Politics* (New York: St. Martin's Press, 1981), esp. pp. 18–19, 25.
43   In 1981, *Zhurnalist,* published a story involving a typical contretemps between developmental and environmental interests in Tiumen', a crucial oil and gas producing region, where a radio station aired two stories on the pollution of the Ob' River caused by intensive energy development. The head of a fish-processing combine complained about the broadcasts to the provincial radio and television broadcasting authority. The head of the local Gosteleradio committee duly reprimanded the editor of the radio station. Seeking vindication, the editor sent an account of the two broadcasts and the reprimand it had provoked to *Zhurnalist.* *Zhurnalist,* in turn sought the opinion of specialists at the Siberian branch of the Academy of Sciences; the State Committee for Hydrometeorology and Environmental Oversight *(kontrol');* and the Ministry of the Fishing Industry. All those to whom the materials were sent replied that the broadcast had been entirely objective; if anything, some felt that the criticism contained in the broadcasts had been too mild. With this backing, *Zhurnalist,* concluded that not the reporter who had

written the stories, but the chairman of the provincial broadcasting authority, had acted improperly. See M. Kushtapin, "Prikaz No. 11," *Zhurnalist*, 1981, no. 9: 27–29.

44 Joel J. Schwartz and William R. Keech, "Group Influence and the Policy Process in the Soviet Union," *American Political Science Review* 62, no. 3 (September 1968): 840–51, as reprinted in Gary K. Bertsch and Thomas W. Ganschow, eds., *Comparative Communism: The Soviet, Chinese, and Yugoslav Models* (San Francisco: W. H. Freeman, 1976), esp. pp. 240–41.

45 Evidence about the editorial leanings of these newspapers is largely indirect. For *Pravda*, see Mikhail Poltoranin, "Be Bold, Proprietor!" *Pravda*, 15 November 1986, in *Current Digest of the Soviet Press*, 38, no. 46 (17 December 1986), which recounts a conversation with a ministry official favoring the project shortly after the Twenty-seventh Party Congress. *Pravda*'s staff reportedly presented objections to the project but the official dismissed them as irrelevant and too late. Not long afterward, the party leadership ruled against further progress on the project.

  Sovetskaia Rossiia tended to present the viewpoint of those concerned about the project's environmental and cultural impact on Russia. On 3 January 1986 the newspaper published a statement by seven prominent writers protesting the project on the grounds that it would cause irremediable harm to vast fertile territories and ancient villages and towns (*New York Times*, 4 January 1986). After the decision to stop the project, *Sovetskaia Rossiia* published a commentary by an ecologist who observed that the newspaper had received over four thousand letters in response to the debate, and that the decision to stop the project was supported by the "widest circles of society." See "Sibaral: An End to the Great Debate?" *Soviet Analyst* 15, no. 17 (27 August 1986): 6. See also the companion piece to this article, "Sibaral: An End to the Great Debate?—2," ibid., no. 18 (10 September 1986): 5–8.

  For *Literaturnaia gazeta*, see Boris Khorev, "The Volga Empties into the Caspian Sea," *Literaturnaia gazeta*, 1986 3 September (a review of the newspaper's interest in environmental preservation) in *Current Digest of the Soviet Press* 38, no. 48 (31 December 1986): 5–6, which recounts the newspaper's interest in opening a discussion that developers wanted to prevent; and which calls attention to the scathing attacks on the project by Russian writers at the Eighth Soviet Writers' Congress, abridged transcripts of which had been published by the paper.

  Information about *Trud* comes from a conversation with a staff correspondent for the newspaper.

  Background information about the river project is provided in Thane Gustafson, *Reform*, ch. 5, "Technology Assessment Soviet Style." See also, Gary Thatcher, "Diverting Soviet Rivers," *Christian Science Monitor*, 16 January 1985, pp. 14–15.

46 *Sovetskaia Rossiia*, 15 March 1987.

47 B. Paton, "The Safety of Progress," *Literaturnaia gazeta*, 29 October 1986, *Current Digest of the Soviet Press* 38, no. 48 (31 December 1986): 1–4.

48 A respected nonparty writer and, since summer 1986, the editor of *Novyi mir*, Zalygin has been one of the leading intellectuals taking part in the heated cam-

paign to defend environmental causes such as the preservation of Lake Baikal and the effort to stop the river diversion project. His articles on the latter struggle are wide-ranging and revealing analyses of the politics of development projects. He is regarded as the most outspoken of the project's public foes. See Sergei Zalygin, "Proekt: nauchnaia obosnovannost' i otvetstvennost'," *Kommunist*, 1985, no. 13: 63–73; idem, "Povorot: Uroki odnoi diskussii," *Novyi mir*, 1987, no. 1: 3–18.

Another harsh attack on the Institute of Water Problems, and particularly on its director, G. P. Voropaev, is Vadim Leibovskii, "Bespovorotno!" *Ogonek*, 1987, no. 40: 24–27. Also see Sergei Voronitsyn, "Renewed Debate Over Canceled River Diversion Project," *Radio Liberty Research Bulletin*, RL 205/87, May 27, 1987.

Responses to Zalygin's attack on the river diversion forces appeared under the title "Kak sovershaetskia povorot," *Novyi mir*, 1987, no. 7: 181–235.

49 For the material bearing on the debate over population policy, I am indebted to Steven H. Koval, "The Soviet Population Problem: The Formation of a Policy," M.A. thesis, Emory University, 1983, esp. pp. 53–54.

50 In his recent monograph on Soviet energy policy in Western Siberia, Han-ku Chung finds close interaction between policy proposals from the coalition seeking substantial increases in national investment in regional energy development and favorable national policy decisions. He finds that in most cases, media discussion occurred in anticipation of the adoption of a favorable decision, and then afterward to mobilize support for the new policy. See Han-ku Chung, *Interest Representation in Soviet Policymaking: A Case Study of a West Siberian Energy Coalition* (Boulder: Westview, 1987), p. 118.

51 *Pravda*, 22 August, 1986.

52 See the comments on Frolov in Jerry F. Hough, "Gorbachev Consolidating Power," *Problems of Communism* 36, no. 4 (July–August 1987): 31, n. 30. Hough observes that "Frolov made his name fighting Lysenkoism in genetics, but then began emphasizing more broadly the importance of factors other than class in human affairs."

53 "Na uroven' partiinykh trebovanii," *Kommunist*, 1986, no. 14: 4.

54 T. Zaslavskaia, "Chelovecheskii faktor razvitiia ekonomiki i sotsial'naia spravedlivost'," *Kommunist*, 1986, no. 13: 61–73; idem, "Tvorcheskaia aktivnost' mass: sotsial'nye rezervy rosta," *EKO*, 1986, no. 3: 3–25. (*EKO* is a relatively specialized journal published by the Institute for the Economics and Organization of Industrial Production of the Siberian Division of the USSR Academy of Sciences in Novosibirsk.) The *Kommunist* article essentially repeated the earlier article, making the same arguments in favor of greater use of market forms and material incentives to spur productivity. The fact that she simply recycled the article for the prestigious theoretical journal of the Central Committee suggests that the editors actively sought to give her ideas the legitimacy that publication in *Kommunist* could confer.

A number of other cases when a publication's editor was removed to make room for significant changes in editorial line could be cited as well, such as the 1970 removal of Anatolii Nikonov as editor of *Molodaia gvardiia* after its phase of

Russian nationalism. This coincided with the removal of Alexander Tvardovsky as editor of *Novyi mir*, an action clearly intended to curb the journal's liberal line.

55 Her previous publication in *Kommunist* was a co-authored book review in 1961 calling for higher wages for kolkhozniki.

56 Cf. "Mneniia i predlozheniia," *Kommunist*, 1986, no. 17: 61–68.

57 L. Legasov, "Problemy bezopasnogo razvitiia tekhnosfery," *Kommunist*, 1987, no. 8: 92–101. A number of other unusual and reform-oriented articles appeared in the same issue.

58 *Pravda*'s editor, V. G. Afanas'ev, pointedly clarified the implications of the new Andropov line for the media with an article in *Zhurnalist*, in February 1986: "When you read mail from the readers, you see that no one is calling for new rights or freedoms: people are pleading for order. In enterprises, in institutions, on the streets, everywhere." As a result, Afanas'ev argued, journalists may be assured that public opinion will back them when they call for stronger labor discipline; nor may editors get off with a few pro forma responses, such as a new rubric or an appropriate title, as if this were just another campaign. Driving the point home, the next month, *Zhurnalist*, appended an unusually frank report on problems connected with low labor productivity to its syllabus for political self-study by journalists. See V. G. Afanas'ev, "Initsiativa, otvetstvennost'," *Zhurnalist*, 1983, no. 2: 1–3; "Aktual'nye voprosy politiki KPSS i pressa," *Zhurnalist*, 1983, no. 3: 30–33.

59 Three articles are V. Orlov, "Okh uzh etot validol . . . ," *Pravda*, 28 January 1985, about a Buriat district party leader who suppressed media criticism; An. Makarov, "Muzhskoi razgovor," *Nedelia*, 1985, no. 8: 12, the premise of which is the insincere, ceremonial quality of public speech; and A. Druzenko, "Glasno o glasnosti," *Izvestiia*, 19 January 1985, a review of reader mail complaining about the lack of open and truthful information in everyday life. Both the *Pravda* and *Izvestiia* articles led to follow-up articles that generalized about secretiveness in the media.

60 Vera Tolz, "The Soviet Press Under Gorbachev," *Radio Liberty Research Bulletin*, RL 38/86 (21 January 1986).

61 The annual total number of announced media appointments is as follows:

1974	46	1981	46
1975	51	1982	60
1976	53	1983	70
1977	47	1984	135
1978	22	1985	129
1979	62	1986	116
1980	36		

62 See Thomas F. Remington, "Gorbachev and the Strategy of *Glasnost'*," in idem, ed., *Politics and the Soviet System: Essays in Honor of Frederick C. Barghoorn* (London: MacMillan, forthcoming).

63 Dina Spechler's treatment of the evolution of "permitted dissent" in *Novyi mir* under Khrushchev suggests the dangers Khrushchev faced in cultural de-Stalinization. Dina R. Spechler, *Permitted Dissent in the USSR: "Novyi mir" and the Soviet Regime* (New York: Praeger, 1982).

64 For example, compare these two quotations from regional party secretaries. One characterizes *glasnost'* as the key to the "psychological restructuring of our cadres" and the activation of the masses. Another, while calling *glasnost'* "as necessary as air," also states firmly that "it goes without saying that all our work in expanding *glasnost'* and improving informedness is not an end in itself. In the last analysis it should actively contribute to the fulfillment of tasks set by the Twenty-seventh Party Congress and the June 1986 plenum of the Central Committee of the party, and develop the initiative of labor collectives and raise in people the aspiration to attain higher results." The first is from an interview with A. Khomiakov, first secretary of Saratov obkom, entitled *"Glasnost'*—oruzhie perestroiki," *Zhurnalist,* 1986, no. 10: 2–5, quotation on p. 2; the second is from an article by the Rostov obkom first secretary B. Volodin, entitled "Rasshirenie *glasnosti*—vopros politicheskii," *Partiinaia zhizn',* 1986, no. 17: 23–28. Quotations on pp. 23, 27.

65 Gorbachev reportedly commented that "between the people, who want these changes, who dream about these changes, and the leadership there is an administrative layer—the ministerial and party apparatus—that does not want changes, does not want to be deprived of certain rights and the privileges they entail." Aaron Trehub, "Gorbachev Meets Soviet Writers: A Samizdat Account," *Radio Liberty Research Bulletin,* RL 399/86, 23 October 1986, p. 1. Compare this language with that cited by T. Samolis in his famous article, "Ochishchenie" ("Cleansing") in *Pravda,* 13 February 1986: "Between the Central Committee and the working class there continues to sway an immobile, inert, and glutinous 'party-administrative stratum,' which does not particularly want radical changes. Some only carry party cards but have long since ceased to be communists. From the party they want only privileges but do not themselves hasten to give back to the people either their effort or their knowledge." The similarity of the two statements would signal to an audience as adept at reading Aesopian hints as the writers that Gorbachev did not accept Ligachev's repudiation of *Pravda* for its article.

66 *Sovetskaia Rossiia,* 15 March 1987.

67 *Pravda,* 15 July 1987.

CHAPTER 6 POLITICS AND PROFESSIONALISM IN SOVIET JOURNALISM

1 See Michael Schudson, *Discovering the News: A Social History of American Newspapers* (New York: Basic Books, 1978); Bernard Roshcoe, *Newsmaking* (Chicago: University of Chicago Press, 1975).

2 This point is treated well by Anthony Smith, *Goodbye Gutenberg: The Newspaper Revolution of the 1980's* (New York: Oxford University Press, 1980), pp. 158–59.

3 See Herbert J. Gans, *Deciding What's News* (New York: Vintage, 1979), pp. 281ff.; see also George Comstock, *Television in America* (Beverly Hills, Calif.: Sage Publications, 1980), pp. 43–55. The concept of structural bias, in distinction to political bias, is originally that of Richard Hofstetter, *Bias in the News* (Columbus, Oh.: Ohio State University Press, 1976).

4 See, for example, A. V. Grebnev, "Sostavnaia chast' partiinoi raboty," in K. K. Barykin et al., eds., *Problemy nauchnoi organizatsii zhurnalistskogo truda: ocherki teorii i praktiki* (Moscow: Mysl', 1974), pp. 82–83.

5 *Chetvertyi s''ezd zhurnalistov SSSR. 1–3 marta 1977 goda. Stenograficheskii otchet* (Moscow: Pravda, 1977), pp. 255–56. Hereafter this publication will be cited as Fourth Congress.

6 *Zhurnalist*, 1982, no. 7: 26, 53, 54.

7 Fourth Congress, p. 256; *Zhurnalist*, 1981, no. 11: 6.

8 A. T. Gavrilov, "O partiinom rukovodstve podgotovkoi i vospitanieum zhurnalistskikh kadrov v sovremennykh usloviiakh,' *Voprosy istorii KPSS*, 1982, no. 5: 54.

9 Gavrilov, p. 55.

10 Ibid., pp. 45, 56; M. V. Shkondin, "Soiuz zhurnalistov SSSR v edinstve organizatsionno-tvorcheskoi i ideino-vospitatel'noi raboty," *Vestnik moskovskogo universiteta*, Journalism Series, 1982, no. 2: 3–8; A. G. Mendeleev, *Chto za gazetnym slovom?* (Moscow: Mysl', 1979), p. 23.

11 The nine *kafedry* are: theory and practice of the party-Soviet press; radio and television broadcasting; editing and publishing; technology of newspaper and mass literature publishing; history of the party-Soviet press; history of Russian journalism and literature; literary-artistic criticism; history of foreign press and literature; Russian stylistics.

12 All information derived from the *Spravochnik dlia postupaiushchikh v moskovskii universitet* (Moscow: Izdatel'stvo moskovskogo universiteta, 1978), pp. 40–43.

13 *Zhurnalist*, 1982, no. 2: 26–29.

14 Ibid., pp. 29–32; ibid., no. 11: 38–39.

15 Ibid., no. 2: 29

16 The classic study of the importance of on-the-job occupational socialization is Warren Breed, "Social Control in the Newsroom," *Social Forces* 33 (May 1955): 326–35. See also the pithy aphorism offered by Leon V. Sigal "Shop Talk Lays the Basis for Consensus on News Judgements," *Reporters and Officials: The Organization and Politics of Newsmaking* (Lexington, Mass.: D. C. Heath, 1973), p. 46.

17 *Spravochnik dlia postupaiushchikh*, pp. 42–43.

18 S. M. Gurevich, "Partiinyi, tvorcheskii, proizvodstvennyi," in Barykin et al., *Problemy*, p. 54; Iu A. Sherkovin, "Zhurnalist v redaktsionnom kollektive," in ibid., p. 76.

19 On *raspredelenie*, see Mervyn Matthew, *Education in the Soviet Union* (London: George Allen & Unwin, 1982), pp. 170–74.

20 *Zhurnalist*, 1982, no. 12: 52.

21 L. G. Svitich and A. A. Shiriaeva, *Zhurnalist i ego rabota* (Moscow: Izdatel'stvo moskovskogo universiteta, 1979), p. 173; *Zhurnalist*, 1982, no. 7: 27–28.

22 These figures are drawn from a variety of sources and represent the best estimates from several conflicting assertions in the Soviet and Western literature. See *Zhurnalist*, 1983, no. 8: 60; ibid., no. 7: 51–52; ibid., no. 5: 14–15; see also Laszlo Revesz, *Recht and Willkuer in der Sowjetpresse: Eine presserechtliche und pressepolitische Untersuchung* (Friburg, Switzerland: Universitaetsverlag, 1974), pp. 201–2; Bruno Kalnins, *Agitprop: Die Propaganda in der Sowjetunion* (Vienna: Europe Verlag, 1966), p. 102. Note that the estimates provided by Mervyn Matthew are somewhat lower: the income of the editor of a republican newspaper is estimated at 500–600 rubles and the base salary only 240 rubles. Mervyn Matthews, *Privilege in the Soviet Union* (London: George Allen and Unwin, 1978), p. 26. These figures seem too low, particularly since *Zhurnalist* gives the base salary of a journal editor as 350 rubles, which may be increased to 500 rubles for a holder of the doctor of science degree. *Zhurnalist*, 1983, no. 8: 60.

23 Svitich and Shiriaeva, *Zhurnalist*, p. 127.

24 Ibid., pp. 52–53.

25 Ibid., p. 63.

26 A. A. Shiriaeva, "Zhurnalistskie kadry kak ob'ekt sotsiologicheskogo issledovaniia," in E. P. Prokhorov, ed. *Sotsiologiia zhurnalistiki* (Moscow: Izdatel'stvo moskovskogo universiteta, 1981), pp. 161–62.

27 Ellen Mickiewicz, *Media and the Russian Public* (New York: Praeger, 1981), p. 68.

28 Jan S. Adams, "Critical Letters to the Soviet Press: An Increasingly Important Public Forum," in Donald E. Schultz and J. S. Adams, eds., *Political Participation in Communist Systems* (New York: Pergamon, 1981), pp. 113–15.

29 Svitich and Shiriaeva, *Zhurnalist*, pp. 53, 54.

30 Ibid.

31 Discussion summarized from Christine Kunze, *Journalismus in der UdSSR* (Munich: Verlag Dokumentation Saur KG, 1978).

32 Revesz, *Recht und Willkuer*, p. 197.

33 Kunze, *Journalismus*, pp. 210–11.

34 Ibid., p. 107.

35 Cited in Paul Roth, ed., *Die kommandierte oeffentliche Meinung: Sowjetische Medienpolitik* (Stuttgart: Seewald Verlag, 1982), pp. 186–87.

36 See Frederick C. Barghoorn, *Politics in the USSR*, 2d ed. (Boston: Little, Brown, 1972), pp. 123–26.

37 Roth, *Kommandierte oeffentliche Meinung*, p. 190.

38 Idem, *Sow-Inform: Nachrichtenswesen und Informationspolitik der Sowjetunion* (Duesseldorf: Droste Verlag, 1980), p. 174.

39 Ibid., pp. 179–80.

40   See Dina R. Spechler, *Permitted Dissent in the USSR: "Novyi mir" and the Soviet Regime* (New York: Praeger, 1982).

41   M. V. Shkondin, *Pechat': Osnovy organizatsii i upravleniia* (Moscow: Izdatel'stvo moskovskogo universiteta, 1982), p. 101.

42   F. I. Agzamov, *Leninskie printsipy zhurnalistiki v deistvii* (Kazan': Izdatel'stvo kazanskogo universiteta, 1980), p. 103.

43   *Zhurnalist*, 1981, no. 11: 4–5.

44   Ibid., pp. 2–4.

45   Ibid., no. 12: 62–3.

46   V. I. Novikov, "Chetkost' i distsiplina," *Zhurnalist*, 1987, no. 4: 18.

47   Fourth Congress, pp. 56–65, 69–72, 84, 132.

48   Ibid., pp. 73, 133; *Zhurnalist*, 1982, no. 3: 13; *Zhurnalist*, 1987, no. 4: 15.

49   *Sovetskaia Rossiia*, 15 March 1987.

50   "O merakh po ukrepleniiu material'noi bazy i uluchsheniiu uslovii deiatel'nosti Souiza zhurnalistov SSSR," *Pravda*, 20 August 1987. The resolution authorizes the union to form a discretionary fund from a percentage of the honoraria paid to authors of publications. It directed the Mysl' publishing house to form a division devoted to media studies. Gosplan was instructed to direct maximum possible capital investment into facilities for journalists. The Council of Ministers was told to provide for new housing construction for journalists, and the Moscow city executive committee was directed to finish the capital repairs on the Central House of Journalists. These provisions rather closely matched Afanas'ev's litany of complaints in his 1987 address to the Congress.

51   F. Fedotov, "Kto boitsia glasnosti," *Pravda*, 12 April 1985.

52   *Zhurnalist*, 1982, no. 7: 26 and no. 9: 53.

53   Harry Gelman, *The Brezhnev Politburo and the Decline of Détente* (Ithaca, N.Y.: Cornell University Press, 1984), p. 87.

54   Lilita Dzirkals, Thane Gustafson, and A. Ross Johnson, *The Media and Intra-Elite Communication in the USSR*, Rand Report no. R-2869 (Santa Monica, Calif.: Rand Corporation, September 1982), pp. 18–19; *Zhurnalist*, 1982, no. 7: 26.

55   Iurii Borin and Mikhail Fedotov, "Pravo na informatsiiu," *Zhurnalist*, 1986, no. 11: 24–25.

56   *Sovetskaia Rossiia*, 15 March 1987.

57   Two recent collections of his articles are: *Umet' i ne umet'* (Moscow: Sovetskaia Rossiia, 1979) and *Detali i glavnoe: ocherki* (Moscow: Sovetskii pisatel', 1982).

58   "Deistvovat' aktivno, smelo, tvorcheski," excerpts from speeches at the Sixth Congress of Journalists, *Zhurnalist*, 1987, no. 4: 23. Also, on the institution of "commentators with the right of free comment," see Victor Zaslavsky, *The Neo-Stalinist State* (Armonk, N.Y.: M. E. Sharpe, 1982), p. 178.

59   S. N. Kondrashov, "Tochnyi obraz mira," *Kommunist*, 1987, no. 14: 51.

60   Sergei Dovlatov, *The Compromise*, trans. Anne Frydman (New York: Knopf, 1983). The Russian-language edition is *Kompromiss* (New York: Serebrianyi vek, 1981).

61 Valentin Kuznetsov, "Nenastoiashchie," *Zhurnalist*, 1983, no. 8: 20–23.

62 Information from a senior Soviet correspondent based in the United States.

63 V. M. Gorokhov, "Politika KPSS—ideinaia osnova tvorchestva sovetskikh zhurnalistov," *Vestnik moskovskogo universiteta*, Journalism Series, 1987, no. 2: 4–5.

64 *Sovetskaia Rossiia*, 15 March 1987.

CHAPTER 7   BUILDING THE SOCIALIST COMMUNITY

1 Ellen Mickiewicz, *Media and the Russian Public* (New York: Praeger, 1981), surveys the Soviet literature on media consumption extensively. Only a few illustrative data will therefore be presented here.

2 B. A. Grushin and L. A. Onikov, *Massovaia informatsiia v sovetskom promyshlennom gorode* (Moscow: Izdatel'stvo politicheskoi literatury, 1980), pp. 126, 130, 179, 216–17.

3 Vs. Vil'chek, "Pod znakom TV," in E. Efimov, comp., *Televidenia vchera, segodnia, zavtra*, vyp. 1 (Moscow: Iskusstvo, 1981), p. 208.

4 V. A. Losenkov, *Sotsial'naia informatsiia v zhizni gorodskogo naseleniia* (Leningrad: Nauka, 1983), pp. 44–45.

5 M. F. Nenashev, "Nasushchnye voprosy sovershenstvovaniia organizatsii i stilia ideologicheskoi raboty," in Zh. T. Toshchenko, et al., comps., *Voprosy teorii i praktiki ideologicheskoi raboty*, vyp. 17 (Moscow: Mysl', 1985), p. 6.

6 Grushin and Onikov, *Massovaia*, pp. 112–13; M. F. Nenashev, *Effektivnost' ideino-vospitatel'noi raboty* (Moscow: Izdatel'stvo politicheskoi literatury, 1974), p. 65; Grushin and Onikov, *Massovaia*, p. 138.

7 Ibid., p. 145.

8 Ibid., p. 219.

9 G. T. Zhuravlev, "Opyt konkretnogo sotsiologicheskogo issledovaniia kompleksnogo podkhoda k ideino-vospitatel'noi rabote," in *Voprosy teorii i metodov ideologicheskoi raboty*, vyp. 11 (Moscow: Mysl', 1979), p. 233; G. Maksimenko, "Tsentr ideologicheskikh usilii—trudovoi kollektiv," *Partiinaia zhizn'*, 1984, no. 18: 58.

10 P. V. Pozdniakov and E. N. Marikhin, *Nauchnoe rukovodstvo agitatsiei* (Moscow: Mysl', 1984), p. 33. The authors are discussing agitation, political information, and reports here and excluding political education and Znanie lectures.

11 M. P. Gabdulin, "Rukovodstvo ustnoi politicheskoi agitatsiei," in Zh. T. Toshchenko et al., eds., *Voprosy teorii i praktiki ideologicheskoi raboty*, vyp. 14 (Moscow: Mysl', 1983), p. 41. According to Gabdulin, surveys of agitators show that only 7 percent report coordinating their work with the party committee; 11 percent claim they draw up their own plans; and 82 percent do not plan their work at all.

12 Cf. Thomas Remington, "The Mass Media and Public Communication in the USSR," *Journal of Politics* 43, no. 3 (August 1981): 803–17.

13 A. A. Kozunov, "K probleme koordinatsii sredstv massovoi informatsii," in V. S.

Korobeinikov, ed., *Sotsiologicheskie problemy obshchestvennogo mneniia i deiatel'nosti sredstv massovoi informatsii* (Moscow: Institut sotsiologicheskikh issledovanii, 1979), p. 28.

14 *Pravda*, 3 September 1981.

15 V. V. Voronov and I. P. Smirnov, "Zakreplenie molodezhi v zone BAMa," *Sotsiologicheskie issledovaniia*, 1982, no. 2: 17.

16 L. G. Svitich and A. A. Shiriaeva, *Zhurnalist i ego rabota* (Moscow: Izdatel'stvo moskovskogo universiteta, 1979), p. 47.

17 T. P. Arkhipova and V. F. Sbytov, *Voprosy teorii i praktiki politicheskogo rukovodstva: opyt deiatel'nosti raikoma partii* (Moscow: Izdatel'stvo politicheskoi literatury, 1981), pp. 232, 233; Alex Inkeles and Raymond A. Bauer, *The Soviet Citizen* (New York: Atheneum, 1968), pp. 174–77.

18 Grushin and Onikov, *Massovaia*, p. 329; also see Tamotsu Shibutani, *Improvised News: A Sociological Study of Rumor* (Indianapolis: Bobbs-Merrill, 1966).

19 Losenkov, *Sotsial'naia*, pp. 79–81. This was also suggested by Inkeles and Bauer, who found that the urban elite placed highest credence in rumor. *Soviet Citizen*, p. 176.

20 Losenkov, *Sotsial'naia*, pp. 61–63.

21 M. K. Gorshkov, "Ispol'zovanie oprosov obshchestvennogo mneniia v praktike partiinoi raboty," *Sotsiologicheskie issledovaniia*, 1984, no. 3: 32.

22 An. Makarov, "Muzhskoi razgovor," *Nedelia*, 1985, no. 8: 12. I am grateful to Vladimir Shlapentokh for bringing this article to my attention.

23 I. E. Kokorev, "K probleme tipologii auditorii massovoi kommunikatskii," in A. G. Volkov, ed., *Materialy nauchnogo seminar 'Semiotika sredstv massovoi kommunikatskii'* (Moscow: Izdatel'stvo moskovskogo universiteta, 1973), pp. 114–18. This survey is also discussed in Remington, "Mass Media," pp. 807–8.

24 See esp. Grushin and Onikov, *Massovaia*, pp. 232, 379–80.

25 T. M. Dridze, "Lingvosotsiologicheskie aspekty massovoi informatsii," *Sotsiologicheskie issledovaniia*, 1975, no. 4: 159. The discussion is based on Thomas Remington, "Soviet Public Opinion and the Effectiveness of Party Ideological Work," *Carl Beck Papers in Russian and East European Studies*, Russian and East European Studies Program, University of Pittsburgh, no. 204 (Pittsburgh, 1983), p. 12.

26 T. M. Dridze, *Organizatsiia i metody lingvosotsiologicheskogo issledovaniia massovoi kommunikatsii* (Moscow: Izdatel'stvo moskovskogo universiteta, 1979), p. 247. This book was intended as a textbook for a special course in the distinctive "linguosociopsychological" methodology that Dridze seeks to introduce, but it outlines in great detail the nature of the sample she constructed, her methodology, and her findings.

27 See Mickiewicz, *Media*, pp. 133–36.

28 O. T. Manaev, "Vkliuchennost' lichnosti v sferu vliianiia sredstv massovoi informatsii," *Sotsiologicheskie issledovaniia*, 1984, no. 4: 43.

29 A recent article suggesting rather widespread consumption of information from

"bourgeois propaganda" among the intelligentsia is V. S. Komarovskii, "Metodika sotsiologicheskogo issledovania vozmozhnogo vozdeistviia burzhuaznoi propagandy," in Toshchenko *Voprosy teorii*, vyp. 17, pp. 186–97. The author cites an interesting study showing that guarantees of anonymity are (not surprisingly) likely to produce much more accurate findings in surveys about listening to foreign radio and the like; and also that where the survey is administered makes a difference in the findings. Three categories of respondents were differentiated: ITRs, nonproduction intelligentsia, and students. Asked whether they *never* attended to channels of bourgeois propaganda, substantially higher proportions of respondents gave the ideologically correct response when questioned at their home than when asked at their place of work or study. In nearly every case, a minority of respondents said they never consumed bourgeois propaganda.

30 Jonathan G. Mark, "The Private Zone: A Development in Soviet Political Communication since Stalin," Ph.D. thesis, University of Oklahoma, 1981, pp. 158–85.

31 Ludmilla Alexeyeva, *Soviet Dissent: Contemporary Movements for National, Religious, and Human Rights,* trans. Carol Pearce and John Glad (Middletown, Conn.: Wesleyan University Press, 1985), pp. 269–70, 351, 307–9.

32 Vladimir Shlapentokh, *Love, Marriage and Friendship in the Soviet Union: Ideals and Practices* (New York: Praeger, 1984), pp. 218–38.

33 See chapter 2, section on the ideological aktiv.

34 John H. Miller, "The Communist Party: Trends and Problems," in Archie Brown and Michael Kaser, eds., *Soviet Policy for the 1980's* (Bloomington: Indiana University Press, 1982), p. 7.

35 Zh. T. Toshchenko et al., comps., *Nravstvennoe vospitanie v trudovom kollektive: opyt sotsiologicheskogo issledovaniia* (Moscow: Profizdat, 1981), p. 90.

36 The report on the poll first appeared in an article in the *Rheinische Merkur/Christ und Welt,* 24 September 1981, under the pseudonymous authorship of Viktor Maksudov. It is translated in Radio Free Europe/Radio Liberty, Soviet Area Audience and Opinion Research (SAAOR), "Attitudes of Some Soviet Citizens to Andrei Sakharov: Comparison of SAAOR Data with Unofficial Soviet Poll," AR#11-81, December 1981. See esp. p. 13.

37 On the method SAAOR employs for its surveys, see R. Eugene Parta, John C. Klensin, and Ithiel de Sola Pool, "The Shortwave Audience in the USSR: Methods for Improving the Estimates," *Communication Resarch* 9, no. 4 (October 1982): 581–606. On the validity of SAAOR's results and how they compare with the results of other surveys, see SAAOR, "A Study of SAAOR Data Validity: Behavior and Opinion Measurement," AR 5-84 (April 1984).

38 SAAOR, "Attitudes," p. 7.

39 RFE-RL SAAOR, "Soviet Citizen Attitudes toward Poland since Martial Law: *Agitprop,* Western Radio and the Evolution of Opinion," AR#6-82 (September 1982), p. 5.

40 Alexander Zinoviev would modify Orwell's vision of totalitarianism by em-

phasizing the importance of the social cell as the site where support for communism is constantly generated. Although in Zinoviev's view children, pensioners, and members of free professions lie outside the influence of the cell, cells are not necessarily based in workplaces. Unfortunately, Zinoviev does not develop his concept of the cell further. See Alexander Zinoviev, *The Reality of Communism,* trans. Charles Janson (London: Victor Gollancz, 1984), pp. 59–60.

41 N. N. Bokarev, "Sotsiologicheskie issledovaniia v deiatel'nosti partiinykh komitetov," *Sotsiologicheskie issledovaniia,* 1982, no. 1: 44; Toshchenko, *Nravstvennoe vospitanie,* pp. 13–14.

42 See, for example, Louise I. Shelley, *Lawyers in Soviet Work Life* (New Brunswick, N.J.: Rutgers University Press, 1984), p. 96.

43 Robert W. Campbell, "Statement," in U.S. Congress, Joint Economic Committee and House Committee on Foreign Affairs, *The Political Economy of the Soviet Union* (Washington, D.C.: U.S. Government Printing Office, 1984), p. 11.

44 Quoted in Elizabeth Teague, "The USSR Law on Work Collectives: Workers' Control or Workers Controlled?" *Radio Liberty Research Bulletin,* RL 184/84 (10 May 1984), p. 14.

45 *Sputnik partgruporga, 1979* (Moscow: Izdatel'stvo politicheskoi literatury, 1978), pp. 129–34.

46 Zinoviev, *Reality,* pp. 168–69; Toshchenko, et al., comps., *Nravstvennoe vospitanie,* p. 197.

47 One study showed that the ideological work of workers' immediate job supervisors, trade union leaders, and party group leaders—the local triangle—was most likely to be rated "fully satisfactory" among the channels of ideological influence by the general work force. Ibid., pp. 94–95.

48 Cf. "The political and economic mechanism as a whole produces a fragmentation of social groups and institutions which, in its turn, weakens any potential opposition." Mary McAuley, *Politics and the Soviet Union* (New York: Penguin Books, 1977), p. 317.

INDEX